AUTHORS SERIES · VOLUME VI

COURTESY OF STATE HISTORICAL SOCIETY OF WISCONSIN

Svein Nilsson

AUTHORS SERIES · VOLUME VI

A Chronicler Of Immigrant Life Svein Nilsson's Articles In *Billed-Magazin*, 1868–1870

Translated and Introduced By

C. A. CLAUSEN

C. A. Clausen

1982
The Norwegian-American Historical Association
NORTHFIELD · MINNESOTA

ISBN 0-87732-067-5

PRINTED IN THE UNITED STATES OF AMERICA AT THE NORTH CENTRAL PUBLISHING COMPANY, ST. PAUL, MINNESOTA

The figure that appears on the cover and title page of this book is one of the twenty-four letters in the older Germanic runic alphabet used in the Scandinavian countries from about 200 to 800 A. D. In addition to representing the sound "m," approximately as in modern English, it also has a name, meaning "man" or "mankind." It thus serves here as a symbol for the humanities.

Preface

AS EDITOR of *Billed-Magazin* 1868–1870, the first illustrated monthly in the Norwegian language published in America, Svein Nilsson wrote a series of articles about the arrival of the early Norwegian immigrants and their pioneer settlements in the Midwest. These articles constitute an important landmark in Norwegian-American historical research; they have been consulted by scholars and by lay people interested in the period and have had a significant impact on later historical literature. Based as the articles are on personal interviews with the immigrants themselves, they provide a highly individual and human dimension to the story—they are the oral history of their day—but Nilsson's interest encompassed the historical background as well as the possibilities for advancement in the new environment, and in his hands the accounts become sober and balanced records of the historical situation during the founding phase of immigration which lasted until shortly after the Civil War.

Nilsson belonged to the group of gifted rural youth in nineteenth-century Norway whose educational opportunity was limited to the normal school; as a graduate and a schoolmaster Nilsson became a devoted progressive and a champion of enlightenment, which is reflected in his sensitive portrayal of his countrymen in America. Indeed the permanent value of *Billed-Magazin* rests largely on his series of articles, researched at considerable sacrifice of time and labor. *A Chronicler of Immigrant Life: Svein Nilsson's Articles in* Billed-Magazin, *1868–1870* contains in full Nilsson's articles in *Billed-Magazin* published under the heading "De skandinaviske setlementer i Amerika" (The Scandinavian Settlements in America). We are indebted to Dr. C. A. Clausen for translating Nilsson's intricate nineteenth-century Dano-Norwegian into accurate and readable English, one of Dr. Clausen's many credits in our publication program. We present these records as volume six in our Authors Series. This series has room for many more studies of men and women whose creative writing or careers in immigrant journalism bring to light and interpret a Norwegian presence in the New World.

In the translation the modern forms of Norwegian place names are used; farm and personal names are, however, save for changes to assure uniformity, as in the original text. A special thanks is due my assistant Mary R. Hove, who performed the detailed work of editing, researched and drew the map of early Norwegian settlements, and indexed the volume. Elaine Kringen, assistant secretary of the NAHA, typed the edited manuscript.

St. Olaf College ODD S. LOVOLL

Contents

CHRONICLER OF IMMIGRANT LIFE

Introduction

SVEIN NILSSON, who may justly be styled the father of Norwegian immigrant history, was born into a family of freeholders in Namdalen, Norway, in 1826. After receiving the rudiments of education from itinerant schoolmasters, as was then the custom in rural Norway, Svein had the opportunity to attend a newly opened normal school in nearby Klebu; when he had completed the course he returned to his home community as a teacher. Following the usual pattern of nineteenth century *seminarister* (normal-school graduates), Svein Nilsson did not confine his efforts just to the teaching of children but became a real community leader who established a local library, organized a young people's society, agitated for better farming methods, and aroused interest in home industries and the manual arts.[1] Later he moved to the larger community of Namsos, partly, one may suppose, because his annual salary was increased from $40 to $150 plus free housing. But the very next year, 1856, he left for Oslo, where he studied at the university and supported himself by private tutoring and working for *Morgenbladet* (The Morning Paper), which at the time was Norway's largest and by all odds most influential newspaper. Under the leadership of its conservative and controversial editor, Christian Friele, "it assumed during the 1860s and far into the 1870s a position which is absolutely unique in the history of the Norwegian press."[2]

Friele's young assistant, Svein Nilsson, may have played some small part in the attainment of this unique position. According to Johannes B. Wist in *Norsk-amerikanernes festskrift*, Nilsson for a long time served as the editor's "political detective and colleague. It frequently surprised the political world how well informed *Morgenbladet* was concerning all sorts of political cabals. Little did anyone suspect that it was Svein Nilsson who, in his own shrewd manner, kept Friele abreast of the many important things which took place behind the scenes so that in the next morning's issue he could tell to a word what had happened without *Morgenbladet* having been at all in evidence."[3]

Nilsson's apprenticeship with *Morgenbladet* evidently stood him in good stead in later years, because after he came to America in 1867 most of his life was devoted to journalistic work. On his arrival in this country, he settled in Madison, Wisconsin, and there secured a position with *Emigranten,* probably the leading Norwegian newspaper in America at the time. He did not remain long with *Emigranten,* however. In late 1868 there appeared the first issue of *Billed-Magazin* (Picture Magazine), a weekly published by B. W. Suckow, a Madison bookseller and printer, and edited by Svein Nilsson. The very first article, "Hvad vi ville" (Our Objectives), states the aims of the fledgling publication, one of the earliest attempts at publishing a Norwegian-American literary magazine. The art of clarifying the written text by means of illustrations had by that time reached such perfection, they explained, that all the important countries had publications which helped by this means to spread information and enhance the appreciation of the beautiful. Even a country like Norway, with a smaller population than the state of Illinois, had illustrated magazines with some 18,000 subscribers.

Despite the many obstacles in their way, the publisher and the editor felt that the Scandinavian population in the United States had reached such proportions that a Dano-Norwegian illustrated magazine should have a chance of survival. They had been warned that most of the Scandinavians in America had now mastered English and would prefer to read illustrated magazines in that language even if a Norwegian publication could compete with them in excellence of contents, illustrations, and make-up. In reply to this claim they pointed out that *Billed-Magazin* would cost a bit less than two cents per issue (one dollar per year) while its American rivals cost from ten to fifteen cents. Furthermore, a magazine directed at Scandinavian readers should have more appeal for them than American publications aimed at circles "whose interests in many respects are different from our own." Then follow eight paragraphs which summarize what Suckow and Nilsson hoped to offer their readers. There would be articles on history and folk life, as well as mythology and legends from all parts of the world—especially such topics as would be of interest to Scandinavians. The present-day reader must admit that in this respect they kept their promise. Material was literally garnered "from Greenland's icy mountains, from India's coral strand" and from practically every other clime. They also promised to introduce the readers to their new homeland through articles and illustrations dealing with important places and personalities. Here again they kept their promise. The total of 102 issues published carried biographical sketches and portraits of about seventy prominent American political and military leaders ranging from Lincoln and Grant to minor figures now remembered only by history professors or Civil War buffs. Peculiarly enough, only eight contemporary Scandinavians rated *Billed-Magazin*'s hall of fame—probably because of the difficulty of obtaining woodcuts. But many illustrations of scenic areas in Norway, and many Norwegian as well as some Danish short stories and poems were printed. Furthermore, every issue contained brief news reports from the Scandinavian countries.

Considering the fact that Scandinavians occupied large rural settlements in Wisconsin and neighboring states it was reasonable for the editors to state that "agricultural life and the many aspects of soil cultivation can not be ignored in a periodical which has set as its aim to work for 'the enhancement of useful knowledge.'" In this connection Mr. Paul C. Johnson, long-time editor of *The Prairie Farmer*, was asked if he would take the trouble to examine the illustrations and articles dealing with rural life. He was kind enough to comply with this request, and summed up his impressions in the following paragraphs:

"I have looked through Svein Nilsson's *Billed-Magazin* with much interest because it is one of the very few attempts at providing the pioneer Norwegian-American farmers with information in their mother tongue on how to farm in America. After all, a large majority of the immigrants were farmers, and farming in this country was in many respects different from what it had been in Norway. Nilsson worked hard at accomplishing his purpose. He covered horticultural and livestock subjects fairly well. He borrowed illustrations from several farm publications of his time, probably *The Prairie Farmer, Breeders Gazette, Wisconsin Agriculturist*, and an eastern publication, *The Cultivator*. Since these are rather crude woodcuts (possibly some are hand-done copper engravings) it is hard to tell whether he borrowed the cuts direct or had access to an engraver who copied them without credit, a common practice among publishers of the time.

"While research could probably determine exactly where the farm articles came from, it is clear that Nilsson used what might be called textbook information, probably gleaned from English-language farm magazines or agricultural textbooks. Nilsson seems to have translated directly, prefacing the translations with general philosophic remarks of his own. Two notable examples are a horticultural piece which he introduced with some excellent paragraphs on the value of beauty to the farm family and another, introducing a piece on windmills, in which he made some remarks on energy conservation that could have been made by an ecologist today."

The sixth declaration of purpose is of particular relevance to this English translation of Svein Nilsson's articles about "De skandinaviske setlementer i Amerika" (The Scandinavian Settlements in America). It will therefore be given *in toto*: "The history of the Scandinavian emigration: one of *Billed-*

Billed-Magazin.

No. 6.] Madison, Wisconsin den 5te Februar. [1870.

Gartnerboligen i Christiania.

Christiania Slotspark hører nu til de smukkeste Anlæg i Christiania, medens denne Del af Byen en Menneskealder tilbage i Tiden var en Udkant, en slet opdyrket Mark og kun undtagelsesvis en Del af en Løkke. Kunst og Natur have i Forening omdannet det Hele, og især er Haven paa Syd- og Vestsiden af Slottet det vakreste offentlige Anlæg, der staar aabent for Almenheden. Vort Billede viser Gartnerboligen med nærliggende Drivhus; rundt omkring ere mange Blomsterpartier, der fremvise ligesaa sjeldne som vakre Planter, medens et almindeligt velordnet Haveanlæg giver det Hele et venligt, hyggeligt Præg, saa at man med Glæde dvæler under de høie, skyggefulde Træer. Baade Formiddag og Eftermiddag er denne Del af Slotsparken meget besøgt; de mange Spadserende nyde her Synet og Vellugten fra de talrige Blomsterbed eller gjør sig en liden Tur

Gartnerboligen i Christiania.

rundtomkring og betragter Svanerne, der svømme om i Dammen, og som opfange de Hvedebrødssmuler, der tilkastes dem. Publikum paaskjønner ogsaa, hvad Parkanlægget yder dem af Hygge og som forfriskende Opholdssted; thi neppe nogetsteds ser man i eller udenfor Anlæggene saa lidet Spor efter et uhindret Besøg af en hel Del forskjellige Mennesker: Publikum er her selv Politi og passer selv paa, at Blomster, Buske og Træer forblive uantastede og at ingen Uorden begaaes. Saaledes burde det være overalt; de offentlige Anlæg burde overlades Publikum, og dette burde overtage et almindeligt Politiopsyn.

De skandinaviske Setlementer i Amerika.

(Fortsættelse fra No. 5).

Pleasant Spring.

Men saa fik jeg efter to Ugers Forløb Besøg af Nykommerens farligste Fiende, Klimatfeberen, der i hine Dage sjelden gik nogen forbi, og her, blandt lutter Fremmede og ubekjendt med Sproget, blev jeg for nogen Tid fængslet til Sygeleiet. Til Forladthedens Kvaler sluttede sig Længsler efter Venner og Hjemland, idet Minderne fra Ungdommens glade Dage i vexlende Skikkelser fremmanedes for mit aandelige Blik og op-

Magazin's publishers will during the course of the summer [1868] travel through the Scandinavian settlements of the Northwest. He will then seek out the oldest still-living persons among the first emigrants, and from their narratives it will be possible to gather material for an immigrant history. . . . We will converse about the causes leading to the migrations, about the sorrows and privations of the newcomers in their new homes, about their progress and their present situation, about the natural resources of the settlements and about economic and moral conditions among the people.'' (They should also have added that comments would be made about the religious and political ideas of the settlers.) How well the editors managed to realize this purpose the present readers will judge for themselves.

It can be added that later historians have found Svein Nilsson's articles to be real ''grass-roots'' history—valuable source material for more sophisticated historical writing. Ever since Rasmus B. Anderson drew liberally on and quoted extensively from the *Billed-Magazin* material in his book, *The First Chapter of Norwegian Immigration* (1896), many other students have gone to the same source. Theodore Blegen says of Svein Nilsson: ''. . . he understood the lasting value of original accounts by those who themselves had been a part of the movement. He was not so much a historian as a collector of the materials of history; and all historians of the Norwegian migration have found his materials a treasure house of information.''[4] Some years earlier Wist spoke along the same lines: ''. . . that which lent the periodical its lasting value was a series of articles about the first Norwegian immigration and the first settlements in New York, Illinois, and Wisconsin. These articles were written by Professor Svein Nilsson, who with no small sacrifice of time and effort gathered material during long and arduous trips afoot through the older Norwegian settlements. For those who have given some attention to the study of Norwegian-American history, these narratives in *Billed-Magazin* have been a priceless source.''[5]

The magazine also carried two other contributions which are of interest to students of immigrant history. John A. Johnson, a well-known figure at the time, wrote a series entitled ''Om udvandringen'' (About the Emigration), wherein he discussed the pros and cons of emigration, a question which was then heatedly debated in practically every Norwegian community. He assured his readers that he was not trying to induce anyone to emigrate. ''My aim is solely to give a true picture of America as a dwelling place for Norwegians . . . I can not promise to give you anything but that guidance which emigrants and newcomers need, and the information I give shall be permeated by the spirit of truth; if it can be of service to my countrymen, then its aim will have been realized.''[6] Also, Elise Wærenskjold wrote a series of three articles entitled ''Beretning om de norske setlementer i Texas'' (Account of the Norwegian Settlements in Texas).[7]

Despite the fact that *Billed-Magazin* contained much valuable material and hoped to appeal to a variety of tastes, despite the reasonable price, it suffered an early demise. The great majority of Norwegian-American attempts to found similar magazines failed, no doubt because the immigrant communities were not fertile ground for such literary endeavors. And there were other obstacles in the way. As the founders of *Billed-Magazin* had realized, the many English-language magazines would prove formidable rivals, especially among the younger generation. Probably even more formidable rivals were certain Norwegian-American newspapers, many of which achieved wide circulation; besides news they contained articles, stories, and poems, features which one more often associates with magazines. Some of these newspapers also had a type of literary supplement which aimed especially at giving their subscribers entertaining reading material. Thus, *Decorah-Posten* had its *Ved Arnen* (By the Fireside) and *Skandinaven* had its *Husbibliothek* (Home Library), which carried both Norwegian stories and poems and similar material translated from English. Many a person now up in years can well remember from the days of his youth with what expectancy the whole family looked forward to the weekly arrival of these newspapers and their literary supplements.

The last issue of *Billed-Magazin* appeared on December 10, 1870; immediately afterward, Svein Nilsson became associate editor of *Skandinaven*, and in 1872 he became its editor-in-chief, a position he held until 1886. Of the 400 or so Norwegian-American newspapers which appeared during the course of the years, *Skandinaven*, established in Chicago in 1866, was one of the most successful and possibly the very most influential in molding popular opinion. Its founders, John Anderson and Knud Langeland, threw themselves with vigor into the political, social, and religious debates of the day. It was strongly Republican but of a liberal persuasion, always sympathetic toward "the common man," something which came naturally to young men who had grown up in poverty.[8] The founders were decidedly low church in outlook and got into heated debates with certain leaders of the "Norwegian Synod" whom they regarded as high church and undemocratic. Although Nilsson was not as belligerent as Langeland, his predecessor in the editorial chair, "with his whole character he fitted perfectly into *Skandinaven*'s program, and this he sought to carry through at every point," to quote Wist again.[9]

This is not the place to discuss at length Nilsson's activities as editor of the Chicago paper. It need only be mentioned that one of the most heated topics of debate during part of his term was the so-called "common school question." Like Langeland, Svein Nilsson made *Skandinaven* the main organ for the defense of the American common school system against the attacks of certain Synod pastors who held it to be "religionless," if not anti-religious, and felt

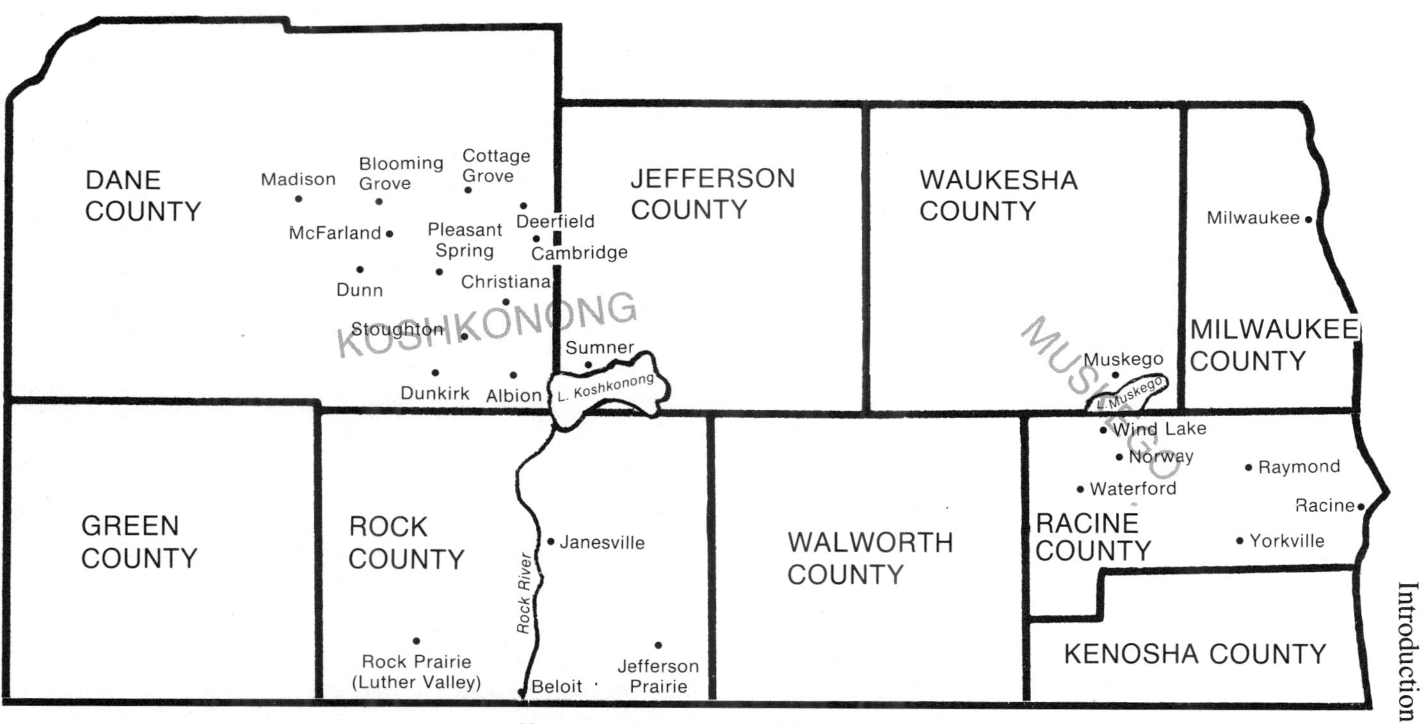

Norwegian Settlements in Wisconsin

that it was a threat to the preservation of Norwegian language and culture in this country. Influenced by the German Missouri Synod they urged that the Norwegians should set up their own school system. Nilsson, and numerous other champions of the common school, declared that such an act would cut the Norwegians off from the main stream of American life and prevent them from playing their proper role in the affairs of this country.[10]

After leaving *Skandinaven*, Nilsson spent some time in St. Paul, where he edited *Nordvesten*, another Norwegian-American newspaper; but he returned to Chicago in 1894 to assume the editorship of a labor newspaper, *Fremskridt* (Progress), founded by Norwegians. D. G. Ristad met Nilsson two years later and "found him to hold very liberal, if not radical, opinions concerning labor and capital and the almost unbounded range of problems connected with the relations of the two." Even though *Fremskridt* is said to have been a well-edited newspaper, it failed to make the desired progress and soon merged with another publication.[11]

Svein Nilsson died in 1908, a lonely and practically forgotten man. He evidently felt that he had been a failure. He did not live long enough to learn that in later years he would be gratefully remembered as "the father of Norwegian immigrant history."

The Oldest Norwegian Settlement in Wisconsin

ONE OF the most remarkable phenomena of this century is the emigration that has taken place from Europe to the New World which Columbus discovered.* The inhabitants of Ireland together with the Germans have furnished the largest number of emigrants. A smaller number of French, Italians, Swiss, and other nationalities have joined these emigrant hosts. Even the sparsely populated Scandinavian countries have participated actively in the emigration, and the number of Scandinavians in America now must be close to 300,000.

The significance of this movement to the history of culture in America is strikingly evident to anyone who travels through the northern half of this western continent for the purpose of collecting historical information. A comparison between the present time and a time less than a generation ago reveals the rapid change. The progress from wilderness to fertile fields, the steadily increasing prosperity of the settlers, the development of industry and other sources of subsistence, and the almost unparalleled advance on all fronts must of necessity strike the visiting stranger with surprise. From the East the stream of immigrants has flowed westward over the great plains. The untamed son of the wilderness has fled before the advancing civilization. The natural resources so generously supplied by Providence have been made available; an industrious and virile people have become the possessors of the soil; immigration has brought a steady supply of energetic workers; the use of machinery to an extent unapproached in other countries has raised industry and agriculture to a level impossible without these aids; free institutions and free choice of

**Billed-Magazin*, October 3, 1868.

occupation have allowed practical talent to flourish among the people; immigrants arriving from the most enlightened and advanced countries of the Old World meet in rapidly growing cities and pioneer settlements, where ideas are exchanged, where everything is tested, and only the best is retained. These are some of the outstanding results of immigration, and they furnish the key to the nation's marvelous progress in economic well-being, in industry, education, and commerce.

The same causes that brought the blessings of civilization and an enterprising people to North America have also benefitted the countries of Europe most involved in emigration. Emigration has furnished a natural release to the overpopulated sections of these countries; it has relieved enforced idleness and the evils due to unemployment. Discontented elements in Europe have found on the other side of the Atlantic a home that richly repaid the diligent toiler, where political freedom held him secure against the encroachments of the ruling powers. Those who in the home countries had suffered persecution on account of their religious beliefs found in America a haven of safety. From the countries where the people suffered most from oppression and poverty came the largest number of immigrants, especially from sections of Germany and unhappy Ireland. Again we have confirmation of the fact that where real misery exists, real help is also at hand; it seems as if Providence intervenes at the right moment to offer the underprivileged relief from rampant poverty and its attendant moral degradation.

Having offered this introductory statement, we call the special attention of the reader to the settlements in North America established by the Scandinavians. The probable causes of emigration, the sorrows and privations of the first years, the growth of the settlements, the gradual economic improvement, the natural resources, and the prevailing social, religious, moral, and political conditions in these settlements will be discussed.[1]

In the year 1839 a vessel from Skien made its way through the Langesundfjord. Aboard the vessel there were, besides the crew, forty people, most of them in their best years, who were prepared to leave the fatherland and their home districts of Tinn and Hjartdal in Upper Telemark. There were about an equal number of men and women but there were comparatively few children in the party. According to the standards of that time these emigrants could be considered well-to-do people. All of them had enough money to defray travel expenses, and most of them even had a little more. Many in the little group were connected by bonds of kinship; and the Luraas family—represented by the heads of four households—included no fewer than twenty individuals. The Luraas group had been joined by four other families from Hjartdal and three from Tinn as well as by some unmarried persons.

In the mountain districts in those days the strangest stories were told about

America and the dangers of a trip across the ocean. Some of the mountain people had heard that skippers often sold emigrants as slaves to the Turks; others maintained that the ocean swarmed with horrible monsters capable of devouring a whole ship—cargo and all. But according to some accounts, an even worse fate awaited those who were not swallowed by sea-beasts or crushed between towering icebergs. In America, so the stories went, the natives commonly captured white men and ate them on festive occasions to the glory of their gods. These and similar tales circulated in the mountain valleys and many of the inhabitants crossed themselves in sheer amazement at the reckless daring of the emigrants.

In spite of all the solemn warnings, the emigrants clung to their decision. To realize the dream of departing for America in those days must surely have required great willpower. America was but little known in Norway thirty years ago, and even short trips were seldom undertaken in the mountain areas. It seems that scarcity of tillable soil and shortage of profitable employment were the factors which caused the emigrants from these regions to shoulder the knapsack. One of them, John Nelson, now a respected, prosperous farmer in Koshkonong, has spoken about these matters: "I was my father's oldest son and as such was entitled to inherit the Luraas farm, which was held to be one of the best in the community; but it was encumbered with a debt of fourteen hundred dollars. I worked at home until I was twenty-five years old and consequently was unable to save any money. It was obvious that I would assure myself a hopeless future by taking charge of the farm with its heavy indebtedness, buying out my brothers and sisters in such a fashion that they suffered no injustice, and, finally, providing a pension for my father.[2] I noticed with apprehension how one farm after another fell into the hands of the sheriff or other moneylenders. This increased my fear of getting involved with any kind of farming. But I got married and had to make some provision for the future. Then it occurred to me that it would be best to leave for America. I was strengthened in this resolve by letters from Norwegian settlers in Illinois, and the idea ripened into firm determination when I read a book written by a Norwegian immigrant who had spent some time in the United States.[3] What I have just said explains what brought me to leave my native land, and I presume that the other members of our party were led to their decisions by similar reasoning."

Here a clarifying note may be in order. Two years previously, in the year 1837, a small group of three families had left Upper Telemark for the sea in search of passage to America. They reached their destination without mishap and settled in the Fox River valley in Illinois. At that time people looked at this undertaking with suspicion and pity. The emigrants were considered foolish daredevils; it was even hinted that they acted upon the inspiration of the Evil One himself who thus sought to lead them to destruction. No one had any inkling at the time that with their journey these farmers from Tinn were shattering the wall of custom which made people lie at home in poverty rather than seek work and food elsewhere. Despite all the horror stories and the loud talk about the sinfulness of leaving the spot where one was born, the America fever gradually spread in wide circles; and, during the following years, every spring saw large groups of emigrants from Telemark trudging through the valley of the Skien river toward the sea.

The incident mentioned above undoubtedly seems very insignificant. But soon the contemporaries of the first emigrants will have passed away; and it may well happen that our children and grandchildren, when they hear about the great number of Norwegians in America, will listen with interest to the stories which seem of little importance to us and be grateful for any information which may throw light on the history of Scandinavian emigration.

There is always some distinction attached to being the first person who performs a deed which later is imitated by many others. Thus it is with these emigrants from Tinn. Their departure can be regarded as the beginning of a whole series of like events which have had decisive influence on the way of life of thousands of people. None of these first emigrants have become noted in other respects nor have they been especially favored by fortune in their adopted country. However, by hard work, thrift, and self-denial they have gradually attained a position in life which can be described as fairly prosperous and which promises a better future for their children.

One of the leaders of the advance guard from Telemark was Erik Gautesen Midbøen. With his large family he settled in Illinois. He did not do particularly well there. Later he converted to Mormonism and undertook a trip to Norway as a minister of that faith; he died some time after his return to America. Thor Kittilsen Svimbil, also the head of a household from Norway, died as a farmer in Blue Mounds, Wisconsin. The only one of the three family fathers in the group who is still alive, John Nelson Rue, lives on a farm in Winneshiek county, Iowa. A bachelor, Tosten Ingebrigtsen Gulliksrud, who also was a member of the party, died many years ago in Illinois.

Soon people back home received letters from those who had left Tinn in 1837. Thus information circulated concerning conditions beyond the ocean, and consequently many people began talking of emigrating. Additional stimulus was given by the publication of a book entitled *Sandfærdig beretning om Amerika* (True Account of America) which appeared in 1838 in Christiania. It was written by the well-known Ole Rynning and seen through the press by Ansten Nattestad from Numedal. The latter had spent about a year in America, after which he returned to Norway to escort some relatives and friends to the New World. Ansten Nattestad's arrival in Norway caused as much stir at that time as if a man had suddenly reappeared after a trip to the moon. And Ole Rynning's book, which gave an attractive picture of conditions in America, was rapidly circulated throughout the whole land. From that time on emigration became a common topic of conversation in both town and country.

We will now return to our friends, those forty emigrants from Upper Telemark whom we have already learned to know. We find all of them in good spirits and full of eagerness to begin the journey. On May 17th (Norway's independence day), 1839, the ship was carried by a strong breeze out through the fjord, and soon the open sea lay spread before them. Gradually the land disappeared in the distance, and when even the highest mountain peaks sank below the horizon, one of the party reports that they grew sad at the thought of the uncertain future which lay before them and the realization that they might never again see this land to which they were bound by so many memories. But the decisive step had been taken and regret was pointless. They made good progress, and after a few days the Norwegian captain brought the passengers to Gothenburg, Sweden, in accordance with the agreement. There they met several families from the Stavanger area—about twenty people in all—who also were going to America. The two groups combined and an American captain, whose ship lay in the harbor loaded with iron, agreed to take them across the ocean to Boston for forty-two *speciedaler* per person.[4] The crossing was made without any mishap, health conditions were good, and after nine weeks of sailing they caught sight of the other shore.

In Boston these newcomers aroused considerable surprise. Few people had ever heard of Norway before; crowds of citizens rushed to the landing place to see the ship which brought immigrants from the far North. The speech, dress, and habits of the strangers undoubtedly caused wonderment; but what puzzled the Bostonians most was that people from a land so close to the polar ice as Norway could look like any other human beings. They reasoned that men and women alike would be dressed in fur from head to foot and that they would eat raw meat and drink train oil like Eskimos. The good citizens were, however, soon convinced that there was no essential difference between themselves and the newcomers and consequently received them with much friendliness and helpfulness.

From Boston the immigrants continued on to New York, and thence westward—mostly by horse-drawn canal boats—to Buffalo. There they met a skipper who agreed to take them across the Great Lakes to Milwaukee. They boarded his miserable vessel which twice came near sinking. One woman was washed overboard. The rest escaped with only a scare—and after three weeks of tossing on the waters landed at Milwaukee. There the city officials talked of prosecuting the skipper because it seemed indefensible to have carried so many people aboard a ship which "took water like a sieve." When, in addition, we learn that the ship was loaded with gunpowder, we must admit that the lives of the passengers had been placed in jeopardy.

Seventeen weeks had now passed since the emigrants had weighed anchor in the harbor of Skien, but they were still far from their intended destination. Their plan was to continue, by way of Chicago, to the above-mentioned Fox River settlement. That plan was given up, however, and in this connection one of the immigrants told me the following story:

"The day after we reached Milwaukee we began preparing for our departure. Then several men from the town came aboard. They asked what we intended to do in America. We replied that we were farmers who wished to get land to cultivate and thought of going to Illinois. 'Go wherever you please,' said one of the visitors. 'This is a free country; but if you are concerned about your own welfare, you had better take my advice.' Then he showed us two men: one of them was a large, heavy-set man of good appearance; the other one was a living skeleton with every sign of sickness and degeneracy. 'Look,' said our self-appointed adviser. 'That fat man is from Wisconsin where there is a healthful climate and abundant food; the skinny one is from Illinois where people dry up in the hot sun and die like flies from swamp-fever. Well, friends, choose as you think best.'

"It was a hot summer day and the rays of the August sun added strength to the man's arguments. Perspiring heavily in our homespun clothing, we thought with horror of the heat in Illinois which would soon turn us into skeletons like the sorry figure we saw by the side of the vigorous specimen from Wisconsin. We held a consultation and decided unanimously in favor of Wisconsin."

So the immigrants went ashore in Milwaukee. That city, which now numbers about 70,000 inhabitants, was then in its infancy. Only a few stores and a few small houses were scattered about the place, without any order to indicate that a town with regular streets was planned. Interestingly enough, the man who had been presented to the immigrants as a representative of Wisconsin was none other than the later well-known Mr. Walker in whose honor a section of the city, Walker's Point, has been named.

The inhabitants of Milwaukee had never before either seen or heard of Norwegians.* The newcomers were therefore scrutinized with inquisitive eyes, but they also received many tokens of goodwill and helpfulness. After their interpreter, a Dane who had accompanied the immigrants from Gothenburg, drowned in the lake near Milwaukee, there was no one able to speak for the immigrants, who now, as best they could, had to resort to signs and

*_Billed-Magazin_, November 14, 1868.

mimicry to express their thoughts and desires. The town councillors evidently reasoned that cattle-raising, fishing, and hunting were the pursuits most familiar to the newcomers. They appointed a guide to accompany the men whom the immigrants had chosen to inspect the available land. He took them to the north end of Lake Muskego in the southern corner of Waukesha county, about fourteen miles from Milwaukee. The summer heat had dried up the swamps, and the large marshes, covered with grass, were taken for prairies by the newcomers. There were woods in great plenty and the rivers swarmed with fish. The men returned well pleased to their companions in Milwaukee whom they told about all the glories they had seen. As a result, the whole group, except two men who took jobs in town, left to settle in the township of Muskego, the name by which the colony is known. There the newcomers bought government land for $1.25 per acre. They immediately began clearing and building, but then came the autumn rains and much of the land was soon under water. Many of the settlers then realized that they had made a bad bargain. It was obvious that the low-lying marshes and sloughs could not be made tillable except at great expense, but they made excellent pasture and land for raising hay. The settlement was, therefore, suited for animal husbandry but not for grain production. The woodlands were difficult to clear and the soil was of a clayey texture which yielded poor crops. The newcomers, however, worked tirelessly to improve their homesteads despite the fact that many of them found it difficult to provide for their families. The number of settlers gradually increased, primarily through the arrival of new recruits from Tinn and from Illinois, where the first settlers had been unfortunate in their choice of land and therefore found it advisable to seek new homes elsewhere.

An elderly, respected man, Postmaster Jacobsen in the township of Norway, has furnished this additional information about the oldest Norwegian settlement in Wisconsin:

The forests consisted of gigantic oak trees and the land was consequently difficult to clear. The area swarmed with game, such as deer and various types of birds, while the lakes and rivers were full of fish. The smoke from the Indian wigwams floated up over the trees of the ancient forest. Friendly relations existed between the red men and the immigrants; the latter never suffered any injustice at the hands of the natives. But the earliest settlers encountered great hardships. Supplies had to be transported great distances over trackless areas; and worst of all there was the ague, which, almost without exception, sent newcomers to the sickbed for months. Despite these tribulations the colony increased in size, and the axe in the skilled hands of the immigrants made clearings in the forests. Thrift and industry were the main characteristics of the first settlers. Usually they bought only forty acres, but as they became more prosperous they found that this was too little: many sold out

A Settler's Cabin
From *Billed-Magazin*, September 4, 1869.

to their neighbors or to newcomers and went farther west to newer settlements in Wisconsin or even Iowa. Consequently, we find throughout the Norwegian settlements many people who, after their arrival in America, spent a short time in Muskego. The settlement served as a temporary stopping place and a point of departure for many of the early immigrants. It was only later, after disease became a scourge, that people went directly from the old country to the newer areas of Wisconsin, Iowa, and Minnesota. During the years 1849 and 1850 Muskego was ravaged by cholera, which wrought great havoc in the little community. The settlement fell into disrepute; many of the survivors moved to other regions, and thereafter it was seldom that newcomers dared visit ill-starred Muskego.

Kittil Nilsen Lohner and his brother Halvor Nilsen Lohner, both from Hjartdal, still live in the old settlement. Gitle Danielsen's deserted family (from Skjold) are still on the old homestead.[5] With these exceptions there are no Norwegians left in the once populous frontier settlement. The others have either died or moved away, and the fields cleared by our countrymen are now tilled by Irishmen or Germans. Two other Norwegians, Knud Johnson Bækhus from Hjartdal and Ole Kjønaas from Bø, have settled farther west, in the township of Vernon, beyond the borders of the original Norwegian settlement. In a few years there will probably be no Scandinavians left in Muskego, but the saga of the oldest Norwegian settlement in Wisconsin will be long remembered. For years to come many people in the Northwest will be able to relate how either they or their forefathers first settled at old Muskego, but left in order to find more healthful and fertile homesteads in other parts of the country.

Now I wish to say something about Scandinavian (primarily Norwegian) settlements in the townships of Norway, Raymond, and Yorkville, which are frequently referred to by the name of "Muskego" even though that title, strictly speaking, should be applied only to the district located several miles farther north, by Lake Muskego in Waukesha county.

The name Muskego was originally written Muskeego, which is derived from the Indian word Muskeeguiac, which means cranberry. These berries are abundant in the lowlands around the lakes and along the rivers in the region. It appears that in times past the Indians found here conditions exactly answering to their hearts' desires. Flocks of deer and other animals roamed the forests; the openings provided space for small fields of corn; and if everything else failed, there were always fish in the streams and lakes. Under the protection of a gigantic oak tree the sons of the wilderness would pitch their tents. Hardened to the hunter's life, they roamed the wilds in search of prey, and even "the king of the forest," the bear himself, sometimes fell to their well-directed arrows. The industrious Indian women took care of things around the tepee: prepared and cooked the game, tended the cornfields, ground the grain between stones, sewed clothes, and looked after the children. Meanwhile the old men, who had tired of the chase, and the youngsters, still too weak for such arduous pursuits, busied themselves with fishing. In this manner these children of nature passed their time; only moves to new hunting grounds or expeditions against enemy tribes altered their routine.

But now everything is changed. The red men have vanished from these regions and of their trails there is scarcely a trace left. Only legends, certain place-names, a few grave mounds, and occasional stone weapons found in the fields remind us that once another race possessed this land—the land now occupied by the immigrants to whom the sons of the wilderness reached a welcoming hand. Thus it happened here—and in many other places. The Indians retreated when confronted by another civilization, and a race further advanced in agricultural skills now till the soil and enjoy the fruits of those resources which the natives did not know how to utilize. In eastern Wisconsin this transition has taken place during the last thirty years. In the same regions where the Indians had their hunting grounds only three decades ago there are now cities of the size of Christiania, Bergen, and Trondheim; and between them, as far as the eye can reach, are golden fields of grain, sturdy farm buildings, and pleasant little villages. When a stranger sees these things and at the same time hears the old settlers tell about the life led by the natives and about their friendly associations with them, then it all strikes him like stories from *The Thousand and One Nights*.

But we must return to our topic. We have already related that the attempt to found a Norwegian settlement on the shores of Lake Muskego failed. Later immigrants from the Scandinavian countries, however, built homes several miles farther south, and the name Muskego, as we said before, was popularly extended to include all the settlements founded by our countrymen in the neighboring townships of Norway, Waterford, Raymond, and Yorkville—all of them located in Racine county. But on the maps and in official usage only the earliest Norwegian settlement, farther north in Waukesha county, goes by the name of Muskego.[6]

The name of Norway township would indicate that this part of Racine county was first settled by Norwegians. And so it was, as one of the earliest settlers tells us: in the year 1839 Søren Bache, son of the merchant Tollef Bache in Drammen, together with the well-known Haugean, Elling Eielsen, left for America in order to study conditions in the New World. The cautious father let one of his trusted employees—a man named [Johannes] Johannesen—accompany the son, whom he evidently thought immature for such a journey. Johannesen, at that time about forty years old, was a man of firm character and stern moral principles who had become acquainted with the English language during a stay in England. The following winter these three men came to the Fox River settlement in La Salle county, Illinois, about seventy-five miles southwest of Chicago. The pioneers there lived in straitened circumstances and, in addition, the winter storms and the chill prairie winds inspired the travellers with such a fear of the plains that early the following spring they set off to the north and reached Wind Lake, where they found one lone settler, an Irishman. They liked it there in the woods by the shore of the little lake, so they bought the plot of ground which the Irishman was tilling and Bache chose this place as his home. It had been agreed that the three should write to relatives and friends in Norway. Even Heg, a hotel owner in Drammen, and a large number of interested people from the surrounding area were ready to leave at the first suggestion from America. The signal was given from Wind Lake; and in the fall of 1840, Heg and company arrived and settled in the neighborhood. Bache was well supplied with money and bought a large plot of government land which he permitted the newcomers to till. The larger part of the township of Norway was thus settled very soon and, before long, later immigrants spread over the adjoining areas.[7]

Fuller information can be given about several of the founders of this settlement. Søren Bache was, it seems, a man of better heart than mind, kindly disposed, helpful, and honest. When his means had been exhausted, primarily through loans to poor countrymen, he went to Norway and returned with more money. This he used for the purchase of more land, which he turned over to newcomers on easy terms. These transactions were usually taken care of by his adviser and companion. Johannesen had started as a printer in Kristiansand but later entered the office of Tollef Bache in Drammen and, finally, accompanied the latter's son to America. He is spoken of as a sincere Christian, an earnest Haugean, and a thoroughly dependable man. As the number of inhabitants in the settlement increased, Bache and Johannesen set up a little trading center. An Indian mound was excavated, the walls lined with boards, and the place fixed up as store, kitchen, and living-room. From the none too ample supplies in Milwaukee they secured their meager goods: several pounds of sugar and coffee, some cloth, a little salt. The Indian mound became, in many respects, the heart of the settlement. Here was the seat of culture and learning, the center of pomp and luxury, the stronghold of finance. It has not been reported that the two cave-dwellers ever took offense at the knuckles and bones which occasionally worked their way through the wall panelling. After two years' stay in the settlement Johannesen died. At about the same time Søren Bache suffered a serious accident; the two events together caused him to sour on life in America. Before leaving for Norway he entrusted his business affairs, including $6,000 invested in land, to his friend Even Heg and a certain Reymert (now a lawyer in New York).[8] Matters went well as long as Heg lived, but after his death Reymert took complete charge and managed affairs in such a manner that Bache recovered little or none of the money invested, despite the fact that the land rose steadily in value. Since his return to Norway Bache has lived on his father's farm, Valle in Lier.

As founders of a Norwegian settlement in the township of Norway, Johannesen and Bache have earned a name in the history of Scandinavian immigration. Undoubtedly many of the settlers in this and surrounding towns would have left the land of their birth without encouragement from these men. Nevertheless, they were the ones who first acquired land here and induced many friends both in Norway and elsewhere in this country to follow them. These two men, then, deserve credit for the fact that so many of our countrymen have settled in the townships of Norway, Waterford, Raymond, and Yorkville that today they form two congregations. I cannot say what may have moved the rich Tollef Bache to send his son on such an adventuresome trip. It seems, however, that the religious movements of the time had an influence on his decision. The followers of Hauge were not actually persecuted but they were exposed to much scorn and ridicule. The aged Bache may, therefore, have thought of sending his son and the experienced, cautious Johannesen to America to buy land for a prospective colony where the so-called "readers" could settle beyond the reach of Norway's established church. At any rate, it is true that the first ones who came at the suggestion of Søren Bache were Haugeans.[9]

The above-mentioned Even Heg from Lier, leader of the group from the Drammen district, is said to have been a very sensible and good man. After Johannesen's death the settlers usually turned to him for advice and help. And Even Heg's barn has become famous throughout the Northwest, because here the many emigrants who then came by way of Milwaukee could rest, after the strenuous ocean voyage, before moving farther west. The settlers then lived in small log cabins of one room which served as kitchen, living-room, and bedroom. Hence there was but little space left for strangers. A somewhat larger building, even though a barn, was viewed as a curiosity; and hundreds, if not thousands, of our countrymen—now scattered over the state—found lodgings and hospitality here while en route to their new homesteads. Probably no Norwegian in America has been more admired than Even Heg's oldest son, Hans [Christian] Heg. He was in charge of the state prison, but when the Civil War broke out he left this lucrative position to organize a regiment composed exclusively of Scandinavians. As colonel of this force he took the field against the rebels. The Scandinavians fought like heroes and their achievements aroused general admiration. Though the brave colonel fell, his memory lives. With the point of the bayonet he has carved runes which time cannot erase.[10]

Accompanying [Even] Heg on the trip to America were his relatives Johannes Evensen Skoffstad and Sivert Ingebrigtsen Nærverud from Eiker. The latter is one of the few members of the party still living in the settlement. Most of them have died and a few have moved away. His farm is located near the so-called Muskego church, a simple log building, presumably the first sanctuary built by Norwegians in America.

It has already been reported that Elling Eielsen accompanied Søren Bache and Johannesen to America and farther up through the country to Illinois.* We do not intend at present to write this man's biography. There will probably be an opportunity to do this in a later series under the title of "The Church History of the Norwegian Settlements." Only a mere mention of Eielsen's activities can be made here. He was born in 1804 on the farm Sønve in Voss. As a young man he joined the friends of Hauge and began to expound the scriptures to his fellowmen. After traveling through Norway, Sweden, and Denmark he migrated to America in 1839 and spent some time in the Norwegian settlement at Fox River. From there he made long trips to various settlements in both Wisconsin and Illinois. During these trips, at the request of the settlers, he performed the duties of a pastor. As opportunity afforded, meet-

* *Billed-Magazin*, November 29, 1868.

ings were held either in a farmer's cabin, in the schoolhouse, or in some other building. Soon the Scandinavians began to scatter over the vast western plains, but Eielsen followed them—sought them out in their new homes and preached the gospel of salvation to them. There is probably no other Scandinavian who has covered America so thoroughly as this man. There is hardly a Norwegian settlement of any importance where he has not been. He now lives on a well-equipped farm in the township of Yorkville, Racine county, but the fervor of his faith often pulls him away from the homeplace, and despite his sixty-four years he seeks out his countrymen even in the distant West. Five years ago Elling Eielsen visited Norway, where he was welcomed by his many friends. He is at present the real leader of the denomination frequently called "Ellingians" but whose members, as far as I know, refer to themselves as "The Friends of Hauge."[11]

The Norwegians were not fortunate in their choice of land in the township of Norway. One must have seen an American forest in order to comprehend how much work is involved in clearing such an area. The soil consists primarily of poor clay; during dry spells it cracks and becomes hard as brick. Even newly broken land yields only 10 to 12 bushels per acre while the prairies a few miles to the south yield 30 to 40 bushels the first years. Some stretches, however, are better and the lowlands provide excellent pasture and meadows. It is peculiar that the earliest settlers chose this inhospitable region when an abundance of fertile land was then available nearby at a low price. The similarity between the area and certain districts in Norway—the forests interspersed with marshes, the crystal-clear lakes and the rivers—presumably had some influence on their choice.

At present about forty Norwegian farmers are located in the northern and western part of the township of Norway. If we figure five persons to a family, there are some 200 countrymen of ours in the township. The local congregation includes five families of the original Muskego settlement as well as the Norwegians in the township and village of Waterford. Five families belong to the Augustana Synod. The rest have joined the Missouri Synod or the Norwegian Evangelical Lutheran Church.[12] The people are good-natured, plain, sober, and hospitable. They are in good financial circumstances. Most of them own, free of debt, the land they cultivate, together with buildings and animals. The primitive log cabins have gradually given way to more comfortable houses. Moral conditions are commendable. An older settler says: "During the twenty-five years I have lived here no Norwegian has been charged with violating the law; theft is unheard of; and only one illegitimate child has been born—to a woman seduced by an American. In politics all are Republicans, with the possible exception of three doubtful ones."

As one of the most prominent men in the township we must mention

Postmaster Peder Jacobsen. He was born in the parish of Holden and was for some time located in Larvik as a wheelwright. Good reports from America induced him to emigrate. Concern for his children's future was a particularly potent factor in this connection. He set off with 400 *speciedaler*, half of which went for tickets. Soon after his arrival he was taken sick, and times were hard for him and his family. But amidst all the hardships he was comforted by the fact that generous countrymen reached him a helping hand. After a year and a half he regained his health, and his economic situation gradually improved. Now Jacobsen is a well-to-do man who is highly respected and has held many positions of trust. He has given much care to the upbringing of his children and all of them have received a good education. The youngest son, who has been trained for business, has attended schools in Milwaukee and Chicago. A daughter is married to Pastor Tobias Larsen and a son, who lives in the township, is married to a daughter of Mathias Himoe, the first emigrant from Overhalla in Namdalen.

If we were to sketch the life story of each settler we would find that the great majority of them managed to attain their present independent position through strenuous toil and hardship, often mixed with sorrow and privation. When we listen to the stories of the old settlers and consider the vast areas they have cleared, we are forced to wonder at the toughness and determination which have produced such a remarkable result: the transformation of miles of wilderness into meadows and grainfields and all this in less than thirty years by a comparatively small band of immigrants, many of whom brought no other capital than willingness to work and a pair of strong arms. Their industry and determination have been well rewarded. Despite unfavorable natural conditions the economic situation within the township is now such that, without exception, all the farmers can be described as well-off—not one of them is poor or dependent on public aid.

As one of the pathfinders for the migration from Upper Telemark we must here make mention of Gunder Gautesen Midbø. He had been a schoolteacher in the parish of Tinn before he came to the Fox River settlement in 1837. There he worked as a day laborer until he moved to Norway, Wisconsin, in 1842. He now owns a farm of 200 acres and is respected as a sociable, prudent, and enlightened man.

The reader has, no doubt, noticed that Upper Telemark—especially Tinn and neighboring areas—very early sent large groups of emigrants to America. We may assume that various conditions worked together to lead people in these parishes to emigrate rather than remain in their homeland. A native of Telemark, now living in America, has this to say on the subject:

"You ask about the causes of the considerable migration from Telemark which began in 1837 and continued in the following years. In order to give a satisfactory answer to this question I feel that we must go fairly far back in time. At the beginning of the present century, Bernt Blair of Brevik and Didrich Cappelen of Skien already owned vast acres of land in those districts.[13] Even many of those who in theory owned their land had signed contracts for the sale of their timber on such terms that they actually were nothing but leaseholders. Cattle-raising, the natural industry for these regions, was neglected—as was agriculture. Most of these farmers gained nothing from the exploitation of their forests except what they earned through contract work, timber-cutting, hauling, and floating timber to the mills. The pay was so poor that practically everything went 'from hand to mouth.' A great number of people—possibly the majority—were thus dependent on a few wealthy proprietors; and when business conditions were such that work in the forests ceased or was curtailed, then poverty and misery stalked through the communities.

"That was the situation up to the time when emigration began, and presumably it persisted much longer. Recurring unemployment and poverty, debt and discontent—these were the social phenomena produced by such conditions. For moneylenders, bill-collectors, and sheriffs, these years were a golden age. Then the America fever began spreading. Numbers of people crossed the ocean in the hope of finding a plot of land where they could build a home and enjoy the fruits of their labor, free from the haunting fear of maturing notes, rents, and mortgages. In Lower Telemark it was the *hoveri* (work obligations) on *Statholder* [Severin] Løvenskiold's estates which drove people away from their native land.[14] In the upper districts it was the insecure economic conditions and a gradual process of impoverishment which induced people to pack their emigrant chests. When the trail had been blazed, then undoubtedly many simply followed friends or relatives.

"I will mention another fact which touches on our present subject. It has been said that just prior to the great inflation Cappelen bought up several properties in Tinn and adjoining areas. He offered such prices and conditions that the owners believed it would be advantageous to sell. But soon the money began to decrease in value, and this decline continued until a dollar was worth no more than two Norwegian shillings.[15] Thus people sold their inherited lands for sums often amounting to hundreds of dollars—but after the inflation they had nothing left but an equal number of two-shilling pieces. Their discontent was intensified by the belief that Cappelen had had 'inside information' about what would happen and had taken advantage of people's ignorance. How far these stories are true, and how much these matters were responsible for bringing on economic ruin and general poverty I am unable to say. I was too young at the time to analyze events with much insight. But some facts are indisputable: the complaints were loud and frequent; poverty increased steadily; even skilled workers were unable to find employment, and the resultant discontent caused people to leave their native land and seek homesteads in the far West. Here, in accordance with my best judgment, is the answer to your question; and I flatter myself with the hope that my letter gives a true account of the conditions which precipitated that migration from Upper Telemark which has increased through the years."

Yorkville and Racine

TO THIS congregation belong the inhabitants of the southern part of the township of Norway, the Scandinavians in Raymond, and those few of our countrymen who live in the township of Yorkville. Settlement in this area began somewhat later than around Wind Lake because it took some time before the newcomers realized that the prairies not only are easier to put under cultivation but also are usually more fertile than the forested regions. As a consequence the first settlers from Norway preferably settled in wooded areas, near lakes, swamps, and marshes, permitting the more experienced Americans or later emigrants to occupy the plains, which only needed to be plowed and seeded to yield a rich crop. If the Scandinavians right from the beginning had known how to choose the best land, much muscle power would have been saved and many misfortunes and sorrows avoided. Most of the newcomers would quite soon have reached that level of prosperity and general contentment which they managed to achieve only after disappointments and years of struggle. "Experience is the best teacher," we are told. So it proved to be here; later emigrants knew how to profit by the mistakes of the first arrivals, and it was not long before our countrymen began to settle in regions where nature generously offers the impecunious stranger the good fortune which he seeks.

The area occupied by settlers belonging to the above-mentioned congregation consists of woodland, prairie, and marshlands in favorable proportions and must be classified as fertile in comparison with Muskego. It contains forty-four farms belonging to Norwegians and the population must approach 250. The church, a white frame building, is located near the center of the settlement, and a talented young man, Pastor [Chr.] Hvistendahl of Muskego, serves both here and in Muskego. The richest Norwegian farmer in the settlement, Mons K. Aadland, has given the congregation an organ, and his son,

Thomas Monsen, is the church organist. Most of the people belong to the Norwegian Evangelical Lutheran denomination, while seven families belong to the Augustana Synod and three are numbered among Hauge's Friends. Each Sunday the children are given instruction in religion by a qualified teacher. During the winter months the singing society gathers once a week in the schoolhouse, and important political or social questions of the day are discussed at the weekly meetings of the debating club. The level of education is rather high, mainly as a result of the influence several progressive men have had on the community. In practically every home there are newspapers, not only Norwegian but also English, and the farmers usually have some dollars to spare for good books. The economy is prosperous; many people even have money out at interest. No Norwegian has been accused of violating the law. Outbuildings are always left unlocked. Theft was unknown in this region until last spring when a newly arrived Danish family was guilty of such a crime. Moral conditions are exemplary. "The cholera took all the drunkards," one old settler related. "So now there are only sober people left, *natløberi* [bundling] would not be tolerated, and only one illegitimate child has been born since the Norwegians came here. Among our countrymen there are no poor people receiving public support. All subscribe to Republican principles with the exception of one fellow who 'eats cabbage soup' with the Democrats."

I wish to add some observations made by one of our countrymen living in the settlement. He says: "The stolidity and slowness which characterize the Norwegians disappear in America. The determination and energy of the American people seem to electrify the newcomer. He soon notices that the saying 'help yourself' is not mere play with words but a slogan to be followed in all the vicissitudes of life. Necessity compels him to become more enterprising; the force of example strengthens and stimulates him; old prejudices vanish; energy awakens; dejection gives place to buoyancy; he tackles one or another worthwhile job; if the first or second attempt does not succeed, he turns to something else, because here work is respected and all legitimate pursuits, except the sale of liquor, are looked upon as honorable. As a result, many who back home might have become a public burden here become useful citizens. All class barriers are broken down. No one asks about birth or family connections. A good character and sobriety are everywhere the best recommendations. The well-informed man is respected, but he is also required to give proof of his ability through the spoken or written word or some useful activity. Emphasis is placed on the practical aspects of life; theories are taken into account only in so far as their utility is demonstrable.

"Formerly I believed that it was the rich and the official classes who impoverished the common man in Norway. I discovered long ago that this idea was wrong. At least it was not the case in that part of the country where I was born. If respect for manual labor could be enhanced back home and things done with more energy and initiative, then Norway would provide her people with their daily bread just as well as any other land. In this country the ambitious young man tries to discover early what type of activity will bring him the best salary; he tackles any kind of work within his range of abilities which promises a good income.

"At home, on the other hand, the knack of living on society like a parasite seems to have been elevated to a science; and the man who does not need 'to struggle for existence' is regarded as fortunate. A bit of schooling, instead of acting as a spur to greater industry, is regarded as a license to lead a life of ease, free from all manual work. This attitude tends to depress and demoralize the laboring class, which, as a consequence, performs its work grudgingly, becomes listless and dispirited, gives up the hope of a brighter future, and looks with envious eyes at the higher classes. The phrase 'only a working man or a peasant from the country' expresses the arrogant attitude taken toward all manual labor. So great is the power of custom that even sensible people often sincerely pity the man who is forced by circumstances to earn his livelihood by the labor of his hands. Friends and relatives deem it their duty to free a person 'who has enjoyed the benefit of a better upbringing' from a position which prejudice looks upon as unfortunate, even dishonorable. Here in America it happens quite frequently that the man who sat behind a desk yesterday is seen out in the field today; the man who recently stood behind the counter in a store can later labor with a spade in his hands; even officers of justice are often seen in a shop, and it does not occur to anyone that these men are to be pitied, nor do they themselves feel that they have been wronged by fate.

"The bonds which fettered economic liberty in Norway have gradually been loosened and it is to be hoped that the authorities there will continue along the path of liberalism. The Norwegian laws are excellent—in some respects even better than the American. But of what avail are good laws when the very source of wealth and progress—labor—is held in contempt. An improved educational system will harm rather than benefit the land, because as soon as a young man has acquired a bit of schooling Prejudice will come and shout in his ears that now he must never dishonor learning by engaging in manual work. Thus there will be one more drone to eat away at the people's accumulated supplies. It is work that has made the northern states rich and powerful. In the South, on the other hand, where labor is held to be a curse, misery and discontent prevail. Education ought to be the friend and adviser of labor; but in Norway intellectual culture breeds dislike of constructive work and a penchant for luxurious living. If someone had the courage to break with old prejudices, retribution in the form of exclusion from 'good society' would undoubtedly be meted out. This prejudice is one of the people's most dangerous enemies. Until labor is elevated to the same rank as those activities which now are held fitting for the 'man of good breeding,' we will always hear rumors from Norway about hard times, hunger, unemployment, discontent, and emigration on a large scale.''

The statements above are included to show how a certain Norwegian American feels about conditions in his home country. The man quoted has seriously followed developments in both Norway and America. It is quite understandable that a stay of many years in the New World should have modified his earlier ideas about the necessary conditions for happiness and well-being. It seems to me, however, that he uses rather too strong terms when describing the contempt in which he thinks labor is held in the old country. His contentions are untenable, at least as far as many regions are concerned. The backwardness of the country, the ever-spreading poverty and consequent discontent must be ascribed to other causes. Possibly agricultural economists and popular writers all the way down to authors of cookbooks and advocates of improvement in porridge-making may at times have misguided rather than guided the public.

In practically every Norwegian settlement there are some men who have become well known, not only in the immediate neighborhood but far beyond its borders, because they played a prominent part in the founding and later development of the community, possessed exceptional initiative and ability, or lived an especially varied life.* Such a man is M. K. Aadland whom we mentioned earlier, and therefore I will give a brief sketch of his life.

Mons Knudsen Aadland, commonly known among the Yankees as Monsen, was born in Os parish in Søndre Bergenhus *amt* (county). I will let him speak: ''I felt that my farm was too small and that the prospects for my children were poor. My uncle, Nils Langeland, was versed in languages and read books in German and English about conditions in America. His accounts stirred in me and many others the desire to emigrate. Knud Slogvigen, from the parish of Tysvær near Stavanger, had been in America and came home for a visit. Some men from Os were sent to talk with him. The information they received further encouraged us to emigrate. Nils Langeland, Nils Frøland, and I joined together and went to Bergen in April, 1837, to seek passage. Eighty-four emigrants—mostly from Os but a few from Voss—assembled there. I had with me my wife and five children, and at the time of departure I had about 1,000 *speciedaler* in my pocket. Ole Rynning, well known in immi-

**Billed-Magazin*, December 24, 1868.

grant history, left Bergen that spring in our party. On the ocean we were rammed by a large East India freighter. Our ship was badly damaged, but after nine weeks at sea we reached New York without further mishap. From there we went on to Chicago. A few immigrants from Fjellberg stopped in Rochester, New York, but later moved to Indiana. Because he lacked the means to continue the trip, Nils Langeland and family left us in Detroit and settled in Pontiac, Michigan. As far as I know, he was the first Norwegian to settle in that state. At present a few scattered Scandinavian settlements can be found there. The rest of us went on to Chicago. Here we agreed to send several men, among them Ole Rynning, to look for suitable land. They struck off in a southerly direction through the state of Illinois, to the Beaver Creek area. On their return they reported that they had found fertile government land which was for sale. We packed our goods and followed the leaders through wild, pathless regions, reaching our destination after a long, arduous trip. Today, transported by the magic of steam-power, passengers can cover that distance in as many hours as we required days. While they partake of all the conveniences which science and art can offer, we were forced to work our way laboriously through the wilderness, dependent exclusively on our own ingenuity.

"The township of Beaver Creek lies about seventy miles directly south of Chicago, in Iroquois county, near the Indiana boundary. The land is flat and low, and as drainage is poor, there are many swamps and marshes. Conditions were miserable and soon discontent became general. Sickness broke out and fourteen or fifteen bodies were buried in a short period of time. About a year after our arrival, Ole Rynning also succumbed to the swamp fever.[16] His death was no small loss to the settlement. The axe was the only tool available for either making coffins for the dead or building houses for the survivors. Many of our group left without reimbursement for either their work or their money losses. No one wished to buy land in a region where the pestilent atmosphere threatened the settlers with death and destruction. They moved to the Fox River settlement in La Salle county, about ninety miles northwest of Beaver Creek. Only a few of us continued for two or three years to risk the dangers of staying on in the region.

"I, Mons Aadland, was one of the last to leave the settlement; in 1840 I moved to the town of Raymond, Racine county, Wisconsin, where I have lived ever since. By that time my earthly possessions had been reduced to three dollars in cash and several head of cattle. When we bear in mind that I had already reached the advanced age of forty-four years, had a large family to care for, and was noticeably declining in physical strength, then it will be understandable that I looked at the future with considerable uneasiness. But the acts of the past could not be altered. Complaints would cure nothing, and the dejection which breeds inertia would assuredly lead to ruin. With industry and thrift as allies I did not give up hope for better times. By the sale of cattle I obtained the means to buy eighty acres of land and some food supplies. Slowly things improved. A simple log cabin was for a long time my family's only accommodation. Our acreage increased through later purchases. The area—a combination of woodland and prairie—was fertile and rewarding to the farmer's toil. Little by little I approached my goal: an independent position in life, free of financial worries. After three or four years I could be called a well-to-do man. My success gave me strength for new exertions, and fifteen years after my arrival in Raymond I owned, free of debt, 800 acres of land equipped with buildings, horses, cattle, and implements."

Thus far Mr. Aadland's own words. It might be added that the value of his possessions, before he began dividing them among his children, would amount to about $40,000 at current prices. The aged gentleman now lives near his two sons on a well-stocked farm surrounded by the comforts which prosperity can afford. The elder son, Knud Aadland, runs the country store and post office at North Cape. He is a respected, dependable man who has been given many positions of trust by the people of the township. The younger son, Thomas, lives on a well-kept farm and is in good financial circumstances. The youngest daughter is married to Pastor A. Preus of Coon Prairie. Another daughter, now deceased, was married to Ole Ellingsen Spillum, the son of one of the earliest settlers in Racine county. Knud Langeland, the able editor and publisher of *Skandinaven* (Chicago), the most popular Norwegian newspaper in the Northwest, is a half brother of Mr. Aadland.[17]

A number of the earliest immigrants succumbed to the various hardships of life on the frontier; but many of those who survived have in the course of years advanced to positions worthy of respect. They have assisted their countrymen who arrived later. The influence which wealth, wisdom, and generosity create have given many of them an honored name in our land; and not a few of them are connected with the most respectable families through blood, friendship, or marriage. Even a seat in the Norwegian *Storting* (Parliament) seldom brings such distinction to a man in Norway as some of the early immigrants have achieved in the New World. The young men listen attentively to stories about the mountainous land far beyond the sea; about father's or grandfather's long journey across the vast ocean; about the vicissitudes, dangers, and hardships of pioneer life. The young girl whose blue eyes and flowing locks indicate Nordic descent has heard from mother or grandmother about the land of her forefathers with its steep mountains on whose peaks the snow never melts, about the deep valleys, the swift streams, and the foaming waterfalls in that land beyond the sea, far toward the rising sun, where her relatives once had their home. Interwoven with these stories is the name of that early settler who, with a letter or even just a greeting sent back to Norway, caused her parents and perhaps a whole group of their neighbors to leave the land of their fathers. Many of the men who preceded the great exodus from the North now rest in their graves; but their experiences form the core of those tales which will pass from father to son through many generations and will serve as sources for a Scandinavian-American immigrant history. Many of our countrymen who crossed the Atlantic decades ago to seek a home in America have founded populous settlements; they have, with their reports, encouraged hundreds, not to say thousands, to pack and leave their native land. The influence they have had on the fate of multitudes of people will preserve their names from oblivion for a long time to come. These observations explain why the lives of certain individuals have been given far more space in these pages than would otherwise be justified.

Several developments closely connected with the settling of the Yorkville area and the emigration from the northern parts of the Trondheim diocese will be discussed now.*

In the year 1837 Hans Barlien emigrated. He was born in Overhalla, lived for some time in Trondheim, then in Christiania, and finally on Overgaard in Namdalseidet, Trøndelag. As a champion of ideas from the period of the French Revolution he attracted many friends, who were commonly referred to as "Barlinians."[18] Endowed as he was with great natural gifts which found expression in literature as well as in technology, he was much admired by the populace while many—especially among the clergy and state officials—opposed his free religious and political thinking. Barlien had his own printing equipment on Overgaard; and the daring opinions which he often expressed in speech and print involved him in many legal entanglements from which he usually escaped with limbs intact thanks only to his exceptional wit and ingenuity. Finally—wearying of the interminable wrangle—he emigrated as an elderly man to America, from which he carried on an active correspondence with sympathizers and friends in Norway. It seems that the institutions in the New World were exactly to his liking. He wrote: "Now at last I can breathe freely: here no one is persecuted for his religious beliefs; everyone can worship God in accordance with his own views; pickpockets, lawyers, conscienceless bill-collectors, morally depraved officials and loafers are shorn of all power to harm the people. No restrictions are put on economic activity, everyone enjoys the fruits of his labors, and a wise, liberal set of laws protects the American citizen against abuses by the authorities. The so-called free Norwegian constitution has as yet merely served to burden the people with

*_Billed-Magazin_, January 2, 1869.

heavier taxes, increase the salaries of officials, and boost extravagance and laziness. The consequences will soon be obvious; such a state of affairs must of necessity lead to general ruin."

His letters generally breathed bitter hatred of Norway; they were reproduced and read in wide circles, but very few people had confidence in the accounts of the old agitator. Not until Ole Rynning's book became known were the masses of people in the northern part of the Trondheim district really struck by the America fever. A long time passed, however, before anyone dared leave the homeland and settle in the distant West. But at last Elling Hendriksen Spillum decided to find out whether conditions beyond the sea were really such as reports would have him believe. Accompanied by his second-oldest son and Lars Evensen Survigen, he left for America in 1844. After having visited various parts of Illinois, all three returned in the fall of the year to Norway, where their reaction to America was awaited with great interest. Survigen advised people not to emigrate, and it was then said that he had been paid by the Norwegian government to spread unfavorable rumors about America. Elling Spillum, on the other hand, sold farm and property and, with his family, prepared to leave. The following spring he set off, accompanied by Ole Ingebritsen Homstad, Mathias Lorentzen Himoe, and Mads Rynningen with their families—a total of twenty people, all from Overhalla. These men were rather well-off financially. It was long-standing discontent with general conditions, as well as Barlien's letters and Rynning's book, which induced them to leave their native country and seek homesteads in the New World. During the years immediately following, only a few people from Overhalla and neighboring regions left—most of these being tied to the earlier emigrants by either blood or close friendship. Since 1850, however, the migration from this part of the country has in some years reached considerable proportions.

Elling Hendriksen Spillum, the leader of the little group from Overhalla which served as an advance guard for the migration from the northern part of the country, was a levelheaded, thoughtful, enlightened, and cautious man. Judged by the standards of his home district at the time, he would be considered well-to-do. With his family, consisting of his wife and three sons, he settled in Yorkville. After all travel expenses had been covered, he had about 1,000 *speciedaler* left, which enabled him to buy 160 acres of land, implements, and cattle. Elling Spillum could thus start in far better circumstances than most of his fellow emigrants. But it should be borne in mind that on his arrival he was fifty-seven years old and his wife sixty, and that two of his sons were almost blind. These were the conditions under which the elderly man had to build himself a new home in this country. Three years later his son-in-law, Peter Anziøn, with his family, came to join them. They agreed to farm on a cooperative basis and share profits in a brotherly manner. Old Elling, however, was not long permitted to enjoy the fruits of his labor. He died after a stay of five years in Yorkville; we will therefore turn to the fate of his survivors. We will not go into details but merely note that his three sons and his son-in-law worked together for six years before they decided to dissolve partnership and operate their farms separately. The oldest son, Ole Spillum, is now a well-to-do man who besides owning his farm with equipment has considerable money out at interest. And I suppose that Elling's son-in-law, Peter Anziøn, can even be called a rich man. At the last census his farm was assessed at $12,000 to which can undoubtedly be added $4,000 or $5,000 extra in order to reach a true evaluation. His annual income, over and above what went to the upkeep of his family, was put at $1,600 by the assessors.

Often long biographies are written of men whom only fate or good connections have elevated to distinguished positions in society, after which they live and die without ever embarrassing the world with inconvenient ideas. After the oratorical bombast due the memory of such a man is over, everybody agrees that the deceased was a great, good, and noble man, though no one can explain exactly why. But if a man is entitled to be enrolled among "distinguished Norsemen" because he led an eventful life and influenced the fate of countless people, then many of the first emigrants deserve such an honor despite the fact that they are little known in their native land because they neither held nor sought public office. What they did, in defiance of all evil prophesies, was to risk the fateful step of crossing the ocean and settling in the red man's land. Soon their good reports of America reached the home community, arousing in others a desire to depart. In time these others were followed by relatives and friends. Thus the emigrant stream, with a few irregularities, has continued to grow steadily until, in the year 1866—because of crop failure and consequent inflated prices—it suddenly swelled to proportions which aroused general consternation. It is clear to me that Elling Spillum from Overhalla must be considered the man who gave the original impulse to migration from areas north of Trondheim. Except for this man's trip to the West, his later emigration, and his extensive correspondence, the America fever would presumably not have struck these northerly regions so early, and many of the men and women who joined the emigrant ranks would still be tilling the old home fields. Certain apparently insignificant events in this man's life thus came to exert a decisive influence upon the future of hundreds of his fellow citizens.

Like their elder brother, Elling Spillum's two youngest sons live on a well-kept farm which not only gives them a good income but leaves them a considerable annual surplus. Both of them have now been completely blind for many years, and a feeling of sadness instinctively gripped me when, during my stay in Yorkville, I had the opportunity to visit these two brothers whom fate apparently had given so heavy a cross. But if it is true that only those are unfortunate who think they are, then undoubtedly many who have the great gift of sight might envy these two men their peace of mind and their trust in the will of Providence. "Our father's hope that he would prepare a better future for his children by going to America has been fulfilled as far as we are concerned," said the younger brother "and we can never thank God enough for the fact that he gives us our daily bread." In these men creative imagination, keen thinking, good memory, and an unbelievably fine sense of touch have combined to take the place of sight. The two blind brothers have built the house in which they live, and no one can deny that everything, even down to the most delicate carpentry work, has been well done. The older brother, Hendrik, now a man of fifty years, is a master of all sorts of woodwork. Not only is he a wheelwright and cooper but also a cabinetmaker. Even experts declare that if anything distinguishes his work from that of seeing artisans it is the greater care with which his products are made. He has invented most of the implements he works with and often employs methods which bear testimony to exceptional keenness. Various works of his reveal the real artist, and some farm implements he has made are both original and practical. This blind man has also tried his talents in the field of mechanics. He has made a model for an original kind of sawmill which has been declared a masterpiece.

It has already been said that the Scandinavian settlers in the Muskego and Yorkville parishes live at present in good economic circumstances.* One of the Norwegians who first settled here reports as follows in this connection: "Most of us were poor when we came to America, and we have also had our share of the trials of pioneer life. But work is the mother of good fortune. Industry and thrift have helped us forward so that all the people I know in the region must be called prosperous and many are rich. Not a few have money out at interest and no one needs public aid. There are among us not only farmers but also others who have put their savings into government bonds; and we have confidence that the government will not bring disgrace upon America by defaulting. The people from 'the high North' in this area hold their own very well in comparison with our neighbors of other nationalities. The assessment lists prove definitely that there are comparatively larger fortunes among the Scandinavians than among others, and this fact gains significance when it is borne in mind that many of us came here empty-handed while many of our neighbors brought means which enabled them to buy land and equipment and build houses immediately.

**Billed-Magazin*, January 9, 1869.

"The creditable position of our people must be ascribed to hard work combined with frugality. Our countrymen who came in the early days were characterized by diligence and plain living. They were satisfied with little and toiled on in the hope of a better future. The women spun and wove what was needed for the family, and the man of the house required but little help, as he not only knew how to till the soil but was usually his own carpenter and blacksmith. Industry combined with sensible economic management will quite definitely lead to wealth in a country like America. It also deserves mention that the Scandinavians in the neighborhood are peaceful people. Lawsuits, wrangling, and quarrels are common among others; but if we are left alone by our neighbors—a mixture of Germans, Irishmen, and Yankees—we offend no one, and legal prosecutions among Norwegians here are never heard of. Before my departure for America the spreading poverty, the many lawsuits brought by moneylenders, the increasing drunkenness and moral laxity often made me think that the Norwegians were declining rapidly; but after observing my countrymen under the more favorable conditions on this side of the ocean, I must say that there is good stuff in the mountain people. The Americans declare with great unanimity that the Scandinavians are welcome above all other Europeans as settlers in the New World. Up to now 'Norwegian honesty' has not been a mere empty phrase in these parts; I hope we will continue to deserve this good reputation among our fellow citizens. To be sure, many a vagabond has joined the migration from Norway—especially in later years—but, fortunately for the country districts, the large cities attract the scum and the sediment of the immigrant stream. The more secluded places are thus generally spared."

Before leaving the Yorkville congregation I will ask the reader to visit with me one of the homes in the settlement. We will call on one of the prosperous farmers. His name is of no importance to us, as we desire only to get a generalized picture of the life led by our countrymen. We are already in front of the house. It has a very fine appearance and in general resembles the homes of well-to-do farmers in the neighborhood of Christiania. On entering, we are hospitably received, and when the people learn that we are countrymen of theirs it is as if old friends have met after a long separation. Very soon we are engaged in an interesting conversation about conditions among Norwegians in America. Nothing betrays the fact that we are thousands of miles away from our homeland. Language, dress, even the furniture and its arrangement in the house are reminiscent of the land beyond the sea. And when, added to all this, one finds familiar Norwegian books on the shelves, then he forgets for a brief moment that he lives as a stranger in a foreign land, far from his native soil. Spinning wheel and loom speak of home industries, and that they are not mere showpieces is proved by masses of yarn and bundles of home-woven cloth whose lively colors and beautiful patterns betray an artistic sense not present in every Norwegian valley.

Our friendly host shows us around the farm; we follow him to the barn where we find twenty cows all apparently contented as they stand there along the limestone walls. We let the farmer speak: "I find that cows pay well for their upkeep, but you must take good care of them if cattle-raising is to succeed. I grind grain with the aid of a windmill and mix the grain with finely-cut hay to make the mash used as fodder. When I get an apparatus for warming water close to the barn door, the work will be easier. It is best for the farmer to tend the cattle himself. We Norwegians help the women too little with work like this which, following our old country ideas, falls to their lot. It takes some time before a farmer can raise a superior herd of cattle which pay for the trouble and expense of keeping them. But once this is done, the cow-barn can become his greatest source of income. I have just barely gotten a start; but still, from a week's milk supply I sell fifty dollars worth of butter. The Norwegians' care of cattle is not to be sneered at. Even the Yankees are beginning to realize this. I have in mind, of course, cattle-raising as it was pursued in those parts of Norway where it was a principal source of livelihood."

We have already mentioned that with Elling Spillum's departure from Overhalla the emigrant movement from that northern area had its beginning. We will now consider the development of the movement in neighboring communities.

Old Elling had given a solemn promise to his many friends in Norway that after his arrival in the distant West he would send back reliable reports about conditions there. True to his promise, he wrote frequently to his acquaintances beyond the sea and this correspondence was later continued by his son Ole. The America letters were widely circulated and copies were sent to distant places. Elling's opinions about the New World were regarded as absolutely reliable because everybody knew him to be a sensible and thoughtful man. They realized that the Spillum family had not left because of need, and any thought of deception was brushed away by the elderly gentleman's honorable reputation. The first mile which leads away from the old home is a long mile. Many talked of leaving, and their hearts were full of longing to see the promised land, but it seemed that for a long time no one had the courage to hazard this game of fortune. Ole Johnson Hallem from Stod, however, finally took the decisive step and left Norway in 1849, leaving his wife and children behind. They followed him to Houston county, Minnesota, the following summer. A year later, in 1850, Isak Olsen Kne and his wife emigrated. She was the daughter of Anders Aasved, representative to the *Storting* from Stod. Their departure was apparently caused by economic pressure and unfavorable prospects for the future. Only a few persons from this parish said farewell to old Norway in 1852, and it seemed as if the migration from the region had come to an end. But then Lars Aasved, one of the earlier immigrants, wished to visit his native sod again. He returned from America to his home district, and in the spring of 1857 he again left Norway, this time accompanied by about fifty of his countrymen, mostly from Stod. They settled in northern Iowa and southern Minnesota, and since then the district of Stod has contributed an annual contingent to the population of the western continent.

The first people from Beitstad who left home for America were Ole Karstensen Mindrum and Nikolai Haugen. This happened in 1851 and 1852. Both of them were heads of families and had lived in poor circumstances in Norway. After this no one emigrated from Beitstad until 1859, and during the Civil War years only a few from this district ventured to come to America. When peace returned, the Norwegian immigrant stream suddenly swelled to proportions previously unheard of. Among the multitudes who turned their backs on their native land in 1866 were some fifty people from Beitstad, nine of whom were heads of families. Only two of these belonged to the freeholding class. The rest were *husmænd* (cotters), *inderster* (lodgers), and day laborers.

Snåsa is one of the districts which up to now has played only a small part in the emigration movement. This is all the more remarkable when we bear in mind that Ole Rynning was from this area and that his book, *True Account of America*, might have been expected to excite wanderlust. The reading of his book did in fact stir up a real America-craze in his home district. "I believe that for a while," says one eyewitness, "half of the people in Snåsa had lost their senses. Nothing was talked of except the land that flows with milk and honey. Our pastor, Ole Rynning's father, tried to cure the fever. Even from the pulpit he admonished people to be calm and pictured the hardships of the journey and the ferocity of the American Indians in the most lurid colors. But this was merely pouring oil on the fire. Ole Rynning was one of those philanthropists for whom no sacrifice is too great if it can only redound to the benefit of others. He was in the full sense of the word a friend of the people, a spokesman for the poor, a man in whose heart there was no guile. Thus his character was judged, and people overlooked his lack of practical ability and his helplessness in the face of reality. But then came the report: Ole Rynning is dead! The woeful news spread sorrow throughout the neighborhood, for very few have been loved as this man was loved. Now the desire to emigrate cooled; and many of those who previously had championed the cause of migration most strongly shuddered now at the thought of America's horrible climate which had taken from them their friend 'Ola' in his prime—a man blessed with all the qualities which arouse the esteem and respect of his fellowmen."

The above-mentioned Anders Aasved, the father of Lars Aasved who went to America, was in many respects a remarkable man. In the *Storting*, he was the Jaabæk of his time and no one can remember that a "yes" ever escaped his lips when the pensioners passed in review before the appropriations committee.[19] It was still regarded as a sign of refinement to make fun of peasant representatives to the *Storting* and Aasved was especially the object of their ridicule. This scorn wounded the proud man. Broken in body and spirit he returned to his home; but there, also, many misunderstood the enthusiasm for reform which got him embroiled in so much trouble. Aasved was richly endowed by nature and was well-informed for a man of his class. He was good-natured, kindly disposed, helpful, and tolerant. When it was a question of relieving the misery of others he would give his last shilling. But not everyone thought or acted as he did. Some of the most unprincipled men in the neighborhood wished to bring about the ruin of the broken and dispirited man. They succeeded only too well, because Aasved knew little about money matters. "I can remember," says one of his contemporaries, "with what infernal glee his maligners gathered about the block when the representatives of the law auctioned off the family possessions piece by piece. One wealthy farmer could not control his feelings but exclaimed—accompanying his words with loud derisive laughter—'now we have fixed Old Man Aasved; he can't run away to Christiania in his bare shirt; and the *Storting* will be well rid of him.' No wonder his children longed to get away from a country where the family had been mistreated and persecuted in the name of the law. The son had fallen heir to some of his father's earlier prestige. This explains why, on his return, he was able to induce so many of his acquaintances to leave their homeland and settle in America."

Racine county is located along the western shore of Lake Michigan and is the second county from the southern boundary of the state.* It comprises an area of only 324 square miles, making it one of the smallest counties in the state, and it contains only nine townships. There is a well-balanced intermingling of woodland and prairie within its borders; and several lakes, combined with many rivers and brooks, do much to enhance the beauty of the area. Along the shores of Lake Michigan are large forests of oak, walnut, beech, birch, and various other kinds of trees.

Settlement in the county began in 1834, after which clearing and cultivation proceeded rapidly. Fertile soil encouraged immigration and the location along Lake Michigan made communication easy. The counties of Racine and Kenosha constituted one administrative district until 1850, when a partition took place.

Billed-Magazin, January 23, 1869.

The topsoil consists of rich mold two to five feet deep with clay or gravel as subsoil. Agriculture pays well and is carried on with skill and understanding. Because of the large grassy openings the farmers have lately taken up cattle-raising. Some areas in the northern part are not well suited to growing grain but there are fine meadows which produce an abundance of hay.

In 1850 Racine county had only about 15,000 inhabitants. This figure increased to 21,000 during the next decade, while at present the population presumably numbers some 30,000. The people are enlightened, considerate, and enterprising. Everywhere you find that they are anxious to introduce new ways of doing things. On the whole, farming is given much thought and home industries are more highly developed here than in most other districts of the Northwest.

The people of the county have good connections with the important trading centers. The Racine and Mississippi Railway cuts through the county from east to west and at the port of Racine it connects with the so-called Lake Shore Railroad (Chicago-Milwaukee Railroad) which runs north and south along the lake. The country roads are quite well maintained and there is lively traffic on Lake Michigan. Some years ago there was talk of constructing a railroad from Burlington on the Racine-Mississippi Railroad which was to follow the Fox River valley through the towns of Rochester and Waterford and farther on along the western shore of Wind Lake to Milwaukee. However, the deceitful actions of those who proposed the plan stopped everything and the project went up in smoke. But the matter will likely be taken up again and carried to completion.

The county seat, Racine, is located where the Root River empties into Lake Michigan, sixty miles north of Chicago and twenty-five miles south of Milwaukee. The Frenchman Antoine Ouilmette is usually held to have been the first inhabitant of Racine. He came from Cross Point in 1834 and settled about half a mile beyond the present boundaries of the city. Two years later, in 1836, lots were surveyed and a post office established. By 1840 about 300 people lived there. Ten years later the population had risen to 4,000 and by 1860 to 8,000. The rapid progress of the city in trade and industry and the consequent influx of people would lead us to estimate that the population at present is over 12,000.

Few places have as beautiful a location as Racine. The broad streets and the avenues lined with trees stretch into the distance along the lakeshore, and from the heights there is a magnificent view of the neighboring landscape. One traveller has given expression to his enthusiasm for the beauty of the city and its surroundings in the following words: "Racine rests in royal beauty on a throne of rolling hills with the mirror of the lake's surface at her feet. Added to this is an excellent harbor, lively trade, great industrial development, an energetic and enlightened population, cultivated social life, excellent schools, a fertile countryside, railway connections and water communications, ever-increasing commercial activity—everything combines to make Racine a pleasant abode for businessmen and investors alike who may wish to enjoy the fruits of their earlier work undisturbed by the pursuits of everyday life."

A great number of Scandinavians are to be found in Racine. At a later opportunity we will visit these countrymen of ours and tell our friends both here and abroad about their condition and their activities in the New World.

Waterford is a town located on the Fox River in the township of the same name. There are some Scandinavians here who have affiliated in church affairs with their countrymen in Norway township. The population of the village in 1860 numbered a little over 400 while it is now about 800. Within its boundaries are three flour mills, a machine shop, and ten stores.

Tobias Egeberg, a goldsmith from Christiania, came to America three years ago and is now doing business as a gold and silversmith in company with watchmaker Sigvart Rastad from Kongsvinger. They have done well during the short while they have been here. Shoemaker Nils Peter Hansen of Christiania also came from Norway three years ago and now has his own shop. Business is good and he is well satisfied here in America. Among the merchants, Ole Heg and Martin Skoffstad are most prominent. They have a larger turnover than any others in Waterford and enjoy general respect. Halvor Olsen from Solør has the largest tailor shop in town; he owns property in Waterford as well as a farm nearby and is said to be well-off. Blacksmith Iversen, a Dane, operates a carriage factory and is an industrious and wealthy man. Colonel Hans Heg's widow makes her home in Waterford, surrounded by the comforts which money can command.

A Little Excursion into the Past

OUR LAST visit was in Racine county, Wisconsin.* Now we will again take to the road and cover the country from north to south, from east to west; wherever we meet Scandinavians we will stop to have a talk with them. We can bring them greetings from countrymen in distant parts, and among them there may even be a near relative, a dear friend, or an old acquaintance. There is something remarkable about the early groups of emigrants. They form a sort of fraternity. They know each other and often exchange greetings even though one may live by the shores of Lake Michigan and the other far west in Iowa. One might be found up north near the Wisconsin forests while the other lives on the farthest frontiers of civilization beyond the Mississippi. No matter whom we may happen to meet—whether on our wanderings we first run into a Norwegian "Ole," a Danish "Mr. Sørensen," or a Swedish "Mr. Swanson"—this we will leave to chance and merely collect whatever of interest we may find along our path which will enable us to tell our friends about old times and new, the lore of the past and the events of the present, the deeds of those who are gone and the achievements of their descendants.

Originally our destination was Jefferson Prairie in Rock county, Wisconsin; but by chance we made a detour to Dane county and there we met a man who, though no Methuselah, was so old that he could not remember his age. He did, however, recall this much from his own past, that he had come with the first ship which brought emigrants from Norway to America. When others confirmed the truth of his story, this chance meeting made us think of the many thousands who have left their native land since that little vessel set its course westward from Stavanger to bring a handful of our countrymen across the vast ocean to a continent which at the time was less known to the average

**Billed-Magazin*, January 30, 1869.

man in Norway than the interior of Africa or Australia is today. We who have undertaken to collect historical data on the emigration movement dwell with special fondness on that particular event. This little group, usually styled "the Sloopers," left their old homes nearly half a century ago as the advance guard of a great migration.

Their voyage across the sea, their arrival in America, and their later experiences in the land of the red man—all these events offer so many interesting details that we confidently invite the reader to look more closely at them and at the results which followed in their wake. We do this so much more willingly because the effects of this original migration can be followed into later decades. If we are to understand fully the contemporary Scandinavian emigration movement, we must make the Sloopers and their story our point of departure. But if we are to set off on the seas of historical research, we may as well begin at the beginning and go back into the dim past when a ship first carried men of our race to the North American shores. After this excursion into history, we will resume our account of the Scandinavian settlements in the United States.

In the old sagas we learn that our forefathers knew the way to America more than 800 years ago. Once when the daring seaman Bjarne Herjulfson set out for Iceland from Greenland, so it is related, he encountered fog and a stiff northerly wind which swept him far to the southwest so that he did not know where he was. The land he saw, when the weather cleared, was beyond all doubt America. He did not explore the land, however, but sailed northward in order to reach Greenland. In time Erik the Red's son, Leif, resolved to visit the regions Bjarne Herjulfson had told about; after sailing in a westerly direction until he recognized the land seen by Bjarne, he continued toward the south. The first land they found appeared very inhospitable. There were large glaciers in the interior, and between the glaciers and the shore there was solid rock. They therefore called the area Helleland (slateland). Presumably it was the shore of Labrador or Newfoundland. As they came farther south, they caught sight of a flat, forest-clad land which they called Markland, meaning "woodland." This must have been the present Nova Scotia. Finally they came to a land with level shores, partly grass-covered, partly wooded; the climate was mild and very pleasant. Since they found wild grapes there they called the place Vinland (wineland). Judging by Leif's accounts we may safely conclude that his last discovery was the coast of Massachusetts and Rhode Island, more particularly the area around Newport. These events occurred about the year 1000, and Leif Ericson is thus the first discoverer of America.

The reports about the glories of Vinland induced others to go there. They found the land inhabited by wild people, whom they apparently did not respect very highly, as they called them *skrælings*, that is, wretches or weaklings. Leif's brother Thorwald set off with thirty men and stayed in Vinland during the winter. They were careless enough to kill several natives. In order to avenge this crime the *skrælings* gathered in great numbers and showered the Norwegians with a rain of arrows, one of which struck Thorwald under the arm, inflicting a mortal wound. He was buried on a ness or headland, apparently the present Gurnet Point immediately above Cape Cod, with crosses at the head and foot of his grave. They called the place Korsnes. Thorwald Ericson was probably the first white man to die and be buried on the American continent.

Leif Ericson had another brother named Thorstein. When he died, his widow Gudrid married an Icelander called Thorfin who, because of his great courage, was given the surname Karlsefni (a model of a man). In the year 1008 he organized an expedition to Vinland, taking along his wife Gudrid and a group totalling 160. They reached their destination without mishap. In the lowlands they found self-sown wheat fields and on the hills quantities of grapes. In the rivers and along the shore there was an abundance of fish. The natives offered pelts for sale, which Thorfin and his people bought with strips of red cloth which the *skrælings* bound around their heads. Shortly after their arrival in Vinland, Gudrid gave birth to a son who was called Snorre. When three years had passed, Thorfin Karlsefni tired of America. With his wife, his son Snorre, and several others he returned to Greenland, taking along a valuable cargo. Later he settled in Iceland where a large family is descended from him and his son Snorre, the first white man born in the New World.

Soon after Thorfin's return a strong-willed woman named Freydis, together with her husband and two brothers from Iceland—Helge and Finnboge—led an expedition to Vinland. But her ambitiousness destroyed all unity. The settlers attacked and murdered each other and in the year 1015 Freydis and her followers left the colony.

After this, little is heard of Vinland despite the fact that apparently not all the settlers left when Freydis and her group departed for home. It seems that not all connections with Greenland were broken. For example, Bishop Erik of Greenland is said to have gone to Vinland in 1121. Even much later than this, Markland is mentioned. By the middle of the fifteenth century, however, all connections between Norway and Greenland had ceased and the Norse colonies in America had been left to their own fate.

In time Christopher Columbus came to Iceland and there became acquainted with the saga accounts of Vinland. They strengthened his belief that beyond the Atlantic Ocean was located a vast continent. After the Northmen abandoned America the continent was so absolutely forgotten that those who later found their way to it were classed as discoverers. Even though we must admire the courage and tenacity with which Columbus pressed on toward his goal, he really did not do anything more than the Northmen had done 500 years earlier. October 12, 1492, is, nevertheless, a great day in the history of humanity. Then it was that Columbus stepped ashore on San Salvador, thanked the Almighty, and unfolded the banner of Spain. Now developments came rapidly, with many new discoveries in the Western Hemisphere.

During the reign of Queen Elizabeth, Englishmen explored the east coast of North America and in time founded colonies at many places within the present borders of the United States. Some Scandinavians also settled in what is now New Jersey and in 1624 founded the town which still bears the name of Bergen. But since the emigration from the northern countries did not continue, it was not long before the Scandinavian element was swallowed up by the overwhelmingly English population and, to the best of my knowledge, there is nothing left now but a place-name to remind us of the settlement founded in New Jersey by our countrymen. No written records have anything to say about these colonists, their number, where they came from, the causes of their migration, or their fate in the New World.

The flourishing colonies on the east coast declared their independence on July 4, 1776, and after a long, hard war, England was forced in 1782 to surrender all her claims to them. The colonies formed a union called the United States, with a republican form of government. Since then the growth along practically all lines has been so phenomenal that the United States is now one of the great powers of the world.

About forty-five years after American independence was declared, the pioneer of the Norwegian emigration left his fatherland. In his book, *True Account of America*, Ole Rynning discussed the events connected with this migration and the results which flowed from it. Despite all my efforts, I have been unable to obtain a copy of that book in this country. But recently there was an article in *Skandinaven* which dealt with the subject. Relying on this source I will give a brief account of the first Norwegian emigrants' trip across the ocean and their fate in the new land.

In the year 1821 a man by the name of Cleng Peerson left Stavanger, Norway, for America by way of Gothenburg. After a stay of three years on this side of the Atlantic he returned to Norway in 1824. His stories about America soon aroused a desire in others to try their fortunes on the distant continent. Our good old Cleng Peerson, who only recently died in Texas, must thus be honored as the real originator and father of the migration from Norway to America. The very next year after his return to Norway, in 1825, an emigrant group consisting of fifty-two people was organized in the Stavanger area. They bought a little sloop (it is claimed that it was merely a Hardanger fishing boat; at least the vessel was built in Hardanger) for 1,800 *speciedaler*, which they loaded with iron for New York. One of the passengers, named Lars Larsen, is said to have been the actual owner, but most of the emigrants as well as the captain and the boatswain held shares in the speculation.

Remarkably enough, they left Stavanger in their little sloop, called *Restaurationen*, on the American Independence Day. They passed through the English Channel and after a few days reached the small English port of Lizard Head [Cornwall]. There they cast anchor and stayed a few days. It is said that they started to sell whiskey, which was prohibited there. When they realized that they might be arrested they scampered aboard their frail little vessel and set out upon the vast ocean.

Whatever the cause may have been—an attempt to follow the tradewinds, ignorance on the part of the skipper, or contrary winds—they went as far south as the Madeiras, which belong to Spain. Down there they found a cask of wine floating on the water. They hauled it aboard and began sampling its contents. As might be expected, the whole force got intoxicated and the ship went drifting into port like a pest ship, without commander or flag. They were notified by a German ship in the harbor that unless they wished to be greeted by the shore battery, which was already trained on them, they had better show their flag immediately. One of the passengers was sufficiently sober to find the flag and get it aloft. Some local officials (presumably revenue collectors) then came aboard and learned full particulars. During the rest of their stay in the Madeiras they were shown much friendliness. The American consul, especially, was very obliging and delegated some of his staff to show them the sights of the town, including the famous cathedral. The consul also supplied the ship with provisions and, before their departure, entertained the whole group at dinner. They arrived on a Thursday and the following Sunday they weighed anchor. As the vessel left the harbor, a salute was fired in their honor.

From then on for ten long weeks the little sloop fought the waves of the Atlantic. The winds were almost always contrary and the weather stormy. One of the emigrants has reported an odd coincidence: "We encountered four cyclone-like storms on four successive Fridays." Otherwise nothing of importance occurred. All felt well and no one died during the trip. But a child was born aboard, who is now Mrs. Margrethe Atwater of Chicago. There were thus fifty-three passengers when the emigrants, after the dangerous and adventurous journey, finally cast anchor in New York harbor at 10 o'clock on a Sunday forenoon in October, fourteen weeks after their departure from Stavanger. It has been said that the passengers, overjoyed at seeing land, again resorted to the cask of wine and that the noble juice so claimed their attention that they again failed to raise their flag while sailing up harbor. Remembering the Madeira incident, one of the passengers ran below to fetch the flag; but failing to find it, he climbed aloft and waved a gaily colored skirt in the wind. The guards on land stared in surprise at this queer banner; none of them could tell the nationality of the ship which flew such a flag. So goes the story, but according to eyewitnesses the whole thing is a fabrication built on accounts of what happened at Madeira.

In New York it caused general surprise that anyone could cross the ocean in such a small and poorly-equipped vessel. Then it was discovered that there were more passengers aboard than the law permitted, and both the captain and the ship with all its cargo were put into the hands of the authorities. But because of the immigrants' ignorance of the regulations the embargo was lifted, the captain freed, and the ship with its cargo returned to the owners. They decided to sell the vessel, but they lost on the deal since it did not fetch more than $600 or $700—a small sum compared with the purchase price.

When they arrived in New York most of the immigrants were without the necessities of life. They had neither food nor money. But their situation was rumored about and a great number of people came to the pier to see the newcomers; many gave them money so they did not suffer any want. A few days after arriving they were fortunate enough to meet a countryman of theirs with whom they could talk, the above-mentioned Cleng Peerson. A Quaker, he turned to his fellow believers, a group to whom those in need seldom appeal in vain. So much was collected on the immigrants' behalf that they were able to go on to Rochester by way of the canal, a trip which at that time cost six dollars per person. The captain, Lars Olsen, remained in New York and the mate, [Nels] Ericksen, from Bergen, returned to Norway. Except for these two the entire crew consisted of emigrants, among whom can be mentioned boatswain Johannes Stene, Niels Nielsen, Gudmund Haukaas, and Jakob Andersen.

A few of the immigrants settled in Rochester, New York. One of these, Lars Larsen, was regarded as the leader of the group and was the only one who understood any English. He died several years ago but some members of his family still live in Rochester, and others in Chicago. The rest of the group bought land five miles from Rochester in Kendall and Murray townships, paying five dollars per acre. They arrived there in November, just as winter was setting in. The country thereabouts was sparsely settled. It was difficult to secure work and still more difficult to find shelter. Twenty-four of the immigrants built a log house which was just large enough to give each person a square foot of floor space. Packed into this narrow hut the newcomers undeniably had need of much patience. Only an unshakable faith in the future could keep their spirits up under such circumstances and make their situation at all tolerable. The threshing machine had not come into use as yet and therefore the newcomers could earn a livelihood by swinging flails for the farmers in the community. As pay they received every eleventh bushel which they threshed. The next year they began clearing the acres they had bought, a slow process since the land was covered with dense forest. The next summer, however, they were able to harvest a crop on two acres, which undoubtedly gave them courage to carry on. It must be said, though, that the first four or five years brought these people many sorrows and disappointments. Like many of their countrymen who have arrived since, they wished themselves back in Norway, and with good reason. But lack of means made it impossible for them to go anywhere. And even the few who might have been able to pay the return fare knew all too well what it would mean to come back from America with empty hands. So they remained in America despite this inauspicious beginning.

Through the help of friendly neighbors and their own industry they managed to clear enough of the fertile land to produce food for themselves.* Prospects for the future became brighter; they realized that America offered the willing worker many advantages; they wrote letters back to their countrymen encouraging them to seek their fortune here. During the next few years quite a number of people did leave Norway; but they usually left independently, not in groups, generally going by way of Gothenburg, Hamburg, or LeHavre, from which ships frequently left for the United States. I will mention one man, Gjert Hovland, who during this early period left by way of Gothenburg. After his arrival he wrote numerous letters to friends in Norway. Copies were made and widely distributed in the Bergen area. Thus he came to exert great influence on the later migration from his native land.[20] One of the earliest emigrants, a man named Knud Slogvigen, paid Norway a visit in 1835. His return aroused great interest and people traveled great distances to talk with him. In this way reports about American conditions were spread among the common people of the Bergen and Kristiansand bishoprics. As a result, two emigrant ships left Stavanger the following year (1836), and in 1837 the first emigrant ship to leave Bergen set its course for America. We will have more to say about these groups later in our narrative.

Before leaving the passengers who came with *Restaurationen* we can not deny ourselves the pleasure of mentioning those members of the group who are still alive, men and women who with such endurance blazed the way for the migration from the Scandinavian countries.

In the old Norwegian settlement near Rochester, New York, are still two families which came with this first group of "America-farers," namely those of Henrik Christoffersen and Ole Johnson. Both of them have, of course, long since passed the hardship stage of pioneering and now live very well. Niels Nielson, one of the crew aboard the sloop, spent twenty-one years near

**Billed-Magazin*, February 6, 1869.

Rochester and then moved to the Norwegian settlement on the Fox River in Illinois. He has now lived there twenty years and owns one of the finest farms in the area.

Perhaps as many as fourteen of the original emigrants are still alive. Of these, four live in Kendall township, New York; eight in LaSalle county, Illinois; one in Dane county, Wisconsin; and one in California. The offspring of these first emigrants are very numerous and can be found in practically every part of the union. Most of the passengers aboard the famed Stavanger sloop came from Tysvær, Skjold parish, near Stavanger.

Jefferson Prairie

THE NORWEGIAN settlement on Jefferson Prairie covers the southern half of Clinton township, which forms the southeastern corner of Rock county, Wisconsin, and extends across the state line into Illinois, where it covers a part of Manchester township in Boone county.* Here we have the second oldest Scandinavian settlement in Wisconsin. This circumstance is of particular interest to us who are gathering material for the history of Nordic immigration, but of even greater significance is the fact that here we will meet the first Norwegian to set foot on Wisconsin soil. Since that event took place thirty years ago, thousands of Scandinavians have sought homes in this state; at present the Nordic element is increasing rapidly because of both a high birthrate and ever-increasing immigration. The number of Scandinavians in Wisconsin at present can not be determined exactly, but there have been estimates of some 70,000. Even if we have to subtract a few thousand, still the Scandinavian element is astonishingly strong when we consider the short time which has elapsed since an emigrant from the far North first turned his steps toward the Wisconsin Territory.

The man who can give the most reliable account of the Jefferson Prairie settlement is its founder, Ole Knudsen Nattestad from Veggli, Rollag parish in Numedal, who left his native land in April, 1837. We will let the man himself tell about the causes of his departure, his travel experiences, and his fate on this side of the ocean:

"As the second of three brothers I had no hereditary claim to my father's farm, which, in accordance with law and custom, went to the oldest son. My heart was set on agriculture and I hoped in time to be able to purchase a farm in my home neighborhood. Then my brother enrolled in a school for non-

**Billed-Magazin*, February 13, 1869.

Ole Knudsen Nattestad

commissioned officers in Christiania, and I was left to run the farm during his absence. I entered into this responsibility with great spirit, worked with enthusiasm to the full extent of my powers, and kept careful account of income and expenses. To my great surprise I soon noticed that, despite all my toil and sweat, progress was very slow. At the end of the year I had little or nothing left as a reward for my work. I then realized that I would get into an impossible position if I bought an expensive farm and went deeply into debt. Farming did not pay in my home district. Then I tried my luck as a tradesman and traveled around peddling goods. I made some money, but the law was against me, and I was ashamed to carry on a business which would force me to sneak about to avoid the sheriff. Next I worked a while as a blacksmith, which went well enough, but money came in very slowly. I could not carry on my craft in a town, as this was also forbidden by law.[21]

"Then my younger brother Ansten and I went to the west coast to buy sheep which we hoped to sell at a profit. While roaming around the Stavanger area we heard much talk about a land called America. It was the first time we had ever heard the name. We saw letters from Norwegians who lived in

America, and we were told that Knud Slogvigen, who had left Stavanger many years before, had recently revisited his homeland and had given such accounts of America that—despite threats of slavery, death, and disease—about 150 emigrants from the districts of Stavanger and Hardanger had boarded two brigs that very summer (1836) in order to undertake the long voyage across the ocean. This was the first large migration from Norway after the departure of the Sloopers. Everything we heard and saw was so new to us and found us so unprepared that we could not easily form a clear picture of conditions in the New World. But while spending Christmas with a member of the *Storting*, Even Nubbru, in Sigdal, we talked about the bad conditions in my home district and I hinted that fortune might favor me more in some other part of the country. Even Nubbru then remarked that no matter where I went in the world I would never find a people enjoying as good laws as the Americans. He had by chance read something on the subject in a German newspaper and greatly admired America's free institutions. This information had a magical effect on me, for I considered it unjust that Norwegian laws could forbid me to find honest employment as a craftsman wherever I wished to settle. I had confidence in Even Nubbru's judgment and added his words to what I had heard about America in the Stavanger area.

"Gradually the idea of emigrating took form in my mind; and it matured into firm determination as I thought the matter over more closely on my way home. I did not need to ask my brother Ansten a second time—he was ready to go with me immediately. He agreed to my plans, and in April, 1837, we were ready for the journey. At the time we left home we shared 800 *speciedaler*. But the sum steadily decreased as payments had to be made, and we lost more when we exchanged our money for American currency. Ansten also advanced money to pay the traveling expenses of Halsten Halvorsen Brække-Eiet, who now lives in Dodgeville and is considered an excellent blacksmith. Besides the clothes we wore, our equipment included skis and knapsacks. People looked at us with surprise, figuring that we must have lost our senses and that we ought to string ourselves up on the nearest tree so as to avoid a worse fate. We went from Rollag to Tinn on skis over the mountains and then more or less directly over hills and through forests to Stavanger, where we expected to find passage across the ocean. We did not worry much about the roads because all three of us were experienced skiers, and our baggage—a bit of food and some little things in our knapsacks—did not inconvenience us seriously.

"In Stavanger we told everyone we met that we were on our way to America and wished to secure passage across the ocean. This frankness came near wrecking our whole plan. Rumors about the three mountainmen spread throughout the town, and the authorities soon came to inspect our passport.

Now we learned that the pass issued by the sheriff was valid only for a trip to Stavanger, though the certificate from the minister, to be sure, did state that we intended to leave for America. We did not understand such matters and thought that everything was in order, especially as the testimonials we brought along certified that we were well-behaved Christians. Nothing was said to arouse our suspicion, but that evening a man came who expressed indignation at the injustice the officials were going to perpetrate. It had been decided, he said, that we should be arrested the next day and sent from sheriff to sheriff back to our home district because we were trying to leave the country without authorization. The authorities here, he said, rage against all emigration and we could not count on any mercy.

"In accordance with his advice we left Stavanger in all secrecy so as to escape the danger which threatened us. Without attracting any attention, we reached Tananger. There we met a skipper who had his boat loaded with herring, ready to sail for Gothenburg. He agreed to take us along; but when we told about our experiences in Stavanger, he became rather dubious. He praised our honesty, however, and agreed to take us aboard after we promised to assume responsibility if he got into any trouble because of us. We took proper precautions while on land and only breathed freely when we were at sea. No misfortunes met us in Gothenburg; there we secured passage on a ship carrying iron from Sweden to Fall River in Rhode Island [sic].

"The trip across took only thirty-two days and each of us paid fifty *speciedaler* for bed and board. From Fall River we went to New York, where we met some Norwegians who assisted us with counsel and advice, enabling us to reach Rochester. There we talked with several countrymen of ours who had come twelve years earlier with the sloop from Stavanger which brought the first Norwegian immigrants to America. Rochester and environs did not exactly fit our conception of the New World. Many of the first group had moved away from the oldest Norwegian settlements in Murray and Kendall townships to seek new homesteads farther west, especially by the Fox River near Ottawa, La Salle county, Illinois. The population of the latter settlement was greatly increased by the large migration from Stavanger in 1836—the year before I came—as most of those people decided to locate there. We were told about this settlement in Rochester, and there also, for the first time, we heard Chicago mentioned. We determined to go west and see what the opportunities might be.

"After we arrived in Detroit, I was out walking one day to have a look at things. There I chanced to see a person whom I immediately recognized by his clothes to be a fellow countryman from the Norwegian west coast. I greeted the man, and our meeting was as if two brothers had found each other after a long separation. He told me that he had left Bergen several months earlier together with about seventy emigrants from the environs of the city, especially from Sandanger and Voss. The whole group—of which Ole Rynning was the leader—had been in Detroit eight days waiting for passage to Chicago. Happy over so fortunate a meeting, we joined the group; now there was someone who understood the English language.

"As we were about to land in Chicago, we met Bjørn Andersen Kvelve from the Stavanger area. He had arrived in America the previous year and had visited various parts of Illinois; but everything he had seen or heard had conspired to give him a distaste for life on this side of the ocean. Broken both in body and in spirit, he stood before us an apparition of misery and conjured up a scene so terrible that it will never be erased from my memory. 'God be merciful to you,' he said. 'Here you can't get work or land or food. By no means should you go to the Fox River settlement; you will die of swamp fever there.' These words had a terrible effect on the little group, many of whom had long since lost courage. We recalled the terrible warnings from our homeland of the horrors which awaited us in America, and even the most courageous of us were, as if by magic, seized by a panic bordering on insanity. In despair the women wrung their hands and uttered heartrending shrieks; some of the men sat like immovable statues with deep despair carved in their faces, while others cursed those who had induced them to leave home. But in this critical situation Ole Rynning's largeness of spirit truly revealed itself. He stood in the midst of the group now on the border of mutiny, reassuring the fainthearted, admonishing the hesitant, and reproving the obstinate. Not for a moment did he waver; his serenity and courage, his devotion to the welfare of others calmed the spirits. The storm subsided, and discouragement gave way to confident trust.

"Some Americans whom Rynning consulted persuaded him to lead the emigrants to Beaver Creek in Iroquois county, Illinois, directly south of Chicago and close to the Indiana line. As there were some who advised against going to Beaver Creek, it was decided to send four men down to inspect the land, namely Ole Rynning, the present narrator, Nils Veste from Etne, and Ingebrigt Brudvig. The rest were to stay in Chicago until our return. After a trip of about ten Norwegian miles we came to Beaver Creek. Personally, I did not like the land, which, according to my judgment, consisted merely of sandy areas and marshes. But as the others thought the region well suited for settlement, we agreed that Nils Veste and I should stay and build a log house where the immigrants could find shelter when Rynning and Ingebrigt Brudvig, who were returning to Chicago, brought the group down. A few had already left for the Fox River settlement in the company of Bjørn A. Kvelve; but most of the party followed Rynning to Beaver Creek.

"All the land thereabouts belonged to the government and could be had at a low price. For miles around, however, there were no inhabitants; thus it was difficult to get supplies despite the fact that many in our group were quite able to pay for things. Several of them were also discontented and grumbled against Rynning and the rest of us. Everyone bought land, however, and before winter came, a sufficient number of log houses had been built. The discontent vanished eventually and everyone worked cheerfully on his own land. In the fall I went twenty-eight miles farther west to secure work. A bit later I returned to visit the settlement. Everyone was in good spirits and looked forward to a happy future. The number of people there was about fifty. But the following summer the swamp fever broke out. Many people fled, others died, and before long desolation and gloom brooded over the homesteads which a short while before had been full of life and bustle.

"In the spring of 1838 my brother Ansten took a trip to Norway while I worked as a day laborer in northern Illinois. On July 1, 1838, I arrived at the place where I now live, near the center of Clinton township in Rock county, Wisconsin. Here I bought land and was thus the first Norwegian to settle in this state. Neither, to the best of my knowledge, had any Norwegian previously set foot on Wisconsin soil nor entered the state to inspect the land. For a whole year I did not see any countryman of mine but lived secluded, without friends, family, or companions. To be sure, eight Americans had settled in the township before me but they lived in about as lonely and isolated a situation as I did. I found the soil very fertile and the dreariness of the prairie was broken by scattered groves of trees. Herds of deer and other wild animals were seen almost daily and the weird howl of the prairie wolf disturbed my sleep until habit armed my ears against it. The next summer I built a simple cabin and in that house I received the group of emigrants from my home district who came with my brother Ansten from Norway in late September, 1839. Most of these newcomers decided to stay on Jefferson Prairie and in that way this region very quickly received a lot of settlers."

Thus far we have had Ole Knudsen Nattestad's own account of his experiences; only a few additional remarks need be made.* Ole Nattestad is now about sixty years old. He lives on a well-cultivated farm of 314 acres—the same farm he has lived on since he came to Wisconsin. It is valued at forty dollars per acre. His house can well be compared with the residence of a *storbonde* (owner of a large farm) in Oplandet, Norway. In the parlor you will find a sofa and other beautiful furniture, and a carpet on the floor. A collection of good books, both English and Norwegian, proves that the taste for cultural values has not been deadened by the hardships of pioneer life and the struggle to procure the basic necessities. He has been very solicitous about

**Billed-Magazin*, February 20, 1869.

Ansten Knudsen Nattestad

the education of his children and the oldest son has studied three years at Beloit College. These facts have been mentioned merely to indicate something about the everyday life of a well-to-do Norwegian farmer in this part of the country.

Closely connected with the founding of the Norwegian settlement on Jefferson Prairie is Ansten Knudsen Nattestad's trip to Norway and the resultant first large-scale migration from Numedal. We will therefore visit this man also; and we do this all the more readily as he lives only a short distance from his brother Ole who has given us so much information about the fate of his countrymen in America. We can be certain of a good reception from Ansten because he is not at all reluctant to talk about the events of former days. His family has been struck by many misfortunes and his body is very frail, but his spirit is buoyant despite the storms of adversity. He has a keen mind and an excellent memory, and he speaks like a man who has been molded in the school of experience. We will listen attentively to his narrative:

"In the spring of 1838"—so he begins—"I left Illinois by way of New Orleans for Liverpool. From there I went to Norway to visit relatives and friends. I brought along letters from practically all the earlier Norwegian emigrants whom I had come in touch with, and in this way information about America was spread to wide circles in the old country. My brother's diary was printed in Drammen, and Ole Rynning's account of conditions in America appeared at the same time in Christiania. I brought the manuscript of this book along from America. Dean Kragh of Eidsvold read proof. He deleted the chapter about the Norwegian clergy, who were accused of religious intolerance and of taking a do-nothing attitude toward social improvements and popular enlightenment. The book aroused much interest and the edition was soon sold out. Rumors about my return ran like wildfire through the country, and an incredible number of people visited me to hear news from America. Many trekked eighteen or twenty Norwegian miles to talk with me. It was impossible to answer all the letters I received.

"In the spring of 1839 some hundred people from Numedal were prepared to follow me across the ocean. Among these were many farm-owners and heads of families. All of them, except the children, were able-bodied people in their best years. Besides, there were many others from Telemark and Numedal who could not come with me because there was no more space on the ship. We went directly from Drammen to New York. This was the first time that the people of Drammen had seen an emigrant vessel. The price of passage per person was 33.50 *speciedaler*. We were at sea nine weeks. Everything went well, and there were no deaths aboard.

"From New York we took the usual route inland. In Milwaukee we met the group from Tinn. They came aboard our ship and urged us to settle with them at Muskego. Scouts they had sent out told them of grass which was shoulder high, and many other wonders. The Americans also used all the arts of eloquence to induce us to stop in Milwaukee. I opposed this idea, and we continued on our way. In Chicago I learned that while I had been in Norway my brother Ole had settled in Wisconsin. Some members of our party went to the Fox River settlement where they had friends, while several single persons got work in or near Chicago. The rest—that is to say most of them—went up north with me. Among them were a few who settled in Rock Run township, Stephenson county [Illinois], about thirty miles west of Jefferson Prairie, and became the founders of a Norwegian settlement in that part of that state. Others of my party went to Rock Prairie (Luther Valley), a few miles west of my brother's place. In the fall of 1839 the rest of the group and I came to Jefferson Prairie, where we bought land and began the toilsome pioneer life. Among the men who came with me to this settlement were Thore Helgesen Kirkejord and his brothers Kittil and Christoffer Nyhus—all from Numedal. All of them still live here and are well-to-do farmers. In my home community in Norway agriculture paid poorly, there was no money in forestry, and craftsmen could hardly keep their families alive. Trade was forbidden; few farmers could keep a hired man all the year round, and day labor could be had only during the summer. I know of nothing that a person without property could do to get steady employment, try as he might. Still, vagrancy was punishable by law. The sheriff, bill collectors, and others who lived off the peasantry were furious when people left the country. They talked of prohibiting emigration and threatened me with jail when I came home to take my friends to America.

"In 1840, or the summer after my party and I settled here, a few others arrived from Numedal, and after that the population continued to increase, primarily with emigrants from the old country. Most of the people from Numedal are in the northern part of the settlement because those of us who came after my brother—the first one here—bought land near his place; and later emigrants from the same district in Norway, who sought us out in the distant West, staked claims here and became our neighbors. That same fall, shortly after we decided to homestead in this locality, a group of emigrants from Voss arrived. They settled farther to the south; in time others from their home area joined them and thus a fairly homogeneous neighborhood grew up. The Jefferson Prairie settlement can therefore be divided into two districts, of which the northern is primarily inhabited by people from Numedal while those from Voss have a decided majority in the south.

"In speaking of emigration from Numedal in the early period, it should not be forgotten that during the spring after my first departure from Norway—that is to say, in 1838—a rich landowner from Flesberg by the name of Ole Aasland came to this country. He brought with him twenty poor people, paying for their passage across. They went from Tønsberg to Gothenburg, and then to America, where he bought 600 acres of land in Indiana. But Ole Aasland fell into the hands of unscrupulous speculators who took advantage of his ignorance about conditions here, and he was shamelessly cheated. The land he bought was barren and marshy. Sickness soon broke out among the newcomers and many died. With the survivors he moved to Murray township, about thirty miles from Rochester, in the state of New York, where he became a prosperous farmer.

"The first time I saw Ole Rynning was in Detroit when I was on my first trip west in the summer of 1837. We chanced to meet him and his group in that city. He soon won my absolute confidence. 'A man who gives such an impression of honesty can not possibly lie,' I felt. And all his actions indicated that he was a true philanthropist. I have never known another man who based his life on such noble principles and was so thoroughly altruistic. His character was as genuine as gold, and a sincere desire for the welfare of his fellowmen was the inspiration for all his acts. He was never dazzled by the will-o'-the-wisp of fame nor led astray by the still worse temptations of greed. A good and great idea was the central fact in all his thinking: to find a happier home on this side of the Atlantic for the oppressed and poverty-stricken people of Norway. To realize this dream he shunned no sacrifices, endured great hardships, and bore misrepresentations, privations, and disappointments patiently. My brother and I accompanied him from Detroit to Chicago. The decision to go to Beaver Creek was unwise. We were not told everything which he had heard for and against planting a Norwegian settlement there. He believed that there was no danger; the rest of us, who were supposed to have as good judgment in such matters as he, shared his views; thus the decision which resulted in so much misery was made, and we set off. Rynning was one of the most active workers there and won everybody's confidence and respect as they learned to know him better. When sickness and trials struck the settlement, he was always willing to help the suffering to the best of his ability. Nothing could destroy his faith that America would become an asylum for those people in Europe who were slaving under the burden of poverty.

"As for himself, he was frugal and endured suffering with remarkable patience. I remember very well when he came home once after a long inspection trip. Frost had set in while he was traveling; the ice on the swamps and the snow-crusts had cut through his shoes. When he finally returned to the settlement, his feet were badly frozen and bloody. They were a terrible sight and all of us believed that he would be crippled for life. Only he remained confident and never complained. It was while in bed after this injury that he wrote his *True Account of America*, which I arranged to have printed in Norway. As he finished sections of the work, he read them aloud to us and we expressed our opinions. Gradually he recovered and resumed his good work among the settlers.

"In the fall of 1838 Ole Rynning was again sent to the sickbed and he soon died, to the great sorrow of us all. During the winter, sickness raged and death struck blow after blow. During the summer of 1839 most of the survivors left the settlement and did not even wait to sell their land. Only the empty log houses remained as silent witnesses to the terrible destruction which had taken place. A few settlers may have remained for a while; but when they too left, silence brooded over the region. The immigrant streams, however, continued to flow steadily toward the west, and many of the areas earlier abandoned were in the course of years again occupied. Thus it went here also. Frenchmen, Germans, and Yankees now plow the fields which previously belonged to the Norwegians; and it is left to these peoples to care for the graves where so many of our fellow countrymen found their last resting place. According to the testimony of eyewitnesses, conditions at Beaver Creek are now excellent. The people there are prosperous; and as soon as the stagnant waters were drained, there was no more swamp fever. Health conditions at present are quite satisfactory.

"Cleng Peerson from Hesthammer, Tysvær parish, Skjold district," thus Ansten Nattestad continued, "was an adventurer in the broadest sense of the word.* Few men were so widely discussed among the earliest settlers as Cleng, and numerous stories circulated about his youth and later achievements in America. According to what I have heard, he was married at a comparatively early age to a wealthy, aging widow of a prominent family in his home area. From then on Cleng no longer belonged to the laboring class but dressed in fine clothes and aped the manners of the upper classes. When on Sundays, spruced up and stately, he paraded arm in arm with his spouse, who was racked by the frailties of old age, he was an object of popular admiration but also the butt of many a sarcastic remark because of his awkward and odd behavior. With the change that this marriage had brought to Cleng's life, he thought he had reached the seventh heaven of happiness.

"But all earthly glory is fleeting and there are no roses without thorns. Cleng's honeymoon was a time of undisturbed peace, but with its passing much of the enchantment vanished for both parties, and dreams of divine happiness were replaced by the dull prose of reality. The woman discovered that the man's love began to cool; and as she could not explain this except by assuming that someone else had taken her rightful place in her husband's heart, she began to see in every younger woman a rival with whom Cleng was not permitted to exchange a glance, much less a word. He could not agree with his wife's ideas about the mutual obligations of married couples; their differing opinions occasioned many a scene, thus further widening the gap between them which was a natural consequence of disparity in age, wealth, and previous habits of life.

"When Cleng became acquainted with the Quakers his spirit, ever yearning for variety, found nourishment for a while; but as soon as the newness wore off he could no longer get the gratification and contentment from association with his fellow believers which he missed at his own hearth. Home no longer held any attraction for him. His wife's nagging and jealousy increased with each passing day; and his former friends let him understand that they looked upon his misfortunes as penalties well deserved because he had tossed away his youth merely to gain his daily bread. It was under these circumstances that 'the father of Norwegian emigration' determined to leave his native land and thus sever all the bonds which made his stay at home so unpleasant. In the company of a person of ill repute from the Stavanger area who had left his family in gypsy fashion, Cleng in all quietness left for Sweden, his original

**Billed-Magazin*, February 27, 1869.

destination. In Gothenburg he heard talk about America, presumably the first time this word had ever struck his ears. He did not hesitate long, but secured passage on a merchant ship bound for New York and landed on this side of the Atlantic, which henceforth became the scene of his adventures.

"Cleng left Norway in 1821. He stayed in various places in New York state and after three years returned to visit friends in the old country. His visit did not arouse particular attention beyond the area around Stavanger, and there he kept company especially with his fellow believers, the Quakers. Cleng's reports about America, however, soon inspired others to try their luck in the homeland of the red men; and in the year 1825 the sloop *Restaurationen*, equipped in Stavanger, brought the first group of emigrants from Norway to America. Most of these immigrants bought land near Rochester, New York, paying speculators five dollars per acre. The newcomers found that clearing fields in the virgin forest was hard work, and their situation remained for a long time anything but attractive. Only the impossibility of securing means for the return voyage bound most of them to their new homes.

"The burdens and monotony of pioneer life could not satisfy Cleng's restless spirit for long. He stayed for a time among his countrymen in the Rochester area but soon headed west, bent on new discoveries. Eventually he returned to his countrymen near Rochester with the report that some seventy miles southwest of Chicago, in La Salle county near Ottawa on the Fox River, fertile land could be had at a low price. Some members of the first Norwegian settlement in America accompanied him to this new location in 1835 and there they founded a Norwegian community, commonly known as the Fox River settlement, which thus became the second oldest Norwegian colony in the New World. Cleng remained here a while also, but his yearning for change and adventure soon lured him on to further travels. In 1837, the same year that I, Ansten Nattestad, came to America, he was all set to leave for Missouri.

"I asked how Cleng could raise money to cover his travel expenses. I was told that he never needed any money. His entire capital consisted of two shillings (twenty-five cents) and this sum neither grew nor diminished with the passing years. He covered thousands of miles across the vast western plains, voyaged on lakes and rivers, lodged in pioneer cabins, in city hotels, or under the open sky; but he retained his two-shilling piece untouched by other hands than his own. It could never be said of Cleng that he was penniless. If by chance he came to a place where the host might drop a hint about pay for food and lodging, Cleng knew how to put on such a funereal countenance that people did not know whether to laugh or weep. He always managed to leave the house just as rich as when he entered. A resolution to set out on a journey was never a financial question with him. If his shoes were worn out or a piece of clothing threadbare, there was always someone sensible enough to realize that Cleng could not continue his travels unless these wants were remedied. He spoke fluent English, understood French, and was not at a loss even among Germans. He told strangers about the mountainous land far to the north and informed his countrymen concerning the soil and topography of distant regions. In saloons, people gathered around the far-traveled man; ship captains took him into their cabins to hear his tales; and dwellers in lonely huts on the prairie or in the depths of the forest usually took a day of rest when Cleng came for a visit. Without being a beggar he led a free life and was seldom in any difficulty.

"At Cleng's prompting, a Norwegian settlement was also founded in an outlying region of Missouri. But what he lacked, above everything else, was practicality and perseverance. He did not know how to select areas suited for their intended purpose; and no sooner had one plan been brought to realization than Cleng tired of the whole matter and began to hatch new schemes. The settlement in Missouri did not last long. The area had been badly chosen: it was too far from older communities which might have lent the newcomers aid to overcome initial hardships. The settlers soon experienced difficulties which bred discontent and discouragement, and in the year 1840 they left Missouri to settle in Iowa.

"Cleng made still another trip to Norway and returned to America with a group of his countrymen whom he accompanied to Pennsylvania, where they arrived without money and, on the whole, in a miserable condition. After a brief stay there, most of them—discouraged and discontented—left Pennsylvania for points farther west, in Missouri and Iowa. It has been said that Cleng undertook even a third trip to Norway. Whether or not this is true I am unable to say. When the Swedish sectarian Eric Janson and his followers settled in Illinois, Cleng Peerson associated with them for a while and married a woman of the Jansonian sect. But again the bonds of marriage could not chain him for long to one place. He yearned to get out into the world, and when certain matrimonial misunderstandings made his position at home unbearable he more than willingly grabbed his staff to roam again across the length and breadth of this vast land. After a long time of wandering he finally went to Texas where, not long ago, full of days and presumably weary of adventures he died at a ripe old age."

The paragraphs above are a brief sketch of the life of that man who had a greater influence on the exodus from Norway than anyone else and whose name therefore deserves a prominent place in the history of Norwegian emigration. The departure of the Sloopers in 1825 was a direct result of Cleng Peerson's first return home: in its wake came the migrations from Stavanger in 1836, from Bergen in 1837, and from Porsgrunn, Drammen, and Bergen in 1839. The emigrations during the decade after 1825 stood in direct relation to each other as cause and effect. How things would have shaped themselves without Cleng's appearance on the scene is difficult to say. No doubt Norway would in time have sent her share of people to the western wilderness even if such an apparently trivial event had not occurred as the departure of one man—and that one an adventurer. But when and from which regions the emigrant streams might then have flowed are questions which no one can answer.

Despite all his shortcomings, Cleng Peerson was undoubtedly the right man to set things in motion. To be sure, he was erratic and capricious, but no one can deny that he was honest and sincere. He was kindhearted and always ready to help others, even though at times he made great mistakes. Despite the fact that he was miserably poor, no one could better induce others to relieve the wants of the newcomers; Cleng Peerson was always the faithful friend of the poor and the oppressed. When it was a question of urging the wealthy to support his needy countrymen, few were as eloquent as he. His communistic ideas concerning the sharing of wealth caused him frequently to depend too much on other people's pocketbooks; and when poor borrowers were unable to repay at the right time, Cleng—who had been their spokesman—had to suffer much unpleasantness because of the unreliability of others. He was consequently rather disliked by the rich; but the masses honored him as an ally and a friend and usually overlooked his weaknesses. His influence was great among the newcomers during the early immigration. He was able to found settlements because wherever he went there were always some who were willing to follow him. His lack of practical sense was the source of misfortune both for himself and for others, but everyone recognized his honorable intentions, and people readily excused a man who had set himself the goal of using all his powers for the good of his fellowmen.

The well-known Elling Eielsen gave the writer of this biographical sketch some information about Cleng Peerson's departure from Norway which is somewhat at variance with the account given above by Ansten Knudsen Nattestad of Jefferson Prairie.[22] Elling Eielsen's report was essentially as follows: "In the year 1821 Cleng Peerson Hesthammer and Knud Eie left Norway to examine conditions in America. They were Quakers, and to defray travel expenses they received contributions from their fellow believers in Norway—possibly also from a Quaker mission fund in England. The motivating force behind this trip was presumably the religious constraint which at that time existed in Norway. In America they received aid from their many fellow believers. After a stay of two or three years, Cleng Peerson returned to Norway and gave such accounts of matters in the New World that fifty-two persons from the Stavanger area and Skjold parish prepared to leave in 1825. Ole Helletveit and Gudmund Haukaas were members of this group. In

America the latter joined the Mormons, thus becoming the first Norwegian to embrace Joseph Smith's teachings. He was a highly respected man in Norway and had a good education. Lars [Larsen] Jeilane from Stavanger was also one of these emigrants and in this country he became a master boat-builder on the Erie Canal. Immediately after the departure of the Stavanger sloop, only a few people left; but in 1836 an upswing in the emigration movement began and when Ole Rynning's book appeared in 1839 emigration became a common topic of conversation in many areas of Norway. The earliest emigrants from Norway settled in New York state. Later, settlements were founded at Fox River and Beaver Creek in Illinois. Not until 1839 did the Scandinavians start looking for homesteads beyond those states, namely in Wisconsin and Michigan."

The origin of the name Jefferson Prairie is uncertain.* It may be that one of the earliest pioneers in the area was named Jefferson and that his name became associated with the prairie and the colony. Many towns and townships are named for a man who played a prominent role in their early history. Other American place-names are of Indian origin or they commemorate presidents, prominent statesmen, or generals. Very often the first settlers gave their new home the name of the town or area where they had lived before. Hence we find in America a multitude of place-names which are well known to us from the Old World. As the original settlers or their descendants moved west from the Atlantic coast, memories of the old home followed them into the wilderness, and they gave their new homes names which were associated with the years of their youth. This explains why names of European localities, which occur so frequently in the eastern states, are in time transplanted westward on the continent with the emigrant stream and are found intermittently all the way to the Pacific. As regards Jefferson Prairie, this name is not officially recognized; the two townships of which the Norwegian settlement forms a part are called Clinton and Manchester—the first located in Wisconsin and the latter in Illinois.

The soil in this settlement founded by our countrymen must, I suppose, be called very good, as the annual wheat yield per acre still averages some 14 or 15 bushels. For many years after the beginning of cultivation, the fertile prairie soil, rich in vegetable nutrients, yielded each fall from 25 to 30 bushels per acre. The accumulated supplies of plant food produced by centuries of decaying vegetable matter freed the pioneers from the need to fertilize their fields. But each annual crop deprives the soil of nutrient substances, with the result that now it is absolutely necessary to fertilize if the farmer wants to

**Billed-Magazin*, March 6, 1869.

avoid reduced crops. The generally clayey soil of the wooded areas gives good yields under favorable weather conditions; but the crops there are dependent upon a variety of circumstances and are deemed less certain than on the prairie.

The main source of income for the people in this area is wheat-raising. The farmers have easy access to market for their products because the town of Clinton lies only a mile or two north of the Norwegian settlement. This town is at a junction of two different railway systems, the Racine-Mississippi line and the Chicago-Northwestern. The distance between Clinton and the city of Racine on the shore of Lake Michigan is only fifty-eight miles and from Clinton to Chicago seventy-eight miles. This fortunate location near such important markets for the Northwest as Chicago and Racine is of great economic significance for the people of Jefferson Prairie. In this respect they are better off than many of their fellow countrymen in America. I have been told that the farmers in this region have gone in more for cattle-raising in recent years than formerly was the case. The high price of meat combined with the necessity of fertilizing for profitable grain crops has caused this transformation. Presumably cattle-raising will, before long, be one of the farmers' main sources of income.

I would say that education among the people of the district is fairly good, even though it seemed to me that the love of reading was not as common here as, for example, in the Yorkville settlement. In most of the houses, however, you will find Norwegian language newspapers. About two-thirds of the people can read English and at least half of the farmers subscribe to newspapers in English. The schools in the district have in recent years been well attended. Religious instruction is given the younger generation by Sexton Anders Andersen from Holden parish in Norway. He conducts parochial school ten to twelve weeks annually, receiving a salary of $18 per month plus free board.

The moral level of the settlement is praiseworthy. No Norwegian has been indicted for violations of the law, and lawsuits between our fellow countrymen practically never occur. Addiction to strong liquor has almost died out. Bundling is a thing of the past. Only two illegitimate children have been born in the settlement. Drinking parties and dances are nonexistent. In many homes family devotions are observed during the holidays when there are no church services. This devout custom is, however, not as general as might be desirable. A singing society has been organized to provide social entertainment for the young people. Nine pianos and melodeons are to be found among Norwegians in the settlement. This last remark may seem unimportant, but it acquires a certain significance by suggesting that the taste for nobler things in life begins to develop among our countrymen when their spirits are released from the ever-gnawing anxiety about making a living.

There are said to be eighty-four Norwegian landowners in this settlement.

Among them are seven who own more than one farm. There are also twenty other families, whose breadwinners do not operate their own farms but support themselves as craftsmen or day laborers. Hence there are about 100 households, and one might safely estimate the total population of the settlement at around 500. The average size of the farms is said to be about 160 acres.

At present the economic condition of the settlers is unusually good. Most of the farmers own, free of debt, everything under their management, and there are many who have money out at interest. It is true here also that the Norwegians, as a rule, are better off than farmers of other nationalities living in their neighborhood under otherwise similar conditions.

Home crafts are not inconsiderable. The women spin and weave; for everyday use, clothes of homespun are usually worn. In many families wine is made from homegrown fruit, and the production of cider takes place on a fairly large scale. Housewives are usually busy from morning till night because only a few employ full-time maids. Neither is it usual to engage hired men by the year. Most of the farmers manage with day laborers.

Forty of the farmers in the settlement, so I have heard, have joined together in a congregation served by Pastor [C. F.] Magelsen from Rock Prairie, who belongs to the Norwegian Evangelical Lutheran Synod (the Wisconsin Synod). There is now talk about the congregation getting its own pastor; they have already bought 140 acres of land equipped with buildings which is to serve as their parsonage. The Norwegian congregations in Beloit and on Long Prairie will presumably become annexes to Jefferson Prairie, which will then be the main parish. A Norwegian church was built as early as 1846, but as the population gradually increased it became too small and the congregation erected a spacious and beautiful new structure near the center of the settlement. Here we find one of the few Norwegian rural churches where hymn singing is supported by an organ and the faithful are summoned to divine service by the tolling of bells.

On Jefferson Prairie there is still another congregation to which twenty-six of the local farmers belong. It has joined the Augustana Synod and its church is located near the Illinois border. Ole Andersen Aasen—here generally known as Andrewsen—from Hjartdal, Telemark, Norway, serves this congregation as minister. He was described to me as an enlightened man of high principles who performs his pastoral duties with great earnestness. Andrewsen is at one and the same time churchman and farmer. He lives the arduous life of a tiller of the soil without thereby neglecting his ecclesiastical work. When we add that four families in the district have joined "Hauge's Friends," then we have given all the information regarding church matters which came to my attention during a brief visit to Jefferson Prairie.

Among the men who enjoy the respect and confidence of their fellow citizens I want to mention Knud Brynildsen Dugstad. An unusually well-informed man, he serves as organist and has frequently held official positions in the township. I also heard Thore Helgesen Kirkejord, Ole Anstensen Møgstue, and Christoffer Nyhus spoken of as men who often take the lead in community affairs and to whom the people frequently delegate positions of trust. In politics practically the whole settlement is Republican. I was told that in the last election only one Democratic vote was cast by a Norwegian.

Rock Prairie

PLYMOUTH, NEWARK, Avon, and Spring Valley townships form the southwestern corner of Rock county; the area of about two and a half Norwegian square miles which lies within the borders of these townships usually goes by the name of Rock Prairie among us Norwegians.* In the same year that our countrymen founded the Norwegian settlement by Lake Muskego others went northward from Chicago and sought homesteads in the southern part of Wisconsin. Some of them settled within the large quadrangle known as Rock Prairie, comprising the above-mentioned townships, while a greater number founded homes on Jefferson Prairie in Clinton township, which forms the southeastern corner of Rock county. These two Norwegian pioneer settlements, which originated almost simultaneously in the southern part of the state, are only about fourteen English or two Norwegian miles distant from each other. And about midway between them lies the town of Beloit where many Scandinavians have settled in recent years.

In few areas of the state do we find so many of our countrymen gathered within such a small space as on Rock Prairie. Hence it is not only the age but also the rapid growth of the colony which deserves our attention. We will let one of the earliest pioneers in the area tell about the founding and later development of the settlement. For the sake of accuracy, however, we must make clear that as we confided the man's oral account to a notebook in condensed form we are unable to repeat his story verbatim. But the essential part of his narrative is here.

Gullik Olsen Gravdal, our informant, emigrated in 1839 from Sandsvær, Norway. The previous year Ansten Nattestad had returned home and taken with him the manuscript of Ole Rynning's book about America. The book was

**Billed-Magazin*, April 17, 1869.

printed and in a short time circulated through a large part of southern Norway. Hardly any other Norwegian publication has been purchased and read with such eagerness as Rynning's *True Account of America*. People traveled long distances to hear news from the land of wonders, and many who before were scarcely able to read began in earnest to practice in the "America-book," making such progress that they were soon able to spell their way onward and master most of the contents. The sensation created by Ansten's return was about the same as we might imagine a dead man would cause, were he to return to tell of life beyond the grave. Throughout the winter he was continually surrounded by groups who listened attentively to his stories. As many came long distances to talk with him, his reports of the Far West were soon spread over a large part of the country. "Ministers and bailiffs," reports Gullik Gravdal, "tried to frighten us with terrible tales about the dreadful sea monsters and man-eating savages in the New World; but when Ansten Nattestad said 'amen' to Rynning's *Account*, all our fears and doubts were removed. More than ninety people, men, women, and children, were ready in the spring of 1839 to follow Ansten across the ocean—there was no space for more people on our ship. Others desiring to emigrate had to seek accommodations elsewhere.

"The Creator's command to humanity—'Be fruitful, and multiply, and replenish the earth, and subdue it'—is being fulfilled like all other divine decrees, but even though we clearly see its effects, the forces which call them forth are not always easily discernible. Most people cling to that plot of earth where they first recognized father's and mother's features, where the happy days of childhood glided by under the parents' tender care, and where mother's kindly voice brought release from the sorrows which troubled the youngster's heart. With bowed head and moist cheeks the otherwise buoyant youth leaves his childhood home to seek a livelihood among strangers, and when the adolescent girl, by force of circumstances, is pushed out into the world, the tears which stream from her eyes bear witness to the heartache caused by the pangs of parting. Reluctantly the still energetic man leaves the fields which he has sowed and harvested by the sweat of his brow; and only the sternest necessity can induce the man of advanced years to turn his steps away from the sod where dear forefathers are at rest in their graves and which, through many years, has been the scene of his joys and sorrows. This is speaking in general terms. To be sure, there are exceptions, but love of the surroundings of one's earliest years seems to be a law of nature that ties people to the place of their birth. Even the emigrant who has acquired wealth and influence in a foreign land often speaks with deep feeling about the happy days of childhood. Memories of adversity and poverty by no means erase from the heart the image of the childhood home which the emigrant carries with him as a beloved treasure to the farthest ends of the earth.

"It is not recklessness or thoughtlessness which has brought the Norwegian immigrant to America. At the outset, religious intolerance undoubtedly played a certain part; but in Norway this has always been of minor importance as a cause of emigration. Worry about securing the necessities of life—a consequence of the scarcity of economic opportunities—is the potent force which, despite ingrained attachment to home and the familiar ways of life, has induced hosts of our countrymen to leave their native land. Instead of searching for the causes of the ever-increasing emigration the Norwegian authorities should rather subject the following question to a thorough analysis: 'What is the cause of the ever-spreading impoverishment?' From the lands where wages bear a reasonable relationship to the price of goods, migration is comparatively minimal. Only in exceptional cases can religious intolerance or governmental oppression overcome attachment to the native soil. Increased taxes, lack of economic freedom, and oppressive labor practices exert an influence only in so far as they may increase poverty and want among the mass of the people. Bread, bread! is the basic requirement for human welfare, and that government is best which through wise laws manages to improve economic conditions so that labor becomes profitable and prosperity flourishes. Only when Hunger is kicked out the door and Poverty is in exile does the common man thrive in the land of his fathers—which he will not then forsake. But if these dangerous enemies of the people gain entry into the peasant's pantry then the tables are turned: then it is the laborer who wanders as an exile among strangers and the freeholder who goes sadly out into the world in search of a living."

We will pick up the thread of our story and let our friend Gullik Olsen Gravdal tell about the founding of the settlement mentioned above, where through the years so many of our countrymen have found a home and, as we hope, the happiness which was the goal of their migration.* A great majority of those who left Numedal in 1839 belonged to "Hauge's Friends." "We were not actually persecuted," says Gravdal, "but the 'Readers' were the subject of much hostile gossip and we had to endure ridicule and scorn on the part of those who did not share our views. I do not mean to say that this intolerance was the cause of our leaving, but it undoubtedly helped ripen our decision to leave a land where we were exposed to so many insults because our religious teachings did not agree entirely with the beliefs of the majority. The hope of finding cheap, fertile land together with reports about good wages were definitely the determining factors for most of us.

"We secured passage from Drammen to New York, whence we went on to Chicago. The ocean crossing cost each person thirty-four *speciedaler*. Some members of our group found work in Chicago and the surrounding area; others

**Billed-Magazin*, April 24, 1869.

went on to Ottawa or the Fox River settlement, while a large number of the emigrants—I among them—accompanied Ansten Nattestad north to Jefferson Prairie where his brother Ole had settled the previous year. Many of these people bought land in the neighborhood and began clearing and building. Others, however, traveled into the surrounding area to look it over before choosing a homestead. Three of the other immigrants and I went westward as far as Beloit, where we were able to talk to a man who told us where government land could be purchased. We therefore continued still farther west. Finally I located a place which was to my liking because it had good spring water and a proper balance between prairie and woodland. Together with Lars Røste, a bachelor from the parish of Land, I bought forty acres and began building on the spot which I had selected as my homestead. I have lived here ever since. The following spring—1840—I went southward more than 100 miles to the state of Illinois and bought cattle. I drove them alone the whole distance through uninhabited regions with sun and stars as guides until I reached my home in what later came to be known as Newark township.

"Gradually we managed to clear, plow, and seed four acres; the harvest was good, and this gave us courage for further efforts. Our field was soon enlarged and it was not long before we were able to buy more land. I had brought some money along from Norway which helped me greatly at first. About a month before Christmas we moved into the log house we had built. Our home was indeed simple, but from then on we had a roof over our heads and were protected against cold and wind. All foodstuffs were expensive and had to be brought from Beloit. There was no road; we had to carry or pull everything we bought all the way to our house. A sack of flour no larger than I could comfortably carry cost five dollars, and other kinds of food were priced in proportion. Both my wife and I escaped sickness, and our two children got along well. Lars Røste eventually returned to Norway and I have heard that he is still living in his home community, the parish of Land.

"One of the other two men who accompanied me to inspect the land west of Beloit was Gisle Halland from Numedal. He settled about an English mile farther east while the second one, Goe Bjøno, bought land for Gunnild Ødegaarden three miles south of my homestead. Gunnild was a rich widow from Nore in Numedal who paid the travel expenses of many poor emigrants. She was accompanied by her children, some of whom were grown men. The cabin built on her land was the first Norwegian house put up west of the Rock River. She lived fifteen years after her arrival in America and died in 1854. That year our settlement was ravaged by cholera, which carried off many victims, among them Gunnild Ødegaarden from Nore.

"When I settled here, the whole region toward the west was a wilderness. I do not know whether any white people lived between me and the Mississippi.

The same was true of the area toward the north. In a westerly direction, however, some Yankees had settled in the wilderness about seven miles away. The Indians were still lords of these regions, but they were always friendly and courteous. We never suffered any injustice from the sons of the wilderness. There was an abundance of game here at the time—great herds of deer and swarms of prairie chicken.

"The population of our community increased slightly in 1841 when Lars Aae (Skavlem) and Gullik Springen settled on Rock Prairie. Both of them had come over on the same ship as I had. Soon afterward Yankees also came into our neighborhood. As time went by more and more Norwegians arrived. Thus the population of the district increased steadily, and Rock Prairie is now one of the largest Norwegian settlements in the whole state of Wisconsin."

Gullik Gravdal's narrative ends here. He has fared well in America and become a wealthy man. On his 160-acre farm we now see a beautiful stone residence and other buildings of the same solid material. Everything about his property indicates that he is not only a prosperous but also a thoughtful and industrious farmer.

Gullik Knudsen Springen was known in Norway as Gullik Laugen. He emigrated from Numedal in 1839, accompanying Ansten Nattestad across the ocean. The writer of these sketches spent a few days last summer (1868) in the home of this respected gentleman. On the basis of some notes I jotted down on that occasion, I will give a brief sketch of Gullik Springen's history, letting him do the narrating in first person. Essentially the following biographical sketch will be in accord with the facts. If any small mistakes are found, they will be of minor importance, as my aim is to give a lucid overall description of early immigrant experiences on this side of the Atlantic.

Gullik Knudsen Laugen (Springen) emigrated from Numedal in 1839.* "My father," he reports, "lived on a little farm and had many children. Income from farming provided us with only the barest necessities of life. We were five brothers, and I worked at home with my father until I was twenty-one years old. In return I could expect nothing but food and clothing. To work for others on a yearly basis was no better; and other types of work were not available to me. When I began to think seriously of the future, the idea of emigrating occurred to me. My father approved and encouraged me to try my luck in America. He even declared himself willing to sell his farm and join me later if, after exploring the glories of the New World, I should think it advisable.

"Ansten Nattestad, who made a trip to Norway from America, stayed in his home area during part of the winter and spring, and it was especially his

Billed-Magazin, May 1, 1869.

accounts which aroused in the rest of us the desire to emigrate. I got a loan of twenty *speciedaler* and prepared to depart. Under Ansten Nattestad's leadership a group of ninety-three persons from Numedal then traveled to Drammen where we had arranged for ship accommodations. This was the first time that the people of Drammen had seen such a caravan and they looked at us with amazement. Many terrible stories were told about the fate which awaited our group. 'Few of you,' we were told, 'will get across the ocean alive, and those are fortunate whose eyes will be closed before they touch that land of horrors called America. There poisonous snakes swarm, and the even more terrifying Indians lurk like beasts of prey to attack you. The pestilential atmosphere works like slow poison, and the glowing breath of summer soon transforms northern people into skeletons.'

"These stories undoubtedly inspired fear in some people; it was with sadness and dire forebodings that we boarded the ship which was to transport us from our native land to the Far West. The crossing went well; seventeen weeks after leaving Drammen the whole group arrived safely in Chicago, which was still an unimportant frontier post. Scarcely anyone at the time dreamed that within thirty years Chicago would be the largest and richest trading center in the Northwest. Some of our group, especially the free and unattached, remained there. Others went to the Norwegian settlement at Fox River, while the rest followed Ansten Nattestad to Jefferson Prairie where his brother had settled the preceding fall.

"At first I stayed in Chicago and worked in the town and surrounding area. The monthly pay ran from six to ten dollars. My fiancée, a girl from Numedal whom I married the following winter, also worked there and we soon saved a bit of money. Then we decided to buy a piece of land, and in the spring of 1841 we went to Rock Prairie. Four Norwegians had already settled there, and I became the fifth. For several days I wandered around looking for a homestead; finally I came to a place near the edge of the prairie where a copious spring welled forth from the ground. Here I decided to stake out my claim and called the place 'Springen.' The land round about was a wilderness. Except for the four Norwegian pioneers there were no other settlers. Toward the west one had to go twenty-four miles before meeting white people. It was fortunate for us that there was a great plenty of game. During the winter, hunting was our surest source of food. When the first snow had fallen that autumn another Norwegian and I went on skis over the prairie to Beloit to buy flour. The Americans later saw our tracks in the snow, and no one could figure out what kind of animal might have left them. The matter aroused much talk and people racked their brains in an effort to solve the puzzle. The most learned naturalist in town finally delivered the verdict that in the forests out west there must be some hitherto unknown monstrosity whose means of locomotion produced the furrows. But even he could not give any satisfactory information as to how this creature moved about during the summer or whether this freak of nature attacked and devoured human beings.

"Beloit was at this time in its infancy. A mill, a hotel, two grocery stores, and a few laborers' shacks—that was the whole 'kit and caboodle'; but even these humble structures seemed impressive to us there in the wilderness.

"My family and I lived near my spring through the autumn and far into the winter in a cabin woven of branches and thatched with straw. The flat cover of a chest brought along from Norway served as a table, and all cooking was done outdoors. Only toward Christmas was I able to build a simple log house, but even this modest social elevation aroused jealousy: a Yankee came and threatened to chase me off my land with physical force. Such a threat could be quite serious out in the wilderness where the fists carry more weight than the written law. But when he saw that I was prepared to defend myself with muscular arguments, he gave up his attempt, and I remained in peaceful possession of my cabin. The following spring, with the help of others, I got some ground broken. On this plot I sowed grain and planted potatoes. Through day labor during the summer I earned so much money that I saw my way clear to buy a team of oxen—and this event I can call a turning point in my pioneer life. What a camel is for an Arabian and a ship is for a seaman, that a pair of oxen is for a man who seeks to make a home in the wilds, far from inhabited regions. Patiently this often despised animal pulls the plow and transforms the western wilderness into grain fields that in the autumn are laden with the Lord's blessings.

"During the summer many acquaintances from Norway arrived. They came to me and I tried as best I could to help them. The influx continued, and already by the third year after my arrival quite a number of Norwegians had come to the settlement. Not until the fourth autumn did I have anything to sell. Milwaukee, seventy-five miles distant, was the nearest market; the trip out and back took eleven days. We received $.50 per bushel for wheat and we could not carry much of a load on the *kubberulle* [primitive wagon with wheels of sliced logs], since we had to travel most of the way over roadless stretches, through woods and underbrush, over swamps and marshes. Nor did I have a large amount to sell, because we older settlers had to lend a helping hand to the newcomers, very few of whom brought any supply of money with them. Eventually, to my joy, my father and two brothers came to join me. I escaped sickness, while most of the newcomers at first were attacked by the 'climate fever.' During the course of the year we made steady progress because no serious misfortune struck the settlement. Only once did a cattle pest cause some loss; and the cholera, which came with the emigrants, closed the eyes of some people. Elling Eielsen visited the settlement now and then as pastor, and C. L. Clausen also conducted services occasionally. A log cabin was used as a church. Later G. F. Dietrichson became our pastor."

The paragraphs above give a brief account of Gullik Springen's life and sketch in part the history of the Rock Prairie settlement. At present Gullik Springen is a prosperous man who owns a 300-acre farm with good stone buildings. His estate can be estimated at about $10,000. Furthermore he has advanced about $2,000 to his sons, two of whom are now established as merchants in Beloit. Through perseverance and diligence he has worked himself up to his present position and now enjoys the respect of his fellow citizens. It is remarkable what a formative influence free institutions have on people's mental development. Like so many of his countrymen, Gullik had lacked the opportunity to go to school in his homeland. Now he is a well-informed man who keeps up with current political and religious questions.

When a person becomes aware of the corruption within our official life, he sometimes grows despondent and may doubt that the republican system is any better than other forms of government. But when he sees the fruits of our free institutions he becomes reconciled, by and large, to the way things are. Where the Lord erects a temple, Satan will rear a structure close by. So it has been and will presumably remain until the end of time. This is true not only in religion but also in other aspects of life. Despite the dishonesty of many public men, the election skulduggery, and the bribery, the many demonstrable benefits of democracy are so obvious that one overlooks the shady portions out of admiration for the bright aspects of our national life. Every good can be misused. Even religion is sometimes a disguise for the grossest crimes. No wonder then that the precious gift of liberty is often used for petty personal gain. This can not be avoided. Many of the more enlightened Norwegians whom I have asked how pleased they are with American institutions have replied that the laws are irreproachable if only they were obeyed. One fact at least can not be refuted: the apathy and sluggishness of our countrymen who migrated to America have given place to intelligent reflection and initiative.

There are 120 Norwegian farmers in this settlement, a few more than on Jefferson Prairie.* Added to these are a few families who do not secure their livelihood from the soil; so the Norwegian population can be estimated at about 900. Emigrants from Numedal are the largest group, with forty-six farmers. Next come those from Hallingdal and Land, with thirty-seven and twenty-two farmers respectively, whereas Sogn has added to the population only three and Valdres two families. The rest, ten in number, emigrated from various districts in Norway, and one came from Denmark.

Economic conditions are especially good, and there is general prosperity.

**Billed-Magazin*, May 8, 1869.

At least the older settlers own their land and all other property free of debt, and many have money out at interest. The high price of wheat in recent years has particularly contributed to their economic progress. Many farmers who began with small plots of land have been able to buy more. Good agricultural implements have been acquired and a number of useful improvements have been adopted.

The soil consists mostly of dark mold, which in places is rich in lime. In most areas the fields have produced crops for fifteen to twenty years, or even longer, without being fertilized. But the natural fertility, no matter how great, must of necessity decrease, because every crop consumes elements which serve as nourishment for the plants. In the early years, yields up to 30 bushels of wheat per acre were not unusual; at present a farmer can not count on more than 14 or 15 bushels during ordinary good years. Grass still grows luxuriantly; and pasturage is, on the whole, better than in many parts of the state.

The region which commonly goes by the name "Rock Prairie" comprises a group of several prairies separated by wooded areas with openings. The whole district is a rolling plain. There are no hills of any prominence, nor does one find miles of completely flat stretches as in several Norwegian settlements in Iowa, Minnesota, and Illinois. The farmers have wood enough for their own needs and many of them sell wood to the townspeople.

The farmers' main source of livelihood here, as it is everywhere in the southern part of the state, is wheat-raising. Despite the fact that the fertility of the soil has decreased, implements have improved so much that farming pays better now than it did when the farmers harvested 25 to 30 bushels per acre. It must be admitted, however, that the coming of the railroad with the resultant ease of communications, combined with higher grain prices in recent years, has done more than anything else to promote agriculture and further the farmers' prosperity. The railway towns of Orfordville, Broadhead, Beloit, Janesville, and Hanover are easily accessible markets where the farmers, at any time, can dispose of their products at the highest going prices. Here, also, people are beginning to pay more attention to cattle-raising than formerly; not a few settlers already regard grazing as one of their main sources of income. The time is presumably not far distant when grain-raising and cattle-raising will be carried on side by side in proportions best suited to a sound agriculture.

On most of the farms we find substantial, beautiful houses. There are more limestone buildings here than in any other Norwegian settlement I have visited. In combination with the white-painted, well-maintained farmhouses, they speak with equal eloquence of the owners' taste and the general prosperity among the people. We may still find an occasional log house, though, which reminds us of the simplicity of earlier years and the frugal life led by the first settlers.

When you enter the house of one of our countrymen on Rock Prairie you will find much food and furniture which remind you of the old country even though the American influence has also made itself felt. As time goes by, the customs inherited from our forefathers disappear more and more in this country. Among the oldest settlers, household matters are patterned largely along American lines. This is due not merely to the force of example but possibly even more to the altered conditions under which our countrymen find themselves after their arrival in America.

It has been said that the hospitality usually ascribed to the Norwegian *bonde* (freeholder) in his homeland is not found among our countrymen here in America. I do not know what experiences others have had in this respect; but it appears to me that this reproach is ill-founded. Usually the traveler is received kindly; and when we consider that characters who misuse people's hospitality frequently roam about in the settlements, we have, it seems to me, reason to admire the trust and the friendly spirit shown the stranger who, as a rule, is denied neither food nor bed. On Rock Prairie I found further proof of the fact that in this respect our countrymen do not disgrace their forefathers. And I take this occasion to give my most sincere thanks to the many people I had an opportunity to visit during my travels through the settlement—by all of whom I was received with sincere cordiality.

Moral conditions in the settlement must be declared good, I would say, in comparison with the way things are in many communities in the old country, even though in this respect there is still much to be wished for. Quite a few illegitimate births have occurred, and among the young people the dancing craze seems to be on the increase. Bundling is by no means eradicated. There is some addiction to drink, and carousals are not at all exceptional. I must add, however, that the statements above are not based on personal observation, but on testimony received from others.

If one is to pass judgment on the degree of enlightenment within a settlement he is often faced with a dilemma, since ideas about matters which can not be weighed or measured or expressed statistically vary so greatly. Many will call a thing great which others find to be trivial, and some people will talk about utter crudity where many discover beauty and perfection. In such a case comparison is the only applicable gauge. With this as my guide I dare to express the opinion that the general level of education within this settlement is lower than among our countrymen in Yorkville, and that the desire for reading is less widespread than on Jefferson Prairie. For the sake of accuracy, however, I must record that there are many people here who have acquired a considerable fund of information through reading, and a still greater number who have achieved in the school of experience a level of education worthy of respect at the same time that they are a credit to our nationality. During my brief stay on Rock Prairie last summer (1868) I had time to visit only a comparatively small number of farmers; but I hope on a later occasion to have an opportunity to become personally acquainted with the many people whom, as yet, I have learned to know and respect only through their reputation and the reports of others.

After I visited Rock Prairie last summer I wrote the following report on the religious situation there:* "The settlement then formed a congregation which in the synodal reports goes by the name of 'Luther Valley.' Reverend [C. F.] Magelsen, son of Dean [Wilhelm Chr. M.] Magelsen of Toten in Norway, has for nine years served as its pastor. His salary amounts to $200 per annum, but in addition an approximately equal sum is collected in offerings and from fees for various types of services. So his total yearly income from this congregation probably amounts to about $400.00. The pastoral lands comprise forty acres, with good limestone buildings. Not far from the parsonage lies the church, a stone structure, which is now too small. Hence there has been some talk of replacing this one church with two new ones more conveniently located for the people in the settlement. The congregation at Rock Prairie was until recently a member of the Norwegian Evangelical Lutheran Church (the Missouri Synod). There probably are a few families that belong to the Augustana Synod, as well as five families that have not joined any congregation. For the instruction of the young in the elements of Christianity there are three teachers, all former students at teachers' colleges in Norway. Two of them, Hans Thingvold and Ole Klevmoen, are from the parish of Land. The third one, Iver Ingebrigtsen Ytterli, who previously taught school in Norway, also serves as sexton in the church. Each of them conducts school about three months during the year at a salary of $20.00 per month plus board while teaching. The pastor on Rock Prairie has also served the congregations at Albany, Janesville, Beloit, and Jefferson Prairie as annexes and Long Prairie, Queen Anne, and Rock Run in Illinois as mission churches."

The account given is, as I said, a sketch of conditions as I found them in the settlement during my brief stay last summer. Since then the situation has changed. The demon of discord has won entry into the congregation, the result of which has been extended controversy ending in a complete schism. That it should come to such an extreme surprises me very much because, as far as I could gather, the utmost harmony existed between pastor and parish. Some members undoubtedly opposed the Synod's teachings about slavery and resented the fact that in this controversy Reverend Magelsen defended the

**Billed-Magazin*, May 15, 1869.

Synod. Still, they spoke with respect about their pastor in whom they saw an earnest and zealous servant of the Lord.

Before I end my account of the Rock River settlement, I wish to tell about still another settler with whom I had the pleasure of becoming personally acquainted. He is L. S. Heyerdahl, a thoughtful man, educated well beyond the average. As a result he has frequently filled township positions and on numerous occasions represented his congregation in synodical meetings. It would have pleased me greatly to give a full account of Mr. Heyerdahl's life. But because of the limited space available, I will restrict myself to some brief remarks—and this mostly so that the many readers of *Billed-Magazin* in the homeland may have still another source of correct information about the prospects for the rural classes in America.

L. S. Heyerdahl emigrated from Høland, Norway, in 1853. He came as a printer to Rock Prairie where the newspaper *Emigranten* was then being published. He was employed for seven years as a typesetter but then bought 120 acres of land. "On this farm," he says, "I can produce, during average years, 350 bushels of wheat, 400 bushels of oats, and 350 bushels of corn." He believes it would be possible to feed thirty cattle, twenty sheep, and three horses on his farm. Heyerdahl, however, does not keep that many animals, but has leased out some meadow land. He does most of the work himself and hires help only during seeding and harvesting time.

"It seems to me," he says "that the farmers in Norway usually make the mistake of keeping too many people. Their methods of work are too laborious and consequently each man accomplishes too little. The soil in Norway is very fertile in many places that I am acquainted with. I feel certain that anyone who has learned how to manage things in America would do very well if he bought a farm in Norway provided he had some capital to start with. It does not take much skill to run a farm profitably in this country. I had been a printer all my life but I soon learned to operate my farm just as productively as the others. Hard work breeds success, and diligence makes a farmer prosperous. During the summer, to be sure, a farmer must carry many a heavy load; but, in return, he has many easy days during the winter. I know a man named Christian Nelson Nyhus from Land parish. Three years ago he bought 120 acres in this settlement for $15 per acre. He made a down payment of $300 against the total of $1800, and he also owned some cattle. Now the whole debt has been cleared. He has also bought machinery for several hundred dollars and made many improvements on the farm. I suppose results like these can not be cited as general, but this one case does suggest how favorable conditions here have been for the farmers."

The great majority of the settlers are with heart and soul devoted to the principles of the Republican Party. There are many who participate actively in discussions concerning the most vital questions of the day, but without indulging in the cheap political palaver or scrambling for popularity which, in certain places, have demoralized more than one of our otherwise reliable countrymen. "All of us on Rock Prairie," said one of my informants, "have in recent years voted the Republican ticket with the possible exception of some ten men who, out of old habit, still follow the Democratic banner. However, we are not 'voting cattle,' but stick by the Party only as long as our convictions tell us to follow its leadership."

Most of the Norwegian emigrants have preferred farming to any other occupation in life. This was especially true during the early years, when the emigrant ranks were filled almost exclusively with people from the mountain regions who from early childhood were accustomed to regard tillage and cattle-raising as the surest source of food and income. The turmoil and instability of city life did not agree with their conception of well-being. They left the old country in order to find a plot of ground on this side of the ocean which they could call their own. With great reluctance a few of them did take temporary jobs in the cities as servants or day laborers but only in order to earn enough money to buy a little land in regions which the red men had abandoned for new hunting grounds in far western wilds still untouched by civilization.

Only in recent years, when city people have also become a part of the emigration movement, has the situation changed somewhat. As might be expected, the latter prefer city life to the rather monotonous existence in the country. But even now the majority of our countrymen scatter about on the plains of the Northwest which lie there ready for cultivation. With the industry and stamina characteristic of our people they soon transform these regions into productive grain fields and flourishing pastures. Therefore the Yankees declare that among all nationalities from the Old World who immigrate to America, the Scandinavians, in relation to their number, are of the greatest service to this country. Their industry makes them excellent clearers of land and their frugality creates prosperity. They are loyal and willingly obey the laws. They have a natural feeling for orderly behavior and there are few criminals among them.

The Irish, on the other hand, form almost a complete contrast to the Scandinavians. They prefer town life, and many of the cities in this country are rimmed by several rows of Irish shanties which surround the business district like a frame. Here the sons of Erin live in complete harmony with the habits of their forefathers. Recognizing that they are no longer under English jurisdiction and are not restrained by the overseers of vigilant landlords, they not infrequently behave in a manner which attracts the attention of the police. Their houses are easily spotted by their crude, often filthy appearance and by the flocks of pigs around them which, to the annoyance of the neighbors, seem to have a still more mistaken conception of unrestricted American liberty than the owners themselves. Pigs and potatoes are important elements of an Irishman's life. He talks about them in the daytime and dreams about them at night. Seldom do two pure-blooded Irishmen meet without their conversation either beginning or ending with "pigs."

But despite the fact that the Irishmen are usually looked down upon by people of other nationalities, they have played an important role in America's economic life. As ditch diggers and railroad builders they are in their right place. With spade in hand an Irishman is unequalled. Very likely the steam locomotive would not for a long time yet have been carrying the products of China from the Pacific coast all the way to the shores of the Atlantic had not the multitudes from the Emerald Isle built the roads which made the "iron horse" one of the great promoters of civilization. It must therefore be admitted that the uninformed Irishmen, as railroad builders, have contributed just as much as their more educated fellow citizens to the development of culture, trade, and industry in this country. Even though the Irishman personally may not be concerned about pure air, he eradicates the danger of swamp fever for others when as a ditch digger he transforms the marshlands into meadows and fields. Cleanliness is not among the main virtues of an Irishman, but he serves the cause of public health by sweeping the streets and cleaning the sewers. It has been said that without the ox as draft animal areas of America's most fertile grain districts would still be unmarked by the plow. Just as truly it may be said that the country's complex railroad system owes its origin in a great degree to the Irishman's skill with the pick and spade. Without the railroads the Indians would still be sole rulers of territories they long ago relinquished to the white men, who, following the railroads, have spread over the country to win from the soil those riches which the red men, interested solely in hunting and fighting, let lie unused.

The industrious German, no doubt, prefers the city to the monotony of country life. But he is, nevertheless, a capable clearer and diligent cultivator of the soil if circumstances force him to live outside the city limits. As a gardener he is unrivalled; no one knows better than the German how to make every plot of ground productive. Because he finds it relatively difficult to master the English language, he prefers to use his mother tongue. And even though, with his whole heart, he hates Germany's many tyrants, both great and small, he does not find it easy to familiarize himself with American ideas of liberty. It takes a long time for the fact to sink into his head that complete equality is compatible with law-abiding citizenship. He loves music and song, while gymnastic exhibits and similar performances are among his favorite amusements. But above everything else he loves his beer; and as hotel manager, saloon keeper, or restaurant owner he is in his right element. The Germans are diligent craftsmen and capable artists; even as scholars they know how to attract attention in this country. Furthermore, they are keen merchants and alert businessmen.

Even though in this country the Finns are offered wheat bread, they cannot forget their Finnish rye; and they talk with enthusiasm about "de tusen sjöars land" (the land of a thousand lakes) which we know from Runeberg's songs. They are hardy and industrious tillers of the fields who combine frugality and respect for the law with their diligence. Apparently the Muscovites have not as yet found their way to America; but the Poles have found here a haven of liberty where, undisturbed by the czar's spies, they can hum their "noch ist Polen nicht verloren." The Frenchman continue to be polite even in this country, and only in the third or fourth generation does the Yankee's cold, restrained social behavior replace the unique courtesy and polished manners so characteristic of the French.

Beloit

THE TOWN of Beloit has been repeatedly mentioned in this series on the history of the Scandinavian settlements.* It is one of the oldest towns in the state. When our countrymen first set foot on Wisconsin soil they found in Beloit a flour mill and some small, timbered shop-buildings which gave hints that a town might later develop here. Located about midway between two of the oldest Norwegian colonies in this part of the country, namely Jefferson Prairie on one side and Rock Prairie on the other, Beloit would necessarily become of great importance for the growth of these settlements during the years immediately following the earliest migration. To be sure, the stock of goods was meager and the prices were high, as the merchants had to purchase their wares far away and haul them in wagons long distances through trackless regions. But the wants of the simple pioneers were easily satisfied; and they considered it great good fortune that they could obtain most of the prime necessities of life fairly close at hand. Thus, at Beloit the newcomers could buy flour as well as the implements most needed for farm work. Furthermore, the presence of a mill was a godsend for the nearby settlements that can be fully appreciated only by people who have had to travel scores of miles through uninhabited areas to get their grain, the gift of Ceres, ground into food.

Barely thirty years ago the whole area about Beloit had the forbidding appearance of a wilderness. The difference between then and now is so striking that even eyewitnesses can hardly believe the transformation when they think back and compare conditions only three decades ago with the way things are at present. A stranger who visits Beloit today and makes a tour of the surrounding area will see everywhere signs of prosperity and progress. Spacious cultivated fields, tastefully planned gardens, neat buildings, com-

**Billed-Magazin*, May 29, 1869.

fortably furnished farmhouses, and excellent equipment speak convincingly of the people's well-being. When one learns that all this has been accomplished in thirty years, his spontaneous reaction will be to recall the magic flute of the fairy tales which, in a moment, could conjure forth great castles, populous cities, and droves of cattle. He would reason that something similar must have occurred here if men still in their best years can really remember this area—now blessed with the fruits of civilization—as a dreary wilderness inhabited only by wild animals and Indian hunters. However, many of the first pioneers to plow these plains are still here to testify, so reason must yield to faith and doubt give place to admiration for a phenomenon which, measured by European criteria, borders on the impossible. Only repeated exposure to such transformations gradually compels one to abandon Old World notions about pioneer crudity and the slow development of culture on the frontier. The speedy clearing of the land, the rapid increase of population, the growth of cities, the increasing prosperity, the thriving industry and flourishing commerce—all these in combination present a picture of vitality, initiative, and energetic development to which the annals of history can not offer even the feeblest parallel.

The first settler came to Beloit in 1837 and the town charter was issued in 1845. The city is beautifully located on both sides of the Rock River, near the Wisconsin-Illinois line, and is surrounded by the state's largest prairie, which, toward the east, extends as far as the eye can reach. Above the fertile plain small elevations of fifty or sixty feet are found along the river banks. These are not only excellent building sites but they also add to the beauty of the city. Beloit is a flourishing commercial center, with a reaper factory favorably known throughout the Northwest, the state's largest paper mill, several woolen mills, and a soap factory. Manufacturing is, on the whole, quite considerable and is the main source of the city's commercial activity. The excellent waterpower furnished by the Rock River is one of Beloit's main assets. The city is famed for its healthful location and its rural, peaceful charm. Many rich men from the East have retired after a successful business life to Beloit, where they have found the cultivated companionship and the tranquility which refresh both body and spirit.

The population of the city at present numbers about 6,000. But first and foremost Beloit College has become famous in wide circles. Without any fear of exaggeration it can be said that, next to the University of Michigan, there is no other institution of higher learning in the entire Northwest which gives its students as thorough and comprehensive an education. The college was founded by the Congregational Church of Wisconsin in 1847. The value of its buildings is estimated at $40,000. The instruction is carried on by eight teachers, each of whom draws an annual salary of $1,500. Last year the student body numbered 391, of whom eight were Norwegians. Protected by shade trees, the park-like campus is located on an elevation near the city overlooking the surrounding country. When they are not attending lectures the students stay in buildings specially constructed for them at the institution. Expenses are met primarily by income from the school's substantial endowments. Besides landed property of 2,265 acres, valued at $19,000, the institution draws interest from accounts amounting to $113,500. The total annual income thus amounts to about $17,000.

However, it is not our purpose to give a description of the city of Beloit, which we have merely mentioned in passing as it lies midway between two of the oldest and largest Norwegian settlements in Wisconsin. But the fact that several of our fellow countrymen have, of late, settled in the city deserves our special attention. Hence we will spend a few extra moments in Beloit to hear what our friends from the land of our birth have to tell us.

John Thompson from the parish of Bjerknes in Norway came to America eighteen years ago and settled in Beloit. Fortune has been kind to him: he owns a wagon factory and is said to be a wealthy man. Carelius Hansen from Grue (born on the Opager farm) emigrated in 1853 and came the following year to Beloit, which then numbered only two Norwegians among its inhabitants, shoemaker Peder Andersen from Voss and John Thompson. Hansen was trained as a gunsmith in Norway and shortly after his arrival got a job as a blacksmith. He has now run his own shop for about eleven years and has won first prize for plows that he has exhibited at the fair. Consequently, orders come to him regularly even from faraway places in Iowa and Minnesota. Carpenter Nils Ingebrigtsen from Hønefoss in Norway likewise settled in Beloit in 1854. He is now in business as a contractor and does work both in the city and in the surrounding area.

Shoemaker Nils Aurdal was the next of our countrymen to settle in Beloit. Then came Carl Ledell from Vardal, who at present is employed in the reaper factory. Both of them arrived in 1854. O. P. Tandberg from Gran, Hadeland, came to this country sixteen years ago with his parents and their four other children. This family was one of the first to emigrate from that part of Norway. After a stay of five years in Muskego, Tandberg came to Beloit where at present, as foreman of a shop connected with the reaper factory, he draws good wages and has steady work.

All of the above-mentioned men are now well-off, own homes in the city, and manage lucrative businesses. But—more important—they have, through their integrity and orderly life, won the respect of their fellow citizens. Consequently the term "Norwegian" has a good ring here, as elsewhere in the state, among all nationalities.

Because many copies of *Billed-Magazin* are sent to Norway, we will add a few more reports which may give still more graphic ideas concerning conditions in the New World. They can be looked upon as messages from America to friends and relatives in Norway.

Ole Jacob Johnson from Hadeland has lived for nine years in Beloit where he earns good daily wages in a blacksmith shop. He owns his home and has other property besides. Johannes Thorstensen Gaarder from Grue came to America nine years ago and is now foreman in a shoemaker's shop where he earns two dollars per day. He also owns a house and is well-off. Brede Hermandsen Lie emigrated from Brandval in 1863 and came to America with a large family. As a laborer in the Beloit paper mill he has a good income. Bernt Bredesen, nephew of the well-known John Bredesen in Solør, came to Beloit in 1867 and works at the reaper factory, earning $1.50 per day. His brother, Ole Bredesen, who arrived from Brandval with his family last year, has a position as a blacksmith. Arne Larsen Hagen from Grue and David Jensen from Nannestad, who have been here two years, earn $1.50 per day at the paper mill. Halvor Bredesen Langbraaten from Brandval has his own shoemaker shop and does good business. Halvor Halvorsen Bjørnstad, also from Brandval, has been in America five years and earns twelve dollars per week at a shoemaker's shop.

Among the Norwegians who settled in Beloit during the years 1866 and 1867 we will mention the following. Ole Gundersen Onsrud from Brandval emigrated at the age of fifty with his family. He works in a paint shop at $1.25 per day and is well satisfied with life in America. Ole Olsen Vestli from Grue and his brother Theodor are employed as painters and earn about $8.00 per week. Both are well satisfied with their position and claim that even the father of a family can save part of such a salary for the future. Two more men from Brandval, Hans Olsen Bingen and Julius A. Fjeld, both heads of families, earn $12 per week each as blacksmiths, while Ole Sivertsen Brandvoldsmoen works in the paper mill at a daily wage of $1.50.

The men just mentioned have been in the country only a short time. They are satisfied, however, and give thanks to fortune which permits them to face the future without any worries. They expressed the conviction that two skilled hands insure against want and that diligence combined with frugality clears the way toward happiness and affluence.

About nine months have passed since the account above was written. It is possible that in the meantime some of the people mentioned have moved or have entered new positions. But even if this is the case, it will not seriously alter the main features of the picture. At least, those people in old Norway who are interested in emigrating and for whom wages in this country are a determining factor will obtain some useful information through these reports.

Before leaving Beloit we wish to tell about the merchant Ole Gulliksen Springen. At the age of nineteen he joined the army as a volunteer at the outbreak of the Civil War and for two years fought with honor in defense of his country. But after the battle of Brantwood Station in Tennessee he, together with some 700 Union soldiers, was taken prisoner to the notorious Libby Prison in Richmond. "The rebel cavalry drove us in forced marches for 120 English miles without any food," he reported. "Consequently many fainted because of weakness and were then pierced, without any qualms, by the bullets of our captors. An even worse fate awaited the survivors, who were exposed in the loathsome prison to the agony of hunger and disease, the persecution of the guards, and the deadly hatred of the rebels." At the exchange of prisoners there were only 400 left of the 700; the rest had succumbed to the brutalities inflicted on them. O. G. Springen was one of those privileged to be reunited with his parents, brothers, and sisters. But he returned home broken in health. Days and years passed before he began to regain his strength. "I realized," said his father, "that my son would never again be sturdy enough to take up ordinary farming. It was therefore decided that, together with his brother Knud, he should establish himself as a merchant in Beloit." They started with a capital of $2,000, have had good business, and enjoy confidence and respect. The firm "Springen" is the only mercantile establishment owned by Scandinavians in Beloit.

George Hamlin from Sweden, who operates a watchmaker's shop, has been in Beloit about twelve years and is now a wealthy man. His countryman, J. C. Björklund, a mason by profession, has no grounds for complaint either, although he has been in this country only three years. There are also a couple of families as well as four or five single persons here from Denmark. They make their living as craftsmen and are held to be dependable, industrious workers. With one exception, all of them are to be accounted newcomers as they have been in Beloit only two or three years.

All told, there are about twenty-five Scandinavian families here and not a few unmarried persons; most of them are craftsmen and only a few are ordinary day laborers. The number of Norwegian servant girls was given to me as 100. The figure is perhaps exaggerated; but this much is clear, that they are preferred to other nationalities and are usually offered better weekly wages than the rest. A servant maid generally earns two dollars per week, with a few receiving $2.50 to $3. In cases where special capability is demonstrated, wages may even reach $4 or $5 per week.

The total number of Scandinavians in Beloit can not be much below 250. As yet there is no Norwegian church here; but services are conducted by the pastor from Rock Prairie in a hall rented for the purpose. Moral conditions are good. The artisans are praised for their competence, the day laborers for their diligence and reliability, and the Norwegian businessmen for their integrity—such is the verdict pronounced by their fellow citizens, whether German, Irish, or American.

Koshkonong

THE KOSHKONONG settlement comprises the townships of Dunkirk, Albion, Christiana, and Pleasant Spring that together form a quadrangle of 144 English square miles (about three Norwegian) in the southeastern corner of Dane county, which borders toward the south on Rock county and toward the east on Jefferson county.* The name—which is of Indian origin, derived from ''Kosh-kaw a-nong''—means ''the lake we live by'' and was originally applied only to a lake near the eastern boundary; but at present, in daily conversation, it is also used as the name for the area of land mentioned above. The local Norwegians, however, frequently pronounce it ''Kaskeland.''

The history of the first Norwegian immigrants is filled with stories of disappointment and sorrow. As is well known, our countrymen did not find the happiness they sought near Rochester, New York. Beaver Creek brought only adversity and misfortune; neither were the majority of the settlers satisfied at Fox River; and Muskego's marshes and pestilential atmosphere soon bred discouragement and gnawing anguish. The settlements at Jefferson Prairie and Rock Prairie, on the other hand, fared well and advanced rapidly in both prosperity and population. The same is true, to a certain extent, of the Yorkville and Norway areas. At about the time when the latter places were settled, our countrymen began spreading over regions known as Koshkonong. But as this term is not recognized officially except as the name of a district in Jefferson county, we will discuss separately the four townships known collectively as ''Koshkonong'' by our countrymen, and begin with Albion township, which is located in the southeast corner of Dane county.

Albion township

Concerning the Norwegian migration to and settlement in Albion township

*_Billed-Magazin_, June 19, 1869.

we will let one of the earliest settlers, Amund Andersen Hornefjeld from Mosterøy, speak:

''Knud Slogvigen, who in 1824 [sic] came to America on the renowned Stavanger sloop, returned to the home country in 1835. He had lived most of the time in Illinois, and the account he gave of conditions in the New World encouraged many Norwegians to seek homes beyond the ocean. The following year (1836) two brigs left Stavanger with a total of about 150 passengers, most of them from the city's environs and some from Hardanger. Knud Slogvigen was the real instigator of this migration and consequently went along as interpreter and guide. This first large emigration was the occasion of much talk and aroused great surprise in town and country. I was one of the passengers. There was no lack of warnings. Threats of slavery, sickness, and death formed the core of conversations with acquaintances and others before our departure. But after a fortunate passage, we landed in New York and went on to Chicago, whence we proceeded to the Ottawa settlement in La Salle county, Illinois. Only a few of our group remained in Rochester, New York, and in Chicago. The majority went to Fox River where we met the 1824 Sloopers from Stavanger as well as a few who had emigrated since that expedition.

''Most of us got work at once; and the wages were acceptable, measured by the standards of those days. During the second year there was much sickness among the settlers and this gave rise to despondency and dissatisfaction. In 1837 many of Ole Rynning's group also came to Ottawa on the Fox River. The number of people increased, to be sure, but the prevailing spirit was far from satisfactory. I stayed in the settlement four years. Then I, together with John Skjærping, a shoemaker from Bergen who had come to America with Ole Rynning's party, and Erik Johannesen from Kvinnherad, who emigrated from Stavanger in 1836, agreed to look about in other parts of the country. During our wanderings we came in the spring of 1840 to Muskego, where Norwegians had settled the previous year. But we did not like the place, so we decided to go farther west. The trip took us through forests and over empty spaces. Only here and there did we see a lonely pioneer cabin and a few other signs of human habitation. In Fort Atkinson, at present a flourishing town, there was then only one log cabin. After a long and wearisome journey we finally came to Koshkonong.

''Here we found a proper combination of woodland and prairie, and since the soil impressed us as especially fertile, we considered this area particularly well suited for the founding of a settlement. Consequently we decided to return to Ottawa and tell our friends about our discoveries. As a result many of them made up their minds to go north and examine the area. Accompanied by Thorsten (Tosten) Olsen, Lars Dugstad, and Bjørn Andersen I paid a second visit to Koshkonong that same summer. Later we went to the land office in

Milwaukee to buy the pieces of land we had selected as homesteads, whereupon we again went to Ottawa to make preparations for the final departure. In order to give the reader some idea about the extent of these travels, we should add that the distance from Koshkonong to Ottawa is more than 200 miles while the distance to Milwaukee is about 70 miles. Furthermore, the trips generally went through uninhabited areas so it was only on rare occasions that we had a roof over our heads at night.

"In 1840 Thorsten Olsen and I again came to Koshkonong and settled in the region which later received the township name of Albion. At the time it was an absolute wilderness. Indians and wild animals held complete sway. The woods were still unmarked by the white man's axe and the plowshare had put no furrows in the fertile prairie soil. Both of us were unmarried and we lived together in a cabin the first winter. The following spring, 1841, Bjørn Andersen with his family came and settled near us. I was thirty years of age on leaving Norway, stayed four years in La Salle county, and have since lived twenty-nine years on my farm in this settlement."

Thus far the man's own narrative. We will merely add that Amund Hornefjeld now owns 160 acres of exceptionally good and well-cultivated land with solid buildings. He is a well-to-do man. But only by hard work, self-denial, and privation has he fought his way to his present position. To be sure, the bitter experiences of life are written in deep runes on his brow. Now, however, he can look forward to an old age free of worries and think with pleasure of the past years which at times brought their griefs and sorrows but also were rich with the Lord's blessings. "I am well satisfied with life," says old Amund, "and have no complaints against the country. I only wish that there was more honesty and less humbug. If this were the case, America would give the industrious worker a still happier home than is true at present."

Thorsten Olsen Bjodland, mentioned above as Amund's companion from the Fox River settlement to Albion, deserves our attention especially because he is one of the few survivors of the fifty-two persons who boarded ship in 1824 [sic] intent on settling in America. He came from Hå, four and a half Norwegian miles south of Stavanger, was thirty years of age when he left his native land, and possessed at the time about 600 *speciedaler*. After an adventurous trip, Thorsten arrived in Rochester but stayed there only a short time. Then he went to Middlepoint on the Fox River where, after a while, a Norwegian settlement was formed. Finally he joined Amund Hornefjeld and settled at Koshkonong. But poor Thorsten: he has not danced on roses during his forty-five years in the New World. After having survived the various stages of pioneer hardship, he acquired a farm in Albion township, and it seemed for a while that he would find there the happiness which for so long had been the object of his striving.

But an unkind fate decreed otherwise. He engaged in trade with one of his fellow Norwegians, was cheated and lost all his property—the fruit of long years of hard labor. He was a ruined man. "Ever since then I have been like one paralyzed," he says, "robbed of all strength and spirit for new undertakings." Poor Thorsten. At present he lives on the liberality of others. Although he is nearly seventy-five years old, he is still capable of doing manual labor; but his mental powers are broken. Despite the fact that his memory is so poor that only on occasion does he recall past events as faint dream pictures, the iron hand of former calamities has impressed on his spirit a tinge of bitterness and world-weariness which expresses itself through melancholy, a desire for solitude, and a distrust of all mankind. His friend from earlier, better days—Amund Hornefjeld—has not forgotten his traveling companion through the Wisconsin wilderness, however, but sees to it that the poor man has his daily bread and a roof over his head.

Bjørn Andersen Kvelve, whom we have already mentioned, was born in the year 1801 at Vikedal, north of Stavanger.* He is said to have been a handsome, strongly-built man equipped with a good mind and a fearless and determined disposition bordering on the obstinate. Furthermore, he was clever with his hands and had an aptitude for technical matters. Bjørn Andersen was exactly the kind of man who was not intimidated by the uninhabited wilderness, while his diversified skills made the difficulties of pioneer life easier to deal with. Some time before he left Norway he was married to Miss Abel Kathrine von Krogh, a daughter of Colonel von Krogh. This marriage caused much resentment, as the wife's relatives could never forgive her that she, a well-born young lady, could condescend to marry a farmer's son. From that time on, the Krogh family regarded her as an outcast while her husband was hated as the instigator of her imagined dishonor. The unpleasantness which sprang from this situation made a further stay in the homeland well-nigh impossible. An added source of vexation for the couple was the fact that Bjørn Andersen was a Quaker, since those who deviated from the teachings of the state church were at that time looked upon as apostates and heretics.

There were, thus, weighty reasons for leaving; and when the young wife, rebuffed by her family, especially wished to get away from conditions which brought her only sorrow and vexation, the thought of emigrating soon ripened into a firm resolution. As already mentioned, two ships left Stavanger in 1836 loaded with emigrants, among whom were a number of Quakers. Bjørn Andersen and his wife had registered as passengers, and after a voyage of six weeks they arrived in New York. Thence they went to Rochester, where many of the Sloopers still resided. There he worked two years as a cooper, and from that time on was generally known as *Tøndebjørn* (Barrel Bjørn). The majority of his fellow passengers, however, went farther west immediately, many of

**Billed-Magazin*, June 26, 1869.

them settling near Fox River in La Salle county, where they met more of the Sloopers, who, disappointed with their stay near Rochester, New York, had sought homesteads in this region. Bjørn remained in Fox River a couple of years, supporting himself with day labor, until he left with Amund Hornefjeld and several others to inspect areas in Wisconsin.

Conditions in the newly-founded community at Muskego were not such as to encourage settling. They decided to examine other parts of the state, and finally came to the Lake Koshkonong area, where they found everything to their liking, and consequently, determined to locate a Norwegian settlement there. The group then returned to La Salle in order to inform their countrymen of the results of their investigation. Ole Rynning's party met Bjørn Andersen in Chicago just as he was returning from Wisconsin. The unfavorable description Andersen gave of the country both to the west and to the north discouraged these newcomers from settling near any of the existing Norwegian communities. The result was the founding of the Beaver Creek settlement, whose tragic story is all too well known among the Scandinavians of the Northwest. In this connection, bitter accusations have been lodged against Bjørn Andersen, whom people have blamed in large part for the fatalities at Beaver Creek. It is generally the case that human beings like to blame others for their misfortunes. This is no doubt especially true of newcomers beset by adversity. At any rate, it is our conviction that in the name of justice we must say that the accusations against Bjørn Andersen have been too grave and even perhaps quite unfounded.[23]

In 1841, a year after Amund Hornefjeld had settled in Albion township, Bjørn Andersen Kvelve with his family came to that district. Hence he and his wife were the first white couple to settle in the township. He bought forty acres of government land in the northwest corner of the township and built a log cabin which henceforth was their home. As a day laborer he had acquired some cattle in the Fox River settlement, and at first these were the main source of sustenance for the family—until enough of the fertile soil was put under cultivation to provide them with food. Implements for cultivating the soil were at that time very inefficient. Until the pioneer farmer was able to acquire a team of draft animals he made but slow progress against the wilderness, which he found in a state unchanged since the creation of the world. Bjørn had to endure all the hardships which were inseparable from frontier life in those days. Six cents was all the cash he had during the first years; and there was no opportunity to earn money in what was then one of the most primitive regions in the state. The couple could merely save some butter, which Andersen carried on his back all the way to Milwaukee. There he exchanged it for flour and other necessities, with which he then had to trudge through thick woods and over lonely prairies as yet seldom trodden by the feet of white men.

But the die was cast. The homeland, where relatives and friends dwelt, lay far away beyond the vast ocean; there was no use dreaming of returning, for the means were lacking. Only courage and endurance could save them from complete ruin. Fortunately, Bjørn Andersen was blessed with these characteristics. Through hard work he succeeded, in time, in achieving better economic circumstances. The surrounding areas were gradually settled, and neighbors could lend each other a helping hand. The easing of frontier conditions which accompanied the growing population naturally benefitted the earliest settlers most. Bjørn finally became a well-to-do man. When he succumbed to the cholera epidemic which attacked the settlement in 1850, he was the owner of 230 acres of especially fertile soil well equipped with good buildings and livestock. His widow is still living. She is spoken of as a charming woman of a pleasant and devout disposition, possessed of all the virtues which are an adornment to her sex.

Her husband, on the other hand, has been variously judged. Some there are who praise him for his helpfulness, honesty, and orderliness, while others describe him as quarrelsome and vengeful. It is easily understood that opinions would vary about a man who differed from his neighbors in religious beliefs. Even in our day, religion is a source of disagreement and misunderstanding among men. As a Quaker, Bjørn was hated to some degree by people of other views. We can also add that he frequently engaged in disputes with Pastor [J.W.C.] Dietrichson, who then served the Koshkonong parish. These two men held views about Christianity which mixed about as well as fire and water. However, this does not concern us here. Our objective is to give a history of the founding and later development of the various Scandinavian settlements. It is in this connection that we have recorded a fraction of Bjørn Andersen's life story. To be sure, he can not be counted among those fathers of emigration who have exerted the strongest influence on the exodus from the Scandinavian countries, such as Cleng Peerson, Ole Rynning, Ansten Nattestad, Mrs. Wærenskjold, Reiersen, Gasmann, and others. But the fact that he was a member of the first large group of emigrants which left Norway and that he was one of the founders of the most populous Norwegian community in America entitles him to a place in the history of our settlements.

Bjørn Andersen did not live to enjoy the fruits of his labors. Just at the time when fortune began to smile on him, the Angel of Death knocked at his door—the sand in his hourglass had run out. The earth took back what it had given, and his body has now for almost a score of years rested in the bosom of our common mother. But his many children are presently living in very good circumstances. One of his sons, Rasmus B. Andersen, has held a position as professor at Albion Academy and is at present connected with the state university at Madison.[24] One of his daughters is married to Pastor [S.S.] Reque in Lemonweir, Juneau county, Wisconsin; and another daughter is married to

*The house built by Gunnul Olsen Vind*æg in Christiana in 1840.

Pastor [T.A.] Torgersen in Worth county, Iowa. The rest of his surviving children are also living in good circumstances. But the father was not granted the privilege of seeing any of his offspring enter the portals of manhood or womanhood. Weary of life's battles he descended into the grave at a rather early age, but his oft-expressed hope of winning "a better future for my children" has been fulfilled.

Christiana township

The first Norwegian to settle in this township was Gunnul Olsen Vindæg from Rollag in Numedal.* He was the son of a farmer, enterprising and active, but of a somewhat restless spirit with a desire for travel and change. When Ansten Nattestad returned from America in 1838, Vindæg was one of those who decided to emigrate the following spring. Because of a child's illness he was separated from his group in Drammen, but a bit later he managed to secure passage from there to New York. Then he followed the usual emigrant route westward to Chicago and thence onward to Jefferson Prairie where a majority of Nattestad's followers had settled during the summer. Next he stayed several months in the neighborhood of Beloit, but in the spring of 1840 he built a little boat in which he rowed up the Rock River and farther on, until he found a region where the land pleased him. This happened

***Billed-Magazin*, November 6, 1869.

to be located in the southeastern part of the present township of Christiana, where he settled. At that time the whole region now known as Koshkonong was practically uninhabited. Merely a handful of pioneers, probably not numbering even half a score, had ventured into the wilderness, all of them Americans who lived far apart from each other. The land still belonged to the wild animals and the Indians, who seemed to have a special love for this area. Under such circumstances Vindæg's trip from Beloit to Koshkonong was no trivial undertaking. He had need of just as much courage as the undaunted pioneer who is our day penetrates deep into the Far West to settle in the wilderness where the sway of the red man is still unbroken.

Amund Andersen Hornefjeld, Bjørn Andersen, and Lars Dugstad—all of whom were mentioned in the account of Albion township—had chosen land on Koshkonong the previous year, 1839, but none of them had settled there at the time when Vindæg first anchored his boat near the place which was to become his home. To be sure, the three others arrived the same year and settled in the neighboring township, but this happened later in the summer; in reality Gunnul Vindæg was the first of our countrymen to settle on Koshkonong. The founders of the three large and thriving settlements at Rock Prairie, Jefferson Prairie, and Koshkonong were thus all from Numedal, and their migration in 1839 was a consequence of Ansten Nattestad's visit to his homeland. Vindæg was a poor man when he came to America; but he was a skilled blacksmith and a tireless worker. It was not his fate, however, to enjoy for long the advantages of life on this side of the ocean. Only eight years after his arrival in America he died as the result of an accident. At the time he owned about 200 acres of land. One of his sons now runs the farm.

Vindæg wrote frequently to his friends in Norway, who were thereby encouraged to emigrate. It seems that he was one of those who at times overshot the mark; there are numerous stories in circulation about the contents of his America letters. Many newcomers evidently discovered that the reality did not measure up to expectations; and Vindæg, who had advised them to emigrate, has on occasion been blamed for letting his friends in Norway see the New World in altogether too rosy colors.

When tracing the gradual development of the settlement, the second man we meet is John Haldorsen Bjørgo from Voss. His father was a farmer and John was the youngest of nine children. Gjert Hovland, one of the Stavanger Sloopers [*sic*], had written home, and a Haugean preacher carried a copy of the letter with him to various communities, among them Voss. The letter was full of praise of America and this was what led John Bjørgo and Nils Larsen Bolstad from the same parish to emigrate. Nils Røthe, also from Voss, had gone the previous year, 1835, by ship from Stavanger to Gothenburg and thence to New York. Bjørgo and Bolstad, however, went directly from Bergen to New York with the first ship which transported emigrants from that city to America. They met Nils Røthe, the first migrant from Voss, in Rochester, where he was living with his family in very poor circumstances. It was Gjert Hovland's letter which had inspired him, also, to tempt fortune in a strange continent. Gjert later moved to La Salle county in Illinois. John Bjørgo worked a week in Rochester, thus earning enough money to pay for his fare to Chicago. Here a few days more of work put some food in his knapsack and three dollars in his pocket, after which his travels continued on foot seventy miles westward to La Salle county, where some of the Sloopers, as previously mentioned, had founded a Norwegian settlement. "Here," so Bjørgo reports, "I soon got work. With my money I bought a scythe and a whetstone and during the fall season I earned a dollar per day cutting hay. From then on things went steadily forward, and after staying there five years I had saved enough to set me thinking of getting a home of my own."

In April, 1840, several men from the La Salle settlement went north to look for homesteads in Wisconsin. Among members of this exploring group I will mention Nils Bolstad (now deceased), Nils Gilderhus (now in Minnesota), and Magne Bystølen (deceased in Minnesota). During their journey they too came to the region now called Christiana, which pleased them very much, and so they went immediately to the land office in Milwaukee where they were allotted homesteads on Koshkonong. When they returned to La Salle they told about their discoveries, and as there was still an abundance of unclaimed fertile land, many of their countrymen decided to leave Illinois and settle in Wisconsin. John Bjørgo did so in the spring of 1841; and a bit later that same season Ole Sivertsen Gilderhus settled a little farther to the north, in the neighboring township of Deerfield. He is a brother of the above-mentioned Nils Gilderhus who, a year earlier, had been exploring in this area. "Now we wrote to our friends," John Bjørgo reports, "and told them about the land hereabouts. No one but Norwegians lived in this region until well into the summer of 1841. Then a few Americans came; and during the years 1842 and 1843 we had the joy of seeing many of our countrymen move in. From then on settlers came rapidly so it was not long before all the land was bought up. We helped the newcomers as best we could and our community became widely known."

During the first winter John Bjørgo lived in a little log cabin he had built three miles distant from the nearest white neighbor. He was unmarried at the time and thus had to cook his own meals and do all the other household work. An Indian tribe had pitched camp near his cabin and lived there from the fall until the following spring. "They were good, friendly neighbors," he reports, "and we always got along well with each other. Frequently they were guests of mine, and I visited them. It never occurred to me to harbor any fear of these red children of the wilderness, nor did they ever give me any reason for doing so. They were peaceful and gladly shared their meagre supplies with those who might need their help. There was an abundance of game at the time, but the wild animals disappeared as the land was gradually put under cultivation and the Indians were driven off.''

John Bjørgo is now a prosperous man. He owns 200 acres of especially good land well provided with buildings, cattle, and farm equipment. His estate probably amounts to about $15,000. He is still able-bodied and mentally alert. He likes to talk about events of past years: he has a good memory and a vivacious delivery which lends his stories a freshness and fullness that make them very entertaining. At the same time he speaks with an authority which can spring only from personal experience and observation.

In the year 1842 Jens Pedersen Vehus from Nore in Numedal came to the settlement. He was the brother of Vindæg's wife and was accompanied by Halvor Funkelien from Kongsberg and Thore Nore from Numedal. Later in the summer many other emigrants from Numedal arrived who became neighbors of their countrymen already settled in the area. These newcomers came by way of New York to Milwaukee and thence to the Norwegian community in Muskego—and finally to Koshkonong. Others came from Illinois by way of Jefferson Prairie. Gunnul Vindæg, as the first settler, was given the honor of choosing a name for the township when it was organized as a separate district. He wanted to commemorate the Norwegian capital, Christiania; but as orthography was not his forte, he unfortunately happened to write Christiana—the name which it still bears.

During the first couple of years health conditions were excellent, but when cultivation of the land began in earnest, cholera arrived. Many families were harried by this pestilence, the most fearful enemy of the pioneers of the time. The soil was extremely fertile and crops of 35 to 40 bushels per acre were by no means uncommon. But Milwaukee was the nearest market place; and it was no joyride to take a load of wheat on a *kubberulle*, pulled by a pair of oxen, over the largely trackless wilderness which then separated Koshkonong and Wisconsin's presently imposing metropolis on Lake Michigan.

The oldest person in the community today is, presumably, Kari Gulliksdatter Mogen from Flesberg, Numedal. She is ninety-three years old and has been in America twenty-one years. Kari came as a childless widow to her relatives in this country. She lives with her nephew, Ole Anderson Lande, can still do some work, remembers well many events of her childhood, and like most old people, prefers to talk about bygone days. The sailing ship *Tricolor* on which she came from Drammen took fourteen weeks and four days to cross the ocean—as far as we know, the longest time ever for any emigrant vessel. The mate aboard the boat at the time, Hans Fries, now lives as a prosperous and respected farmer in Muskego.

Lars Johansen Holo from Ringsaker left Norway in 1839 as the first emigrant from Hedmark. The circumstances which led to his migration seem to be as follows: a self-educated doctor by the name of Johannes Nordboe from Ringebu had travelled far and wide in Norway without finding any place that satisfied him. Hence he left for America where, for a while, he practiced medicine among the Norwegians in La Salle county, Illinois. He was a close friend of Cleng Peerson and probably accompanied him on some of his trips. Both of them later moved to Bosque county, Texas, where they lived as close neighbors until death parted them.[25] Nordboe is said to have died some two or three years ago. He wrote from America to his good friend Lars Holo, who, as a consequence, decided to emigrate. He sold his farm in the old country and, accompanied by a glass blower from Fåberg named Lauman, went from Christiania to Le Havre, France, where they secured accommodations on a ship which took them to New York. Then they went to Rochester, where Lars Holo stayed about a year and worked with his three grown sons on the canal. Next he traveled westward to the Norwegian settlement at Muskego, which had been founded the previous year. There he remained for three years, and in 1843 he came to the township of Christiana which since then has been his home. Lauman, however, settled in Missouri, where he died some years ago.

Seven years after Lars Holo's and Lauman's departure from Norway, Holo's brother, Anders Johansen Tømmerstigen, also came to America. He had been a farmer in Vardal and was thirty-nine years old when he left home in 1846. No one had previously left that community to cross the Atlantic. Consequently Anders Tømmerstigen's emigration aroused much attention and for a long time was a topic of conversation. There was no shortage of ill-omened predictions, the refrain of all of them being that the emigrants who escaped death in the waves would be sold as slaves to the Turks or the still fiercer cannibals. Pastor Borchgrevink in Vardal was particularly passionate. He thundered against all migration and told countless stories about the horrible fate which awaited the daredevils who, despising all warnings, went to the land of lust and corruption called America. "I was always being harrassed," says Anders Tømmerstigen, "and during the last couple of months before our departure my children were very reluctant to leave the house because of all the ridicule and mockery they were exposed to. I did not let myself be discouraged," he continued, "but with my wife and four children left Christiania for Le Havre, France, where I met about 300 emigrants from western Norway, especially from Telemark. In Le Havre we got passage on a ship to New York, and then went on to Milwaukee. There I met my nephew, who took us to Christiana where I have lived ever since."

Measured by the standards of the time Anders Tømmerstigen could be called a well-to-do man when he left Norway. He had about 1,000 *speciedaler*—no mean sum at that time. The fare from Norway to New York was only $25.00 per person, and the trip from there to Milwaukee cost $14.50. The money he had left enabled him to buy 120 acres of land at once. In time this increased to a holding of 345 acres of land which consists largely of excellent soil—a mixture of prairie and woodland. He has fine buildings on his farm, which is one of the best cultivated in the township. Anders Tømmerstigen's estate probably amounts to something in excess of $20,000. "I thank God," he says, "that it was written in my book of fate that I should come to America. Like my brother I have paid the fare for many of my poor countrymen; and I am so pleased with my position in life that with my whole heart I wish many from the old country might come here where nature more liberally rewards a man for his labor." His oldest son, Johannes, operates a silver mine in California, where he was one of a group of Norwegians who discovered a rich lode that is said to be paying well.

In the village of Clinton lives Ole Jacobsen from the parish of Snåsa, Trøndelag. He emigrated in 1853 and was the first man to leave that region for America, with the exception of Ole Rynning. There was much talk about his leaving, the general opinion being that it was blasphemous for a man who could easily earn a living at home to tempt fate in this manner. Jacobsen went by way of England to New York and Chicago. The following winter he worked as a ship's carpenter in Michigan, after which he roamed through Minnesota, Iowa, and Kansas inspecting the land. Next he was in St. Louis and he went from there to Memphis where he was occupied for the next four years as a railroad engineer at a salary of $100 per month. In 1859 Jacobsen left the South for Clinton, which has been his home since then, with the exception of two years when he served as a lieutenant in the war. He has established a brewery in Clinton and is, presumably, doing very well. All told, the migration from Snåsa has been practically nil. As far as we know, only two persons from Snåsavatn have left their home community and native land in recent years. They are now living in Minnesota.

We will mention still another of the early settlers on Koshkonong, namely Anon Olsen Drotning from Vinje, Telemark. He emigrated in 1843 and came by way of Muskego to Heart Prairie where, for a while, he was employed by a Yankee at seven dollars per month. As yet there were no Norwegians living there, and Anon soon left Heart Prairie, after which he worked briefly for an American in northern Illinois. Next he went to Chicago but left there for Koshkonong in the spring of 1844. Here he met many of his countrymen and found work as a day laborer which enabled him to save about $100 per year. During the winter of 1845 he stayed a short while in Madison. At that time Wisconsin's future capital had only two stores and a small number of inhabitants, none of whom were Scandinavians. In 1846 Drotning bought eighty acres of land near Utica for $300. This farm has since been increased to 200

COURTESY OF STATE HISTORICAL SOCIETY OF WISCONSIN

A successful farmer proudly displaying his grain fields, farmhouse, and barn, Dane county, ca. 1875.

acres. He is now a well-to-do man whose estate runs to some $12,000 or $15,000. Only a few people had emigrated from Vinje before Anon Drotning left that part of Norway. As far as we know, Knud Aslakson Svalestuen—now living in Muskego—was the first man who bade farewell to that parish in order to seek a home in the New World.

Great are the changes which have taken place on Koshkonong during the last thirty years. If a person had last seen this region three decades ago, everything would assuredly strike him now as a grand illusion, like stories in Oriental fairy tales. The forests have been cleared, the wild prairies have been plowed and transformed into billowing fields of grain, the Indian trails have vanished, the prairie grass has been replaced by cultivated species, luxuriant orchards surround the homes of the prosperous farmers, good roads have been laid out, well-equipped schools provide education and refinement, factories have been founded, churches with their lofty spires testify to the people's respect for religion, industry and crafts advance steadily toward greater perfection. In sum, the progress is phenomenal, the transformations are like a dream. Less than three times ten years ago poor toilers came to this region; now they are well-off, some of them even rich. They have changed a wilderness into flourishing meadows and fertile fields which give bread to thousands. Most of the immigrants were destitute when they came to a strange land, but their hopes were not put to shame; willing spirits and strong arms enabled them to reach their goal. And the newcomer is no longer a foreigner: the soil he tills belongs to him; he takes part in the governing of the land and enjoys all the rights of a native-born citizen.

Clinton is a little village in the eastern part of the township, located on Koshkonong Creek, which furnishes much waterpower.* As a result there are a flour mill, a carding machine, and a sawmill at Clinton. Even though the village was founded more than a score of years ago it has scarcely more than 150 inhabitants, almost all Norwegians. Two stores, a brewery, a hotel, a post office, and some artisans' shops—this is about all there is to the village of Clinton. The reason for its slow growth is possibly explained, in part at least, by its great distance from railroads or other lines of communication. Formerly Clinton had a bad reputation for drunkenness and other disorders. Of late, however, the moral condition of the village seems to have been quite satisfactory; and a person hears no more about lawlessness in Clinton and its environs than in other parts of the state.

Cambridge is another village with a beautiful location in the northeastern part of the township on Koshkonong Creek, which here also makes waterpower available. The village was founded some twenty years ago. Growth was rather slow to begin with and, after a while, ceased almost entirely. Only recently have there been signs of renewed life and an awakening spirit of enterprise. In the village we find a flour mill and a woolen mill, as well as a few workshops. The number of inhabitants is probably somewhat over 300—among them four merchants, one druggist, and some artisans. More than fifty percent of the inhabitants are Norwegian. The farmers to the north, west, and south—practically all Norwegians—are prosperous; many of them can even be called rich. East of town there is a Scottish settlement. Despite the fact that Cambridge is located far from the great highways of trade, the commercial activity is quite brisk considering the size of the place. Cambridge is about equally distant from the railway stations at Stoughton, Waterloo, Fort Atkinson, and Jefferson—some twelve or fourteen miles. The farmers must take their products to one of these stations. Besides a Presbyterian church there is also a Norwegian Methodist church in the village. The latter, though not large, is a beautiful, well-kept building. It is said that the Swedish singer Jenny Lind gave a considerable sum toward its construction. A Methodist pastor by the name of [Andrew A.] Haagensen lives in Cambridge and a part

*_Billed-Magazin_, November 13, 1869.

of the Scandinavian population in and near the town belongs to his congregation.

The well-known surgeon Johan Christian Dass (Dundas) has his home in Cambridge. He is the son of a landed proprietor on Lurøy in Helgeland and is descended in direct line from the famous Nordland pastor, Petter Dass, whose poetic works have long been greatly admired by the Norwegian populace. Johan Christian Dass first studied medicine three years at the University of Christiania, after which he continued his studies in Copenhagen and in Germany. He served two years as assistant surgeon at the hospital in Bergen and then resumed his foreign studies, spending time at the Universities of Uppsala (Sweden) and Helsingfors (Finland) as well as in Switzerland and Germany. Next he served as a doctor aboard a Dutch man-of-war bound for Java, where he practiced medicine some three years, after which he served as a doctor on an emigrant vessel going to America.

In New York he became acquainted with Consul Løvenskjold, who had recently visited the Norwegian settlement on Koshkonong. He was urged by Løvenskjold to go to the assistance of his countrymen in this pioneer community which was badly afflicted with climate fever. Shortly after his arrival in Wisconsin he performed some highly successful cures, which at once established his reputation as an able doctor. At the same time cholera was spreading through the Northwest. Hence Dass went to Chicago and later to St. Louis where he practiced medicine as long as the epidemic lasted. After stays of two years in China and Japan and nine months in London, he returned to Koshkonong and has since then lived in Cambridge. Dass has performed many operations considered among the most difficult in the practice of medicine; he is regarded as one of the ablest doctors in the Northwest, not only by his countrymen but probably still more by the Americans. Through wide reading and continued study he has also developed an interest in progress and improvements in many fields of endeavor. That he has a large clientele and through his practice has acquired a considerable fortune goes without saying.

Speaking of Norwegian doctors, we will mention a few others who have practiced in this country. As far as we have been able to learn, Hans C. Brandt from Drammen was the first Norwegian-trained doctor to come to America. He first practiced a while in Chicago and in the Norwegian settlements in Illinois. Then he bought a farm in Iowa and later moved to Indiana. At present his practice is exclusively among Americans. He is in good repute as a doctor and is said to have made a fortune of no mean proportions.

Some time later Theodor Schjøtte and Gerhard Paoli left for America. Both of them first went to Koshkonong, but there they did not secure the following they had expected. Schjøtte returned to Norway and was appointed district doctor in Finnmark by the Norwegian government. Paoli, however, settled in

Chicago where he has a flourishing practice, especially among Americans, and enjoys public confidence.

Doctor [Bernhard I.] Madsen had studied medicine several years at the University of Christiania. He came to Koshkonong, where he settled in Cambridge and practiced about eight years before succumbing to typhoid fever. S. [Søren Johan] Hanssen, who had studied medicine in Norway, was also on Koshkonong some nine or ten years and was considered an able doctor. He accumulated a fortune of about $5,000 or $6,000 and returned to Norway where he was appointed district doctor in Romsdal. When the Civil War broke out he enlisted with the 15th Wisconsin Regiment as assistant doctor, but because of illness he soon had to leave the service.[26]

Some years ago Cambridge became a place of pilgrimage for sick people not only from Wisconsin, but also from Iowa, Minnesota, and other places. This time the goddess of healing revealed herself in the form of a woman. A midwife from Norway, who had settled in these parts, began practicing medicine and gained great renown for her miraculous cures. The influx of people was tremendous, and patients often had to wait days before they gained admittance to the lady doctor, who was busy from morning till night. No ailment was so serious that she could not cure it with her "drops," powders, and pills. She was a sorceress in the fullest meaning of the word and was looked upon as an extraordinary being: her fame increased in direct proportion to the distance from her home. Her knowledge of medicine, however, does not seem to have been very extensive. When she went to a drugstore her order usually went about as follows: "give me 'drops' of different colors and tastes, bitter, sweet, and sour; also various kinds of powders and pills, large and small; and some syrup for children." No matter what she gave them, there were many people who imagined that they were healed through her "cures"; and the woman continued her practice for years to the great surprise of those who were somewhat acquainted with her qualifications. For a while she was the American "Mother Sather" among the Norwegians.[27] But in time the illusion was broken. The stream of patients gradually decreased and finally dried up entirely. Now only the memory remains of how bold humbugs can cheat the gullible and the ignorant in this country.

Koshkonong prairie extends from the northeastern part of the neighboring township, Albion, through the central part of Christiana, where at first it contracts to a narrow strip but later expands and stretches out two arms in opposite directions, giving it the appearance of a long, serpentine fjord which toward the north cuts into the township of Deerfield and toward the west reaches an arm into Pleasant Spring.* Toward the east the prairie borders on a

**Billed-Magazin*, November 27, 1869.

belt of woodland through which Koshkonong Creek flows, providing the towns of Clinton and Cambridge with waterpower. In the northwestern corner of the township there is some marshland spreading out on both sides of a brook which flows northward and empties into the above-mentioned creek which also receives the water from a brook flowing along the eastern border of the prairie. In the southern part of the township are also found some smaller marshy areas which are cut for hay. The soil in Christiana and the northern part of Albion is fertile and is considered superior to that in Pleasant Spring. The township comprises 23,000 acres of land, which for tax purposes are assessed at $22.75 each, making a total of $524,000. In all of Dane county there are only three townships where the land is appraised higher, namely Sun Prairie, Madison, and Dunkirk.

In Christiana there are some 220 separate farms, of which twenty-five or thirty belong to non-Norwegians. The average size of the farms here is about 105 acres, somewhat larger than those in Pleasant Spring. Raising of grain, especially wheat, has been the main source of income. In second place comes cattle-raising, which of late has been given increasing attention here. Pastures are good, grass grows luxuriantly, and there are enough trees to provide both firewood and building material. The economic situation is particularly good, and there are a rather large number of farmers who can even be called rich. The assessed valuation of property in the township amounts to something more than $691,000. The general rule for tax assessment makes us believe that this sum should be increased by at least one-third, putting the true value of the people's real and personal property at about $921,000. The population of the township can be estimated at approximately 1,700. Thus, if the total wealth were divided equally among all the people, each person would receive more than $540.00. None of the thirty-five townships in Dane county can show property figures as high as those in Christiana. The richest man is Nils Olsen Smitbak from Numedal. He owns about 600 acres of land of which at least a large part is of good quality. The value of this land, combined with capital out at interest and other real and personal property, presumably amounts to some $40,000 or $50,000—a handsome fortune for a Norwegian farmer. None of the people in the township except two shiftless men require support from the community.

In ordinary good years a farmer can expect an average yield of fifteen bushels of wheat per acre. Whether farming pays under such conditions will be seen from the following figures.

If a landowner bought the seed and let all work—plowing, seeding, harvesting, threshing, and transporting to market—be done by others who provided their own board and implements, the outlay at last year's wages would amount to sixty cents per bushel, figuring fifteen bushels per acre. In other words, the production cost per bushel would amount to sixty cents, not including fencing and taxes. At a market price of $1.00, the farmer will then have a net profit of forty cents per bushel. Furthermore, if he does part or all of the work himself he will save an additional sum.

On most of the farms in this township you will find well-built houses, in many places even elegant buildings tastefully and comfortably equipped. As an example, we will describe the home of Tosten Eriksen Rokne in the northern part of the township. He emigrated from Voss in 1845 and brought with him $500.00 in cash. Rokne now owns 380 acres of good land and lives in a beautiful stone house which bears witness to good taste and a feeling for comfort in both its outer appearance and its furnishings. A guest feels pleasantly attracted to what he sees as soon as he enters the house. There are maps on the walls in the guest room, Norwegian and English books on the bookshelves, and elegant furniture that enhances the appeal of the surroundings. We are received with genuine old-time Norwegian hospitality. We will let the host escort us around the premises so as to get a better look at a farm establishment in this part of the country. The dwelling is a large two-story structure which, besides the guest room, contains a living room, a dining room, bedrooms, and a kitchen, with everything so arranged that full justice is done to the demands of symmetry and beauty. In the barn, also built of stone, ten horses and eight cows are well protected against the severity of the winter weather. Furthermore, Rokne has a well-built machine shed containing a complete set of farm implements as well as other useful equipment. It is unnecessary to add that he cares about the upbringing of his children; it did not surprise us to learn that his oldest son was attending an American high school.

The moral condition within the township is quite exemplary. Lawsuits and disputes between Norwegians hardly ever occur. Illegitimate births are very rare and bundling has ceased almost entirely. There is very little dancing and carousing, while violations of the law are practically unheard of among the Norwegians.

On the whole, education is progressing among the young. The district school is usually well attended; and most of the families send their children to parochial school several weeks each year, particularly to give them instruction in religion and the mother tongue. Furthermore, there are many parents who send their sons to institutions of higher learning, opportunities being conveniently offered at Marshall College, Albion Academy, and the state university in Madison.

Most of the people in the township belong to the Norwegian Evangelical Lutheran Synod (Wisconsin Synod). The East Koshkonong church, as it is called, is a beautiful and spacious stone building, erected in 1858. Anders Knudsen from Vardal is now the parish pastor. Earlier he served thirty years as a schoolteacher in Norway, but emigrated to America because of the unrest which resulted from Marcus Thrane's agitations. The parsonage is conveniently located, and it is undoubtedly the most pleasant building which as yet any Norwegian congregation in this country has erected for its pastor. In Cambridge and the surrounding areas there are some twenty-five Norwegian families which have embraced Methodism. Their pastor lives in Cambridge, where the church is also located. Previously the district superintendent of the Norwegian Methodist Church, O. P. Petersen from Fredrikshald, lived about a mile and a half from Cambridge. He emigrated from Norway nineteen years ago, first spending some time in New York, after which he again spent six years in the old country. Then he came to Koshkonong, but moved to Chicago in 1868. There are also said to be a few Sabbatarian families among the Norwegians in the township as well as three Haugeans and six or seven families that do not belong to any congregation.

As regards politics, the majority in Christiana are Republicans. In the last presidential election 302 votes were cast: 219 Republican and 83 Democratic. Most of the Democratic votes in the township were cast by Norwegians.

Pleasant Spring township

The term Koshkonong also includes the township known as Pleasant Spring.* I will let some of the district's first settlers tell about its founding and early history. We will therefore at once strike up an acquaintance with Knud Hilliksen Roe from Tinn in Telemark, the first white man to choose a place in Pleasant Spring as his future home. Reader, you are invited to listen for a few moments to this countryman of ours as he tells about experiences of earlier days. I feel certain that you will accept this invitation gladly, because one after another of the fathers of emigration are leaving us. Before many years have passed there will not be anyone left among the living who can give eyewitness accounts of the first Norwegian emigrants' departure from the homeland—about their longings and hopes, and their fate on this side of the mighty ocean. Among us there is no one who, like the witch of Endor, can make the dead speak. Hence, while there is time, we will turn to the living and listen attentively to the stories which the first pioneers on the vast western plains have to tell us about events of former years, about conditions in the country when the migration began, and about progress in the various communities founded by our fellow countrymen in the New World. Let us then hear first what Knud H. Roe has to relate.

"In the year 1839 I left Tinn in the company of a group of emigrants from Telemark, among whom was John Nelson Luraas, the first Norwegian settler

Billed-Magazin, January 8, 1870.

in the neighboring township of Dunkirk. About the middle of May the first ship to carry emigrants from Skien glided down the fjord and after a pleasant journey we landed at Gothenburg. There two vessels were lying ready to sail for America. One of the ships took aboard the whole emigrant group from Telemark except two families for whom there was no room—my wife and I being among the latter. Hence we registered as passengers with the other ship. There we fell in with a group from Hardanger, making a total of about fifty America-bound people aboard that ship. During our seven weeks on the ocean nothing remarkable happened. When we landed in Boston all of us were in good spirits and gazed longingly toward the Far West where we hoped to find the good fortune which the stingy soil of our native land denied her toiling children.

"From Boston the journey was continued by way of New York along the usual emigrant route of those days to Chicago. There most of my traveling companions remained, since they secured jobs as day laborers, digging ditches, building dikes, and constructing canals. I learned later that it was not long before many of these immigrants were afflicted with sickness; consequently not a few families became so poor that they were in want of life's simplest necessities. Swamp fever was rife in Chicago at the time and claimed particularly numerous victims among the penniless newcomers who were forced to work hard, live in poor quarters, and exist on short rations. When autumn came, only a few of my group were still alive. Most of them succumbed to the unwholesome climate and closed their eyes in death soon after they reached their long-sought goal. After a while one of the survivors, Endru Rude, like myself, became a member of the Norwegian settlement on Koshkonong. Now he also has been gathered to his fathers. He died some three years ago on his homestead near the West Koshkonong church.

"After staying in Chicago a couple of days my wife and I, with two companions, secured passage to Ottawa on the Fox River in La Salle county. There we met many of our countrymen, most of them from the Stavanger area and a few from Tinn. Conditions in that community could not be called satisfactory either; and there was much discontent among the settlers. Soon after my arrival I became bedridden and was unable to work for about a year. When I had regained my strength I sought whatever work I could get, but wages were low and money a rare article. Ever since I left Norway I had wanted to find a plot of ground to cultivate and call my own. But in La Salle county, at the time, practically all good land had already been grabbed by speculators and the price was consequently very high.

"Then the rumor spread that the people from Tinn and Telemark who had left Gothenburg on the other ship when I emigrated had let themselves be persuaded in Milwaukee to found a settlement at Muskego. We were told that in this community there was a surplus of good and inexpensive land; and rumor had it that the new settlement was in a flourishing condition. Several of the people who were dissatisfied with their stay in La Salle county therefore went to Muskego, hoping to find better homesteads in that part of the country. In the spring of 1842 I also bade farewell to my friends in the Ottawa community with the intention of striking roots in the Wisconsin settlement. I arrived there, but conditions were by no means such that I dared hope for a fortunate future in that area. Marshy ground unsuited for grain-raising, a pestilent atmosphere, and much sickness—all this gave but little promise; and I prepared to leave the settlement as soon as I could. Many of the people there expressed the conviction that other areas offered the immigrants greater advantages than Muskego; and several men had gone westward the previous autumn to look around. They returned with reports that they had traveled about seventy miles through practically uninhabited regions, and that on Koshkonong they had met Norwegians who had come from the south over Jefferson Prairie and lived in the areas now known as Albion and Christiana townships.

"'There,' they said, 'the soil is very fertile, and we have a fine balance between prairie and woodland. Furthermore, there are good hay meadows, fat pastures, and easy access to water.' These reports caused a stir among the settlers at Muskego; and many of them decided to leave the marshes around Wind Lake and seek more productive areas farther west. As soon as the snow began disappearing in the spring of 1843, I went westward on foot in order to see for myself the glories of Koshkonong. When I returned from this trip my wife and I, accompanied by John Luraas and family, decided to leave Muskego. We hired a team, the expedition went well, and a couple of weeks before St. John's Eve our first dwelling was so near completion that my wife and I with our one child could find protection under its roof against wind and rain. The hut was made of leafy branches and each of its four corners was supported by an oak tree. There were no other settlers in the township at the time, so I was the first white man to light his hearth in Pleasant Spring.

"I often had visits from the Indians; the many paths which furrowed the area near my house proved that the sons of the wilderness had passed there frequently. During their wanderings between the charming Lake Koshkonong and the four lakes which have made the region around Madison so widely famed for its beauty, the redskins—often in groups of half-a-hundred or more—frequently pitched camp right next to my house of twigs. At times I went hunting with them. They never caused me any trouble, but, on the contrary, were always ready to lend me a helping hand. There was an abundance of wild game. Practically every day I saw herds of deer and swarms of prairie chickens, and often at night I was awakened by the howling of wolves.

Now things have changed. The Indians, the wild game, the prairie grass, and the poisonous snakes have vanished to the same degree that cultivation of the land has progressed. The same soil which formerly nourished the primeval forest or the relatively worthless prairie grass now brings forth a rich variety of cultivated plants which are a source of wealth and human happiness.

"In the fall of the year I built a log house where my hut of branches had stood, namely in section 22; and there I have lived with my family until this day. When I arrived at my present homestead I did not have a penny. All my money had been spent to pay for transportation. I did, however, own some cows which made a valuable contribution to our household the first two years. To buy flour I had to go to Whitewater, some thirty miles from my home. The distance to Madison, where there were a few stores at the time, is eighteen miles. The nearest sawmill was at Lake Mills, twenty-two miles from my place. When the time came that the settlers in the township had some wheat to sell we were forced to transport it seventy-five miles to Milwaukee. Really to understand the inconvenience caused by such distances you must bear in mind that the *kubberulle* was our only means of transportation; with the axe we had to clear a way through woods and thickets for the oxen that pulled the heavy-laden, clumsy wagons which frequently sank into the mud so deep that only after much exertion and loss of time were we able to get on with our journey.

"A few weeks after me, Ole Trovatten, originally from Lårdal in Telemark, arrived from Muskego and settled on the farm now owned by Gunnar Felland.* He later sold his land and moved to Liberty Prairie. During the months of July and August—somewhat less during the fall—the immigration was considerable, so that by the winter of 1843 I was surrounded by neighbors, even though the distances between the various settlers generally were great compared with the situation at present. Most of these newcomers were from Muskego. Others had emigrated from Norway that same year and, after a temporary stay in Milwaukee or Muskego, had continued on to Koshkonong."

Thus far Knud Roe's own story. The aged man is now living in good circumstances on his 280-acre farm. He is in quite good health, enjoys the respect of neighbors and acquaintances, and is happy to speak of past days, which brought him sorrow and adversity but also contentment and happiness. He talks with unaffected directness about his experiences in America and gives thanks to fate which, with a generous hand, has bestowed blessings upon his labors.

About midsummer last year another of the township's oldest settlers, Knud Aslaksen Juvi from Kviteseid, Telemark, gave me a brief account of his life which I record in the paragraphs below:

**Billed-Magazin*, January 15, 1870.

"I was a farmer in Norway in fairly good economic circumstances. Through letters and pamphlets information about conditions in America was given wide circulation in my native country, and concern about the future of my family induced me to emigrate. I was forty-four years old at the time, and had with me a sum of 600 *speciedaler*. In May, 1844 [sic], I left Skien aboard the brig *Washington* accompanied by eighty-three of my countrymen, most of them from Lårdal and Kviteseid. We landed in New York on the 4th of July, the republic's great day of celebration. Most of the emigrants were fairly well-off: they paid their travel expenses and still had some money left over. In those days the emigrants were treated well on arrival, not only by their own countrymen but by others. There were not then the swarms of plundering 'runners' who now, like birds of prey, throw themselves on the newcomers.

"We followed the usual emigrant route to Milwaukee where we met Norwegians from Muskego and Koshkonong. Originally it was our intention to continue the trip and settle in Illinois. But in Milwaukee people advised against this move. We were told that here in Wisconsin the soil was fertile and the climate healthful, while many of the settlers in the Norwegian communities in Illinois had grown dissatisfied, sold their homesteads, and bought land in Wisconsin. Many of our group, especially craftsmen, consequently stayed in Milwaukee and found work. Others went to Muskego and some to Koshkonong, but no one to Illinois. I, along with my widowed sister, Thone Aslaksdatter, and my brother, Knud Aslaksen Gjøtil, chose to go to the settlement known as Muskego, founded by our countrymen near Wind Lake. What I saw there agreed but poorly with my preconceived ideas about the glories of the promised land. By chance I happened to meet a settler from the township of Christiana, and when he noted my discontent he said: 'Go farther west. Only when you reach Koshkonong will you find America!' I took his advice and set off, accompanied by my sister and brother. The district between Wind Lake and Lake Koshkonong could not at that time really be called a wilderness, because the settling and cultivating of the land had already begun. But generally there was a distance of many miles between the log houses, and no roads led through the forests or pointed the way across the plains whose high, tough grass each fall was transformed into ashes by the all-consuming prairie fires.

"We arrived at Spring Creek on the third of August, 1843, and near the present West Koshkonong church we at once started constructing a shelter out of branches and thatching it with straw. Our furniture consisted of some chests which served as both table and chairs. The beds were spread on the earthen floor atop a layer of twigs and grass. In this altogether too well-ventilated residence, considering the climate, we lived until October, when we built a sod hut which protected us well against wind and snow. Both my brother and I caught the climate fever shortly after our arrival on Koshkonong and we did not regain our health until the following autumn. During my illness I suppose it happened more than once that my spirit was assailed by melancholy longings for home, relatives, and friends in my native land. It was of little avail, however, to look back; I was separated by thousands of miles from the shores of old Norway. Despondency would only make matters worse; hence I mustered up all my courage so as not to make the others dispirited also.

"Despite my poor health I managed to build a log house during the summer of 1844. In time my sister Thone as well as my brother got their own houses where they lived as my neighbors. In our region there was a combination of prairies with marshlands and wooded areas. In those days there could, of course, be no talk of such conveniences as roads and bridges, which come in the wake of progress and civilization. Only a few paths indicated that living beings occasionally came to our neighborhood. Not infrequently we had visits from the original masters of the region, the red men; and they never gave us reason to complain. There was a surplus of game here, and the rifle supplied us with meat; but flour had to be transported from Whitewater. With the money I brought from Norway I soon bought a yoke of oxen as well as a plow and a wagon. In the spring of 1844 I broke two acres of land on which I raised some grain and potatoes. The following summer I produced enough food for our own household; and since then I have had something to sell every year.

"When I came, there was no one living in Pleasant Spring township except Knud Roe, Asmund Lunde, and his brother-in-law, Aslak Aslaksen Kostved—all three from the parish of Vinje—and Ole Knudsen Trovatten from Lårdal. Knud Roe had come some five weeks before me and lived in a hut about two miles south of the place where the western church was later built. He has lived there ever since and now owns one of the best farms in the township. Aslak Kostved had bought land about three miles southeast of the church, and Lunde lived with his brother-in-law at the time. Both of them have since moved to Minnesota. Aslak has a farm, while Lunde lives as a pensioner with his son. Ole Trovatten lived near Aslak Kostved. He became our sexton and schoolteacher. I have never heard as beautiful and powerful a singing voice as that man had. Furthermore, he was an able teacher, high-principled, helpful, and good-natured. The newcomers always found him a sympathetic friend and a dependable adviser. He is now deceased, but many of the early pioneers in this area will remember the name of Ole Knudsen Trovatten.

"Toward the middle of August, 1843, [sic] many people moved into the township. Among these I will mention Tosten Gulliksen Bringa from Seljord and his children, as well as Gullik Torkildsen Sundbø from the same district (now deceased) and his sons, Torkild and Ole, both family men. The latter is now deceased. At about the same time came Halvor L. Fossen, with family, and his brother Ole, as well as Ole Knudsen Dyrland with family—all from Seljord. The whole group filed on land near me and thus became my neighbors. In September, or possibly even later in the fall of the same year, came the following men with their families: Thorbjørn Guttormsen Vik from Seljord; Aslak Evensen Groven from Lårdal; Ole Eielsen from Vinje, who later moved to Minnesota, and his brother Odne Eielsen. The last three settled about a mile east of my place, near the church. All of these newcomers had sailed from Skien to New York on an emigrant vessel and then proceeded on to Milwaukee and Muskego. From there they continued westward, after having taken a rest in Even Heg's barn, which is so famous in our pioneer history as a lodging place for newcomers. The following year the population of the township increased greatly because of immigration, especially from Telemark and to some extent from Voss. Not many years passed before all the land in a wide area round about was claimed and bought by settlers.

"In August, 1844, Pastor [J.W.C.] Dietrichson came to Koshkonong. On an earlier occasion we had a visit from C. L. Clausen, then pastor at Muskego, now in Iowa. Dietrichson delivered his first sermon under an oak tree which is still standing near my home. He also conducted all other ministerial duties under the open sky. Later, services were held in the farmers' log houses. He was a zealous preacher of the Word and gifted with an eloquence that had no equal. The following winter we built a church—merely a simple log structure, to be sure, but the need for an assembly place had been temporarily satisfied. It was later torn down, however, and its place is now occupied by our spacious white stone church.

"When I first arrived I bought only eighty acres of land. Later I bought more, so my farm now covers 140 acres. The soil is very fertile and my property is of the type which people here say is 'handy.'

"You ask me for my ideas about America, and this will be my answer: America is an excellent country for the industrious worker.* Such a man will not lack bread here. I love my native land and frequently think of the place where I spent the happy days of youth, but I know that over there one must work very hard just to maintain himself; and I thank the fate which has blessed my efforts in my new homeland."

The paragraphs above reproduce, in somewhat abridged form, the main contents of Knud Aslaksen Juvi's story. He died recently; and when this news reached me I spontaneously recalled the time when I sat in his house jotting down the old man's account of his experiences. He was a good, helpful man of high principles. Pastor Dietrichson chose him as his assistant; and when the

**Billed-Magazin*, January 29, 1870.

Oak trees on the farm of Knud Aslaksen Juvi where Pastor J.W.C. Dietrichson preached September 2, 1844.

new church was built, Juvi was a member of the building commission as well as of the committee in charge of erecting houses on the parsonage land. Furthermore, many people praised him for the willing assistance he gave his poverty-stricken countrymen during their struggle with the hardships of pioneer life. A helping hand had double value then because of the primitive conditions which existed twenty-seven years ago in those regions which are now among the state's most prosperous and most densely populated districts.

The whole area commonly referred to as Koshkonong was settled and put under cultivation in a remarkably short period of time; and the Norwegians took the lead, ahead of any other nationality. It seems as if here our countrymen first found the America of which they had heard such wonderful stories in their homeland. To be sure, not even on Koshkonong did broiled doves fly into the mouths of the newcomers; but there were so many conditions favoring progress that the plain hard-working immigrant did not hesitate to strike roots here and begin at once, with characteristic toughness and frugality, his pioneer work of preparing a better future for himself and his family. Lovely little lakes with crystal-clear water, fertile soil furrowed by rivers and creeks, large treeless plains which the plow could transform into flourishing fields, fat pastures and lush meadows, plenty of fish and game, forests which gave an abundance of building material and firewood—these were the main elements in the picture which the peasants in Norway's meagre mountain valleys had of the far western land beyond the Atlantic.

Not even on Koshkonong did the immigrant find that reality in every respect corresponded to the ideal America he had conceived of and brought with him from his native land. But he soon discovered that this region offered many advantages lacking in the places where Norwegians had first attempted to found settlements. Hence, when chance led some of our roaming countrymen to the shores of Lake Koshkonong and areas northward, they returned to inform relatives and friends that now they had discovered a region favorable for the founding of new homes. Koshkonong soon came to be generally regarded as the promised Canaan, flowing with milk and honey, which had been selected by Providence as a refuge for the hard-beset Norwegian toilers struggling under the yoke of poverty.

From then on the migratory stream flowed toward the southern part of Dane county. Not a few left Muskego and the communities in Illinois to settle on Koshkonong, but the majority came directly from Norway. Even though most of the newcomers who landed in America at the time intended to settle in Illinois, they changed their minds when the countrymen they met in Milwaukee told them that Koshkonong was a Goshen which promised the immigrant good fortune and happiness. "During 1842 and the following three or four years group after group came in ever larger numbers," says one of the early settlers, "so that all the good land in the area was snapped up unbelievably fast. The great plains, which on my arrival were a wilderness, were transformed as by magic into a densely populated settlement with luxuriant meadows and flourishing fields."

A Chronicler Of Immigrant Life

I wish to tell about a few other men from the township and will first mention Gunder Torgersen Mandt from the parish of Mo in Upper Telemark. He was the youngest of twelve children and lost his father when he was two years old. The father had been a sergeant, and he left his widow in straitened circumstances with a large family to provide for. "When I was some twenty years of age," he told me, "it often occurred to me how difficult it really was for the son of a poor man to gain an independent position. Thoughts of the future frequently disturbed my otherwise cheerful spirits. At that time an able worker in my home community was fortunate if he could earn eight Norwegian shillings a day during the winter season. Not infrequently it happened that vigorous men went about offering to work merely for their board. But then people began to talk much about America, and they would walk long distances in order to read letters from earlier emigrants.

"As well as I can recall, Ole Trovatten from Vinje had left in 1840. He was very popular and much respected as a sincere and reliable man. The well-written and detailed letters which he sent home from America aroused much attention and people believed his words like the Gospels themselves. Before leaving Norway he had been a schoolteacher and sexton and was better educated and informed than most of the people who at that time belonged to his class. The sexton's eulogies of America exerted a tremendous influence among the mass of people in Upper Telemark. For several years the rich as well as the poor, the distinguished and the lowly, talked about Ole Trovatten—some to criticize and revile, others to praise and extol him. The opponents of emigration maintained that he was a dangerous person who would lead people to destruction, while many looked at matters otherwise and declared that they were willing to testify with hand on Bible that in his home community Ole was known to be a dependable man.

"I have no comments to make concerning his reliability; but the common people generally looked upon him as an angel of peace who had gone beforehand to the New World, whence he sent his countrymen—weighed down with economic worries—the olive branch of promise, assuring them a better life in America after all the hardships they had survived in their native land. 'Ole Trovatten has said it; that's what he writes': this phrase became the refrain of all the stories about the Land of Wonder, and for several years he was the most talked-of man in the whole district of Upper Telemark. His America letters gave emigration a tremendous push. It is very probable that hundreds of those who are now plowing the fields of Wisconsin and Minnesota would still be living within the bounds of Harald Fairhair's kingdom had they not been induced to bid old Norway farewell by Trovatten's brilliant accounts of conditions on this side of the Atlantic.[28]

"Several families left Mo parish the same year I did, and when we came to

Skien early in the spring of 1843 we joined a large group of emigrants, mostly from Telemark; altogether we numbered about 100. We went with a Norwegian skipper from Skien to Le Havre in France, where we arrived in very good condition. But we had no assurance that we would be able to secure passage from there to America; and if our luck had not been better than our brains, this carelessness in trusting to chance might have led to disappointment and misfortune. But after waiting eighteen days we were offered transportation to New York on an American ship. The passage was relatively uneventful and we arrived in good shape in Milwaukee where we met countrymen of ours, among them the noted Mr. James Denoon Reymert. Here the group dissolved as chance, kin, or other circumstances might dictate. Together with Gunder Fladland, Kittel Strømmen, and several others, I hired a team of oxen and went directly to Koshkonong in September, 1843.

"In Christiana township we met many Norwegians who had settled there in the two previous years. We were received with all the goodwill and courtesy which we have a right to expect from compatriots; but I soon realized that there was nothing to earn here as a day laborer because the settlers still struggled with the hardships of pioneer life and only with great difficulty managed to obtain the basic necessities. Since in those days we did not reckon a walk of seventy miles or more a matter of any consequence, I decided to return to Milwaukee, where I found work as a carpenter at twenty-five cents per day. According to the expectations of those days such a wage was considered acceptable; and encouraged by this glimmer of light in my future I began to dream of dollars and riches.

"But two weeks later I was visited by the newcomer's most dangerous enemy—the climate fever—which in those days seldom bypassed anyone.* And here, among utter strangers and unacquainted with the language, I was for some time a prisoner of the sickbed. Added to the pain of feeling forsaken was the longing for friends and homeland. In various shapes, memories of the happy days of youth were conjured up before my mind's eye and aroused the melancholy feeling called homesickness. But, aided by the kind treatment given me, I finally regained so much strength that I could strike out west for Koshkonong in the company of several acquaintances from Telemark who had come across with a new group of emigrants from Norway. We went to Pleasant Spring, where eight or ten Norwegian families had settled earlier that year, and there I found work well into the winter.

"The following spring Ole Gaarden and I agreed to try our luck in Chicago. This commercial metropolis, though still in its infancy, was beginning to show signs of future greatness and power. Hence wages were better there than

**Billed-Magazin*, February 5, 1870.

in most other parts of the country. I contributed six shillings to cover travel expenses. My companion increased this sum by four shillings and two silver buckles. With this capital, and a large bag of bread which we carried between us, we began our journey southward with sun and stars as guides. In Beloit we met a Yankee from Illinois who offered us a ride and treated us with great friendliness in every respect. We accepted his offer and went with him to Leland. On parting there we gave him the silver buckles as a token of our gratitude. From Leland we again mounted the 'Apostles' horses' for Chicago, where we arrived in good health and cheerful spirits. To be sure, our sum of ready cash had shrunk to six cents; but we got work at once, earning six shillings per day without board.

"I have dwelt on these apparently insignificant matters to emphasize the difference between then and now. Many of the present-day newcomers will probably smile when they hear stories about the primitive life led by the early settlers in the western wilds. But it was just those men in the advance guard of immigration who blazed a trail for civilization through the wilderness. The immigrants of the present time cover in hours distances which took us days; where we found uninhabited regions they find churches, schools, highways, comfortable homes, plenty of food, good wages, and a fully developed social order. But while they partake of these blessings they usually forget that all this progress has come as a result of the hard work, courage, self-denial, and thrift of the first settlers. When I first came to Koshkonong twenty-seven years ago, a few furrows around the scattered pioneers' cabins were the only bits of earth touched by the plow. Our life was full of toil and we had to manage without any of the conveniences which are basic to well-being and worldly happiness. Now, however, the eye meets immense expanses of cultivated land where, less than three decades ago, the raw forces of nature held undisputed sway. At present we have all the blessings which are bestowed upon the nations by modern progress, inventiveness, and enterprise.

"As for me personally, during the first years after my arrival in this country I sought work wherever the opportunity offered itself. Several times I covered on foot the distance of 130 miles between Koshkonong and Chicago. In the settlements, the farmers at times paid with produce instead of dollars, which in those days were 'rare birds' here in the West. At other times I might well have to rest satisfied with a 'thanks for a good job' and leave without any pay. But even though the wages were very low I was able to put some money aside; and as soon as I was able to buy some acres of land with the money I had saved, my condition improved considerably."

The paragraphs above are a brief summary of the account I obtained from Gunder Mandt regarding his experiences on this side of the ocean. At present he lives on one of the best farms in Pleasant Spring, section 22. The once poverty-stricken newcomer is now one of the most prosperous men in the township. As a child he had but meagre opportunity to attend school because his mother's limited resources made it necessary for Gunder to leave the family home at an early age and earn his bread among strangers. "I could hardly write my own name when I came to America," he says, "and my fund of knowledge was miserable indeed." Now, however, he must undoubtedly be counted among the best-informed men in the district. Through private study and reading he has attained over the years a level of education which very few of his countrymen who labored under similar conditions have been able to equal. Modest, unostentatious behavior, strict integrity and honesty—these are the main elements in Gunder Mandt's character; and his fellow citizens have frequently trusted him with positions of importance in the township.

Peder Simon Aasmundsen Tangen from Sannidal, near Kragerø, left Norway in 1845. Thus he can not be counted among the fathers of emigration, but as the largest landowner in the township he deserves a place in the history of the Norwegian-American settlements. He owns 500 acres of land, valued at about $35.00 per acre, which, in combination with private property and other possessions, amounts to an estate of some $25,000. "In Norway I was a seaman," he tells us, "and as such I sailed for ten years. But the monthly wages were low—an experienced sailor could not earn more than five *speciedaler* per month—and times were bad ashore, with miserable crops and poor wages for the laborer. The news from America, on the contrary, was good, and letters sent home by acquaintances on this side of the ocean encouraged us to leave.

"In 1845 two ships left Kragerø with emigrants. On the ship that I took there were ninety persons going to America, mostly townspeople and landless *strandsittere* (shore dwellers) from the area. For accommodations over the ocean each of us paid eighteen *speciedaler*. The whole group stayed together on the way westward as far as Milwaukee, but there the party dissolved. Some got jobs in town; others went to Skoponong where a Norwegian settlement had already been founded. Four of the emigrant families and I went by way of Muskego to Koshkonong where I claimed eighty acres in the southern part of Pleasant Spring township.

"Since then I have increased my holdings to their present size through purchases. When I settled here all the cash I had amounted to about fifty dollars. This was no great sum, to be sure, but it helped me over the first difficulties; and as I was in good health and had two ready hands, I entered upon my work as a pioneer in good spirits. The life of the early settlers was, naturally, full of toil. But my industry was rewarded with success and things improved during the years: the population of the community grew rapidly as people moved in; markets sprang up close by; and before long Koshkonong was held to be one of the most flourishing districts in Dane county."

As already mentioned, Peder Simon Tangen is now a prosperous man—

yes, we must even say that he is rich. He has amassed an estate of more than $20,000 as a result of his quarter century of activity in this county. There are not many men in the Norwegian setttlements who can boast of similar success. We may add that Peder Simon as an honest, upright, and dependable man enjoys the respect and confidence of his fellow citizens.

As sharks and other predatory fish follow in the wake of ships crossing the oceans, so cheats and adventurers also attach themselves to emigrant groups in the hope of making gain at the expense of their gullible fellow passengers. Even from the earliest period of emigrant history many instances of this kind can be reported. I will now relate the story of such a case on Koshkonong. In the year 1841 a Swede who called himself [John] Smith came to the district and settled in Christiana township, somewhat south of Clinton. He said that he was an Evangelical Lutheran pastor who had served as court chaplain in Stockholm, but had been repelled by the luxurious court life and corruption of the capital city. Therefore—scorning all worldly gain—he had now come to the Far West where, as a humble servant of the Lord, he wished to do missionary work among his brethren of the faith.

There evidently were certain individuals who cast suspicious glances at the self-sacrificing missionary; but with saccharine speeches, feigned condescension, and well-calculated flattery he succeeded in fooling a majority of the people. Many regarded him with awe and trust as a man of God who, forsaking the world and its joys, chose a pioneer's laborious existence in preference to the seductive glitter and sinful temptations of court life. He had a great many champions among the women, and through them he soon gained the support of the men also; when the front wheels of a wagon are set in motion the rear wheels follow in their tracks. With a Bible under his arm Smith went out among the farmers to conduct divine service, as he called it. People listened with deep emotion to stories of the battles he had had to fight against the flesh before he was victorious over the Devil and his own evil inclinations. Even though on several occasions it became unpleasantly evident that the self-declared pastor had by no means mastered the Old Adam in his own flesh, his reputation was so firmly established that the most uncomplimentary rumors—even though supported by facts—could not shake people's confidence.

In the spring of 1844 C. L. Clausen, then pastor at Muskego, visited Koshkonong. On this occasion he preached at Holtan's farm in Pleasant Spring and also officiated at confirmation, baptism, and holy communion. Clausen warned against Smith, but this would likely have borne little fruit except for the fact that, as time passed, more and more people declared Smith unworthy to proclaim the word of God. Smith's stock declined rapidly in value, and when Pastor Dietrichson arrived later in the summer most of the people in the settlement rallied around the new pastor. Smith, however, still had several supporters and continued for some time to preach and thunder against "the heretics in the long black robes." But when he finally realized that his role as a preacher had been played out, the theologian was suddenly transformed into a medical doctor. Strange to say, in this field also he got quite a following, even among those who no longer would accept him as their spiritual shepherd. But this glory did not long endure. A death caused by the "doctor's" total lack of medical knowledge aroused people's anger to such a degree that he found it wisest to pack up and disappear as quickly as possible.

Later he surfaced in Chicago, again in the guise of a preacher. He succeeded in forming a congregation consisting of Norwegians and Swedes. They built their own church, and Smith had the game going his way for a while. He was regarded as an earnest man of God to whom everyone owed respect and deference. But then rumors came from Sweden about a man whose description fitted Smith's appearance in every detail. He was said to have skipped the country, and Smith, smelling trouble, suddenly transferred his activities to points farther west. There, as circumstances might demand, he took the shape of pastor, peddler, doctor, land speculator, or agent, until—so the story goes—his dishonesty caught up with him and he was lynched.

A great majority of the people in the township belong to that branch of the Evangelical Lutheran Church which goes by the name of the Wisconsin or Missouri Synod. Six or eight families belong to the Augustana Synod and one family to Elling Eielsen's denomination. There are also a few families which as yet have not joined any church. Late in the fall of 1844 Pastor J. W. C. Dietrichson came to Koshkonong and organized the first Norwegian Evangelical Lutheran congregation in the district. A Lutheran congregation had already been organized at Muskego. Its pastor, C. L. Clausen, visited Koshkonong in the spring of 1844 and conducted services in the township of Pleasant Spring. According to reports, it was the merchant Tollef Bache of Drammen who, in his concern for the extension of God's kingdom, persuaded Clausen to leave for America. Likewise it was a gift of 1,000 *speciedaler* from Sørensen, dyer by trade, of Christiania which enabled Dietrichson to come to America and organize Lutheran congregations among the Norwegian settlers. Dietrichson was both physically and intellectually a powerful man who performed his duties with untiring endurance and complete sincerity. But he labored under great difficulties, and his hot temper involved him in many troubles. Two of the older settlers on Koshkonong, Thomas Braaten, a miner from Kongsberg, and Halvor Funkelien, also from Kongsberg, especially showed themselves on every occasion to be his irreconcilable enemies. They planned methodically to offend the pastor; and when he—misled by his fiery spirit—let himself be duped and led into their snares, they took advantage of the situation to prepare further difficulties for him. On a couple of occasions violent scenes occurred within the church itself. But the two troublemakers were sly enough to make it appear that they were in the right.

Dietrichson had his enemies; but he also had numerous friends who still speak with reverence about the missionary as being always energetically engaged in fulfilling his sacred duties. As a gifted pulpit orator he has scarcely found his equal among the Norwegian pastors in America. It seems that Dietrichson was one of those personalities whose willpower and definite opinions divide the masses into two parties: one to criticize and slander, the other to praise and extol. Moreover, accusations of miserliness launched against him were probably not without foundation. This weakness, combined with an unbending strictness, threw obstacles in the way of his well-meant efforts. Consequently Dietrichson did not succeed in accomplishing as much either on Koshkonong or in the other Norwegian settlements as people had the right to expect from a man armed with such great intellectual gifts. However, an eyewitness to events of those days said, "Despite all these shortcomings and failings, Dietrichson's untiring efforts succeeded in bringing order into the congregations on Koshkonong. I believe he was exactly the right man to do the grubbing and breaking of the spiritual soil among the western pioneers." When J. W. C. Dietrichson returned to Norway, Adolf C. Preus—now at Coon Prairie—became pastor of the Koshkonong congregations; and when he moved to Chicago, Pastor [Jakob Aall] Ottesen took his place. He has now served these churches some eight or nine years.[29]

At first Dietrichson conducted religious services in various farm homes; but during the first winter after his arrival in the settlement, a simple wooden structure was erected which was dedicated and used as a church. When it no longer could serve the purposes of the congregation, the present large octagonal stone church was built. It defies all the architectural laws and stands there as an ugly, crude object which poorly fulfills the demands of the times and forms a strange contrast to the many beautiful farmhouses found in the settlement. It looks like a half-finished haystack, and it arouses the suspicion that the builders either ran short of materials or else tired of the job before it was finished. The church is light and roomy and has a beautiful location. It lacks an organ but has a bell. Ole Olsen Moe, a graduate of Holt teacher's training school in Norway, serves as sexton and conducts parochial school when the pupils are on vacation from the common school. Besides the Norwegians in Pleasant Spring some of our countrymen in Christiana, Cottage Grove, Albion, Dunkirk, Dunn, and Blooming Grove belong to the West Koshkonong church. Recently a new Norwegian church has been built in McFarland, and as soon as it can be put into use the members of the western church will form two separate congregations.

On the first and second of September, 1869, a celebration was held on

Koshkonong to commemorate the twenty-fifth anniversary of Pastor J. W. C. Dietrichson's first sermon as minister of the congregation.* The attendance was very large and many pastors from the Wisconsin Synod were present. The celebration began with a procession from the parsonage to the East Koshkonong church, where the Reverend H. A. Stub spoke from the altar, using Psalm 103:1–2 as his text. He is one of the Synod's oldest pastors and his life in this country has been rich in trials and tribulations. From the pulpit the Reverend U. V. Koren spoke, with John 15:15–19 as text. He also has served as pastor among the Norwegians in America over a long period of years and has, furthermore, long been a member of the church council.

When the services in the church were ended, the gathering moved on to Amund Endressen's barn where Dietrichson, twenty-five years earlier, had assembled his countrymen then living in the district and delivered his first sermon, using Revelation 22:12 as text. Near the barn, in nature's vast temple with the clear blue sky as vault and tall trees as walls, the gathering sang Luther's impressive hymn, "A Mighty Fortress is our God," accompanied by instrumental music. Then Pastor Nils Brandt read a survey of the congregation's history and remarked that out in the Far West lived people who at one time had been members of the local church and would always bear Koshkonong in fond remembrance as the home from which they had gone forth. Brandt is one of the Synod's most distinguished pastors and despite the fact that age and exertions have taken their toll he is still a vigorous man.

The service near the barn was concluded with prayer by the pastor of the congregation, J. A. Ottesen, whereupon the gathering dispersed, but reassembled the next day at the West Koshkonong church, which had been decorated for the occasion with foliage and flowers. Here the services were opened by Pastor S. Reque, who spoke from the altar with Psalm 68:12 as text. Then he read brief biographies of eleven theological candidates who were present to be ordained as pastors. The ordination sermon was delivered by the Synod president, Herman A. Preus, who chose as text Jeremiah 1:17–19. From the church the people went in festive procession to "The Oak" in whose shade Pastor Dietrichson had conducted his first complete service and cut the sign of the cross.[30] The oak was decorated with foliage which spelled out Dietrichson's name, and nearby a platform had been erected for the musicians and the speakers. Pastor Koren spoke first, followed by Pastor Adolf C. Preus of Coon Prairie, who delivered the main speech. He reminded the audience of Pastor J. W. C. Dietrichson, who, under great difficulties, had organized the congregations, and also reminisced briefly about his own activities on Koshkonong and, finally, congratulated the congregation on having in the person of Pastor Ottesen an able and zealous minister of the Word.

**Billed-Magazin*, February 12, 1870.

We have given a brief account of the twenty-fifth anniversary celebration which took place last year because we felt that this was an historical occurrence which ought to be of more than passing interest to the Norwegian people in America.

Eight or nine years ago the number of Republicans and Democrats in Pleasant Spring was about equal. However, of the 130 Norwegian votes cast in the last presidential election only thirty-five went to the Democratic candidate. There were also two votes cast by Germans and thirty-eight by Americans, a total of forty non-Norwegian votes, of which only one went Democratic. Pleasant Spring thus cast a Republican majority of 134 votes. In the township elections the two parties do not present separate lists. There is a joint list and the voters choose "the best man" irrespective of party affiliation.

In the early years, one of the settlers told me, the English school was well attended; but later the attendance was rather poor. Recently, however, people have become conscious of the fact that a certain amount of knowledge is a necessary requirement of human welfare and that the instruction given in the American schools covers exactly those branches of learning which form the foundation of a general education. When the district school is not in session, a teacher educated in Norway gives religious instruction to the Norwegian children. At least one and sometimes several Norwegian newspapers are found in practically every home, and some people also read English papers. In their associations with each other the farmers here generally make use of the English language, which is also the case in all the other larger Norwegian settlements. They also prefer English reading material rather than Norwegian. It seems that there are fewer good books among the farmers on Koshkonong than in the other old Norwegian settlements. From this fact one can possibly draw the conclusion that people here satisfy their demands for intellectual nourishment by reading newspapers. In this community there is no lending library, no singing society, or any other association for educational, cultural, or social entertainment.

Health conditions in recent years have been exceptionally good. We hear no more complaints about climate fever, which in earlier days sorely afflicted the newcomers; and the community has lately been free of contagious diseases. When Doctor [Søren Johan] Hanssen left the district for Norway, Doctor [J. W.] Magelsen, son of Pastor Magelsen of Aker, near Christiania, took his place and has been practicing medicine on Koshkonong for three or four years.

The name "Pleasant Spring" is said to derive from the early settlers' discovery that within the township several springs welled forth from the earth—of which three were especially large. One of these is found on Tollef Gjermundsen's farm, which explains why he has been called "Springen." A second one sees the light of day near the Aaby schoolhouse, and the third

COURTESY OF STATE HISTORICAL SOCIETY OF WISCONSIN

Immigrant family harvesting grain, Dane county, ca. 1875.

spring streams out of its subterranean source on the farm which belongs to the above-mentioned Peder Simon Aasmundsen Tangen. The township should consequently be called "Pleasant Springs" and not, as is commonly the case, "Pleasant Spring."[31]

The soil, consisting of clay or humus, must on the whole be said to be fertile even though in general it is not of as good quality as in Christiana and Albion townships. On the average no more than 13 to 15 bushels of wheat per acre are raised at present, while yields of 30 to 35 bushels were not unusual in the early years. The terrain is characterized by small rolling prairies interspersed with wooded areas and small marshes. There is enough firewood to satisfy household demands and many farmers can even bring wood to market.

The production of wheat is the main source of income, and in past years the farmers here, with very few exceptions, concentrated all their efforts on the production of this particular crop. The average price of wheat during the last five years has been $1.32; figuring fifteen bushels per acre, this will give the farmers a considerable surplus, as the cost of production, including real estate taxes, does not exceed $.65 per bushel. Thus, if the sum total of the work on a farm is figured at current wages and all other expenses added, the farmer will have a net gain of $.67 from every bushel produced. In relation to outlay, this represents a profit of more than 100 percent.

In recent years several farmers in this community have paid more attention to cattle-raising than formerly, and some attempts have been made to improve the breeds. But the often poor and much too small pastures are a hindrance to cattle-raising which, as a source of income, will never be of the same importance as wheat-raising. Besides the products mentioned—wheat and to a lesser extent other types of grain, as well as wood—many farmers also sell live animals, pork, some butter, and at times wool and hides.

All land in this old settlement has long since been bought up. Prices in recent years have averaged from $30 to $35 per acre. In a few exceptional cases the price of very good farms has even approached $50 per acre. With the falling prices of farm products, the value of land will presumably sink also. There are already signs that the excessive prices are declining.

The average size of farms in this township runs to about 125 acres. The economic situation is very good. No one in the township receives public aid. I would say that many of the farmers are rich while the others, almost without exception, must be classified as well-to-do. Not a few have in recent years built beautiful, well-furnished houses which testify to both the owner's taste and his appreciation of modern conveniences and the comforts of a cultured life. In Pleasant Spring there are a few landless families who sustain themselves by working for others. The wages of a maidservant run from $1.50 to $2.00 per week, while a hired man is paid about $20.00 per month plus board. The wages for day labor vary with the seasons. During the winter it may be difficult for laboring people to secure steady work. As a result some of them leave for the forest areas where they find work in the winter months as lumberjacks. During times of unemployment it may happen that some landless families are forced to seek aid from their neighbors; but actual begging is not heard of, except for the frequent requests by newcomers without means for loans to help defray travel expenses of family members left behind in Norway.

I found 112 names entered on the list of Norwegian farmers in Pleasant Spring. These, together with the Yankees engaged in agriculture, plus the landless families, lead us to assume that there are 180 households in the township. Consequently, the total population can be set at about 900. Last year the real estate in the township was assessed at $393,000 and the personal property at $83,500—for a combined tax valuation of $476,500. Increasing this amount by one-third to account for probable undervaluation for tax purposes, we get the sum of $635,333 as a true estimate of the total value of property in the township. If this figure were equally divided among the 900 inhabitants, more than $700 would be allotted each individual.

Dunkirk township

Dunkirk is the last of the four townships which form the quandrant known among the Scandinavians as Koshkonong.* It is located south of Pleasant Spring and east [sic] of Albion and forms the southeastern [sic] corner of the quadrant.** The soil and other natural conditions are about the same as in the other townships.[32]

The first Norwegian settler in Dunkirk was John Nelson Luraas from Tinn in Upper Telemark. We have already heard about his emigration from Norway and his brief stay in Muskego. Together with his fellow countryman from Tinn, Knud Roe, the first Norwegian settler in Pleasant Spring, he undertook the then difficult trip from Muskego to Koshkonong and came to Dunkirk in June, 1843. A Yankee named Huiler had arrived a couple of weeks earlier. Otherwise the township was a wilderness, and except for some bands of roaming Indians there were no other signs of human beings within its limits. He bought land in the northern part of the township and called his place Luraas in memory of his forefathers' farm in his native valley. Through farming and trading John Luraas has, during the years, amassed a considerable fortune. But the same thing happened to him as to so many other early settlers in the state. It seems as if the words "to the West, to the West!" are always ringing in their ears, and no sooner do they overcome the hardships of pioneer life than they again set forth into the wilderness to blaze a trail for less courageous immigrants.

John Nelson Luraas entered the ranks of these untiring pioneers.*** Even though he had already reached an advanced age, he left his good farm on Koshkonong about a year and a half ago and settled in Webster county, Iowa, which could be called a wilderness in comparison with the region he left. Such migration from the older settlements to the unpopulated areas of the West will likely increase in the near future so that those who sell out will grow steadily more numerous. One reason for this development is no doubt the fact that many people in the old settlements feel themselves hemmed in on all sides. They seek wider spaces in which to move about, where they can enjoy freedom of action without arousing protests from touchy neighbors. Others leave for the West because of the lower land prices and the more fertile soil out there. In many of the older settlements real estate prices are already so high that prospects of making any headway are slight indeed for poor people who buy land while the prices of farm produce remain at their present low level. Furthermore, the soil in many districts has become so impoverished that

**Billed-Magazin*, April 9, 1870.

**The correct location of Dunkirk township is *west* of Albion; it forms the south*western* corner of the quadrant. (Editor's note)

****Billed-Magazin*, April 16, 1870.

a farmer must limit the size of his cultivated area or spend considerable sums of money to put fields back into productive shape. In the regions beyond the Mississippi as yet untouched by the plow, however, the virgin soil is so rich that it yields crops reminiscent of the early pioneer days in this state.

Probably the Scandinavians will also become aware soon of the advantages a milder climate has to offer for agriculture and in the future discontinue seeking homesteads primarily in the northern parts of the country. A winter of five or six months, with much snow, may be of benefit for forestry and timber-floating; but agricultural interests, grain-raising as well as cattle-raising, are best served when a long and moderately warm summer is followed by a short, mild winter.

Soil conditions in Dunkirk are about the same as in Pleasant Spring. A wheat crop of fifteen bushels per acre is considered a good yield, and heretofore the marketing of wheat has been the farmers' main source of income. In tax assessments the average land value is estimated at $24.50 per acre as over against $19.33⅓ in Pleasant Spring and just under $23 in Christiana. The easy access to market accounts in part for this high valuation. The average price of land at present is somewhere in the neighborhood of $35.00 per acre.

Gaute Ingebrigtsen Gulliksrud from Tinn in Telemark, one of the first settlers in Dunkirk township, has related to me some episodes from his life story which I offer below.

"Two of my uncles and a brother," began Gaute's account, "emigrated in 1839, while I remained at home with my father, who was a farmer in the parish of Tinn. But then came letters with good reports from America, and my relatives as well as other acquaintances on our side of the ocean were encouraged to leave. The result was that I and many others from my home community prepared for departure in the spring of 1843. The group numbered about 120. We secured ship accommodations from Skien to Le Havre in France, and from there to New York. The journey continued on to Milwaukee and thence to Muskego, where people from Telemark—mostly from Tinn—had founded a settlement four years earlier. I did not like Muskego. The land was low, marshy, and infertile. The newcomers lived in straitened circumstances, and much sickness afflicted the settlement. Many of my group died shortly after our arrival. I could by no means feel satisfied with what I saw and heard there.

"But rumors about the fertile soil of Koshkonong had reached even this out-of-the-way place, and several men had already gone west to inspect the area. I determined to leave, and in August, 1843, I came to Dunkirk where I met John Nelson Luraas, Helge Grimsrud, and Hans Pedersen Tværberg—all three from Tinn—who had settled in this township five or six weeks before my arrival. I had brought along 600 *speciedaler* from Norway, and for $200 I bought 160 acres of government land near the homesteads of the other men from my native valley. I have lived here ever since.

"Thus, by the fall of 1843, four Norwegian families lived within the borders of the township. No serious misfortune struck any of us; everything went its quiet, peaceful way; and before long we got several other countrymen of ours as neighbors. Pioneer life in those days was difficult and gave rise to many disappointments and privations which are now unknown. But most of us were in our best years, so work came easy; and if at first it might happen that our spirits were saddened with longing for our childhood home, our hopes for a better future soon gave us courage and vigor for renewed efforts. Some of the earliest settlers have already laid down their staffs and are now at rest in their graves, while others have left us to seek new homesteads farther west. At present there are twenty-five Scandinavian farmers in the township, all but two of them Norwegian. Besides the farmers there are a few families who earn their living as laborers. There has always been good friendship and understanding in our neighborhood: no quarrels or disputes have disturbed us, nor have lawsuits or other legal difficulties ever been heard of among the Norwegians."

The paragraphs above give a brief summary of Gaute Ingebrigtsen's account. I will add only that he is looked upon as one of the most thoughtful and respectable men in the township. Gaute Ingebrigtsen has also been able to preserve in this country the dependability and sincerity which, at least in earlier ages, are said to have been fundamental characteristics of the Norwegian mountaineers. His face bears the impress of genuine courtesy and helpfulness. Gaute is undoubtedly one of those fortunate human beings who has few if any enemies but many friends.

In 1844 a group of emigrants left the parish of Vik, in the district of Sogn, under the leadership of their fellow parishioner Iver Larsen Hove.* This group opened the way for emigration from that region in old Norway, and early the following spring a large contingent was ready to bid the homeland farewell. The first party of emigrants from Vik, numbering only a few families, went from Bergen by way of New York to Chicago and then northward to Long Prairie not far from the southern boundary of Wisconsin, where most of them settled.

Ole Olsen Menes has told about the larger emigration which took place in 1845: "The emigrants of the previous year wrote to acquaintances in the home community and encouraged them to leave. They told about the fertility of the soil, the low prices of land, and the good wages for laborers. In a letter I received from Iver Hove he wrote that over here they raised thirty-five bushels of wheat per acre and the grass grew so thick that in a day a man could easily cut enough hay to feed a cow through the winter. This was exactly to our taste, and many of us cast longing looks toward the Far West, where it seemed

*Billed-Magazin, April 23, 1870.

that a kind Providence had prepared a refuge for the toiling, worry-worn masses of Norway. The America fever was nourished anew by every letter which came from the land of marvels. Rumors spread like wildfire through the community, and in both private circles and public gatherings talk about emigration was the first and last order of the day.

"Early in the spring of 1845 about seventy of us from the parish of Vik were prepared to leave. Many neighbors wished us good luck and predicted a happy future, but others considered us a pack of deluded fools who were going to our certain destruction. This comparatively large migration attracted much attention in outer Sogn and perhaps even greater wonder in some more remote places. At Bergen we got ship accommodations for the ocean crossing. A shoemaker named Tollefsen who had lived in New York three years was home in Bergen for a visit. He joined our group and accompanied us all the way to Chicago. There we held a consultation as to where we should go to look for homesteads. Most of the Norwegians we met in Chicago advised us to go north, preferably to Koshkonong in Wisconsin where there was said to be an abundance of fertile land at low prices. Before we had reached a final decision as to our destination, we met Østen Blomhaugen from Tinn, who had been on Koshkonong and owned land there, but was in Chicago at the time looking for work. When he gave us the same advice as so many others we decided to go to Koshkonong, with him as our guide. A few remained in Chicago while the rest of us set off under Østen's leadership. When we reached Long Prairie most of the group decided to remain there where some people from Sogn had already settled the previous summer, but the rest went on to Rock Prairie.

"I, Ole Menes, and my present neighbor, Iver Hansen Bakken, Johannes Olsen Finne (deceased in Minnesota), Anders Ellingsen Aase (now in Iowa), six single persons, and Ingebrigt Ingebrigtsen Næse (later moved to Iowa), all from Vik, continued the journey to Koshkonong and settled among our countrymen in Christiana. Many of the emigrants from Vik were in fairly comfortable economic circumstances and Ingebrigt Næse might even be called a rich man. When we came to Koshkonong in the fall of 1845 there was still some government land for sale; but very soon settlers came from everywhere, and all the land was bought up. I purchased land two miles east of Stoughton in the township of Dunkirk and have had my home here ever since. John Nelson Luraas, Helge Grimsrud, Gaute Ingebrigtsen, and Hans Tværberg, all from Tinn, as well as Halvor Grovum (now in Blue Mounds), Thosten Bakken, and I formed a circle of neighbors. During the fall when I arrived and especially during the following summer, the influx of people was heavy. Very soon we were surrounded by neighbors. Tove Kittelsen from Tinn understood some English and acted as interpreter for us Norwegians. He later moved to Blue

Mounds in Dane county where he died some seven or eight years ago. Østen Blomhaugen, whom I learned to know in Chicago and who accompanied the Vik immigrants northward, has also left Koshkonong and now lives on a farm in the western part of the county."

Ole Menes is probably the wealthiest Norwegian farmer in Dunkirk township. He does not speak much but he thinks deeply; he is a man for whom your respect grows the better you learn to know him. Like most of his countrymen in the township he is a member of the Norwegian Evangelical Lutheran Church. He is an earnest Christian, but he is free of the spiritual arrogance which stamps one's own opinions with the brand of infallibility and the religious fanaticism which expresses itself through merciless condemnation of people with differing opinions. Such tolerance, which is neither indifference nor unconcern, deserves all the more appreciation because our people have long been exposed to forces which tend to stir up hatred and religious fanaticism. A man must be armed with a gentle, humble spirit if he is to avoid the self-righteous opinions which the Prince of Darkness utilizes to arouse dissension within Christendom. Ole Menes has been and still is a Democrat; but he is free of political ambitions himself and has kept away from all political wrangles. He has chosen his party because of conviction but respects the divergent opinions of others and would presumably cast his vote for a Republican if he found him more able and honest than his Democratic rival. No one has ever accused Ole Menes of lacking integrity and dependability. He has traveled through the states of Illinois, Missouri, Iowa, and Minnesota. His trips have given him a clear conception of life and social conditions in these parts of the West. He has sound judgment and a rare gift of looking at life from a rational point of view. Based on a conversation I had with Ole Menes some time ago I have written the following paragraphs which, as far as my memory permits, are given in his own words.

"America offers the poor laborer many advantages. With industry and perseverance he can become wealthy here. The greatest glory of the country, however, is that here penniless newcomers can secure fertile land for practically nothing. With the growth of agriculture come various other forms of industry which give artisans and factory workers an opportunity to earn a livelihood. But in the older settlements, as on Koshkonong, land prices are now so high that they offer the buyer without much cash little hope of progress. I do not mean to say that it would be absolutely impossible for such a man to feed his family and pay taxes and other reasonable expenses even though the prices of farm produce continue as low as at present, but he could do it only if he combined thrift with an unusual willingness to work hard. Even so, it might be that of two persons who attempted such a task only one would succeed.

"Homestead or government land in the western states is the surest refuge for a poor newcomer if he is unwilling to take a job as a laborer or to work another man's land as a tenant. Even a farmer who owns, free of debt, 200 acres of land with livestock and equipment can not live as comfortable and carefree a life here as a wealthy man can in Norway. As a rule he must take an active part in running his farm even though it may be worth some $8,000 or $10,000. The luxurious life of a Norwegian gentleman-farmer would lead to ruin here. The farmers who have grown wealthy here owe their prosperity to the low price they paid for their land, simple living, and hard work. A large landowner from eastern Norway, for example, would soon lose out in America, even though he brought along several thousand dollars, if he tried to lead the life of a loafer and not do anything beyond 'managing the estate.' However, I believe that if a farmer sold his possessions here and returned to Norway with some $8,000 or $10,000 he would have just as good a chance of increasing his fortune there as if he remained in America. As owner of one of the best farms, say in Sogn, with all accompanying resources such as fruit-growing and fishing, he could live a comfortable, carefree gentleman's life and even save a little money each year.

"American institutions and laws in general deserve all praise. It is to be wished, however, that there were more honesty among government officials and more loyalty among people in general. According to the letter of the law, everybody's rights are protected, but it seems that personal influence and money more frequently make justice blind here than in other countries. People, however, have the power of reform in their hands and responsibility rests with the citizens who have the right to vote. The Norwegians in this country have the reputation of being law-abiding and orderly. As farmers they usually attain wealth more rapidly than their fellow citizens of other nationalities. It probably comes easier for Yankees to make money; but they also spend more freely, whereas thrifty management of economic affairs contributes to the success of our countrymen in America."

Helge Sivertsen Grimsrud from Tinn was, so I have been told, the first Norwegian to buy land in Dunkirk township.* He was a well-to-do farmer in his homeland; but he decided to make America his future home when his brother-in-law, John Nelson Luraas, and other relatives who had already emigrated wrote letters encouraging him to leave. Helge died about fourteen years ago, but his widow, now Mrs. Andersen, reported to me as follows concerning the circumstances which led to their departure from Norway.

"My sister's husband, John Nelson Luraas, emigrated from Tinn in 1839 and went first to Muskego where he remained three years and a half. In 1841 both my parents and a sister left the homeland; and the next year, 1842, my

**Billed-Magazin*, May 7, 1870.

first husband and I undertook the long and difficult journey. At that time many well-to-do people were emigrating from Upper Telemark. We left from Drammen and went by way of Gothenburg and New York to Milwaukee. The whole trip from our home community to Milwaukee lasted twenty weeks. In Milwaukee the party dispersed. A few got jobs there while many went on to Muskego and others to Koshkonong, Jefferson Prairie, or other places—all depending on how much influence relatives or friends might have on their decisions. My husband and I settled temporarily in Muskego where I met my parents and other relatives.

"Prospects for newcomers were not of such a nature there, however, that we could feel quite satisfied in Muskego. Some of the early settlers had already left the community and several others spoke of moving elsewhere. Some time during the fall of the year my husband Helge and John Nelson Luraas went to Koshkonong to inspect the area. They found everything to their liking and returned with the report that they had already chosen homesteads in the present township of Dunkirk. Helge went immediately to Milwaukee and bought the 240 acres of land which became our homestead. To the best of my knowledge no other Norwegian had as yet bought land in that community. The following spring John Nelson Luraas moved to Koshkonong with his family and later in the summer we also settled there. The two brothers-in-law, John and Helge, both from Telemark, were thus the first Norwegian settlers in this community. Some time later my sister with her husband and our parents also came to live in our neighborhood."

When Helge Sivertsen Grimsrud died, his widow, Birgitte, married a man by the name of Ole Andersen Køien from Finnskog in Solør. They bought more land and settled on a farm which is known in this area as Stølen after its former owner. Through later purchases Ole Andersen's property has been enlarged until at present he owns one of the largest farms on Koshkonong, approximately 550 acres with buildings, implements, horses, and cattle, worth about $25,000 in all.

I am not certain about the origin of the name "Dunkirk."* It occurs as a place-name in the eastern states, and the early settler who was given the privilege of choosing no doubt suggested this name in honor of his home town or some other place which had meaning for him. In the governmental archives at Madison one could probably find information as to who made the proposal and why the name "Dunkirk" was chosen for the township.

The town of Stoughton is located in the center of the township on the Catfish River, which connects the "four lakes" with the Rock River, a tributary of the Mississippi. In time this whole watercourse will presumably be opened for navigation. From the heart of Wisconsin, in the area around the

***Billed-Magazin*, May 14, 1870.

state capital, there will then be a line of communication through the Catfish and Rock rivers to the nation's great commercial artery. A few years ago a little steamboat was built at Stoughton for traffic on the river and the lakes, but so many problems arose that the project was abandoned. It should be possible, however, to overcome these difficulties, and the realization of the plan should be merely a question of time.

The Milwaukee and Prairie du Chien Railway puts Stoughton in direct communication with Madison, some fifteen miles to the northwest, and with the commercial metropolis on Lake Michigan, eighty miles to the east. I have never seen any other town which has such an active business life in proportion to its size as Stoughton. This is easily explained when we consider that it serves as a market for several of the principal grain-producing districts in the state. Manufacturing is still only in its infancy but the Catfish River offers excellent opportunities of developing waterpower for industrial purposes. If the inhabitants are sufficiently alert to harness this force of nature it will give business such a mighty impulse that Stoughton will undoubtedly assume a prominent place among our inland towns.

What especially has attracted my attention to Stoughton is the strongly marked Norwegian character of the town. A newcomer from Norway who arrives here will be surprised indeed to find in the heart of the country, more than a thousand miles from his landing place, a town where language and way of life so unmistakably remind him of his native land. Only memories of the ocean voyage can convince our countryman that he actually is more than 5,000 miles distant from his childhood home, in that wonderland which an active imagination has furnished with the most curious images. On the streets his eyes will easily recognize faces of Nordic type, and his ears will catch the familiar sounds of his mother tongue. On the store signs are Norwegian names which remind him of his homeland, and at the merchant's desk are customers who dicker and ask for credit, exactly as the custom was in old Norway. Language, way of life, and all the other distinctive features which go to make up a nation are here found in their original purity. I do not believe there is in all America another town—except possibly communities in embryo—with such clear-cut, pure Norwegian characteristics as Stoughton.

The reason for this is easily found. The number of Norwegians is very large in proportion to the total population and, to the east, America's most populous Norwegian settlement extends right up to the edge of town. More than fifty percent of the farmers who do business in Stoughton are Norwegians, and a large proportion of the business men in town are Scandinavians. Thus the Norwegian elements are very strong, and American influence has remained comparatively weak. This explains why we find *norskheden* (Norwegianness), with all its special traits, in a purer form here than anywhere else within the union.

About twenty years ago Luke Stoughton came from Rock county to this region and bought a large area of land for speculative purposes, including the ground on which the town bearing his name is located. Waterpower was there to be used; he therefore built a flour mill and a sawmill. Soon a grocery store and a boardinghouse also appeared. These were the first indications of a town on the site. The aged Luke Stoughton is still alive and has accumulated a considerable fortune. For a long time the town grew very slowly. The isolated location hindered trade, and the farmers in the area had to seek more conveniently situated markets for the disposal of their products. But when the railway from Milwaukee reached Stoughton, these drawbacks vanished, and the town is at present one of the chief wheat-marketing centers in the state. Fertile land farmed by an enterprising people; waterpower which has the potential for producing considerable wealth; railway connections with the leading commercial centers in the Northwest, Chicago and Milwaukee—these foundations for progress and growth give promise that in the future Stoughton will be classed among the most flourishing inland towns of the state.

The population of the town probably numbers some 1,500, of whom about three-eighths are Norwegians. The rest are Yankees and Irishmen. The Germans are represented by only two families. In the actual laboring class—besides Irishmen—you will find many Norwegians, and Norwegian girls outnumber others as housemaids. In late years the town has made steady progress, wages are rather good, and there seem to be fewer professional idlers in Stoughton than in most other towns of its size.

The following business establishments are found in Stoughton: six dry goods stores, three owned by Norwegians; three drugstores, two owned by Norwegians; two hardware stores; three hotels; seven saloons, three owned by Norwegians; three shoemaker's shops, one owned by a Norwegian; one tailor shop, Norwegian; two cooper shops, both owned by Norwegians; one iron foundry, Norwegian; three wagon factories, two owned by Norwegians; two plow factories, both owned by Norwegians; one carpenter shop; one brick factory, Norwegian; three blacksmith shops; two watchmakers, one a Swede; two lumberyards, one owned by a Norwegian; four doctors; two veterinarians, both Norwegian; four grain dealers, two Norwegian; one stonecutter; one printing shop, and one book dealer.

This list gives an idea of Stoughton's commercial and industrial activity, and in the following paragraphs I will give a more detailed account of the town and its people.

Hans Andreas Haaversen was born on the farm Gurslie, in Lunde parish, in Jæren.* His father was a landowner and a rather wealthy man. "I wanted to see the world," Hans Haaversen relates, "and the thought struck me that

Billed-Magazin, May 21, 1870.

America was undoubtedly the land most favorable for a Norwegian emigrant. At the age of twenty-five, in the year 1848, I was ready to say farewell to relatives and friends. To the best of my knowledge no one had as yet left this part of Harald Fairhair's kingdom to strike roots in America. In Farsund an emigrant ship was lying all prepared to sail. I went aboard together with fifty other emigrants, most of them from Lista. The passage across the ocean lasted fourteen weeks. We had the misfortune of losing our captain during the voyage and the mate was in bed with a mortal illness. I do not know what would have happened to the vessel and its passengers under these circumstances but for the fact that one of the emigrants, fortunately, knew something about handling a ship. He assumed command and brought us and the boat safely to New York.

"From there we took the general emigrant route up through the country to Milwaukee. Many of the group remained there while the rest of us went on to Koshkonong. It is now eighteen years since I settled in Stoughton. At that time we had only one store, one tavern, a flour mill, and three or four other houses. Halvor Mathiesen, a mason from Telemark, and Nils Jensen, a gardener from Christiania, were then the only Norwegians in Stoughton. A couple of miles toward the east, however, a number of my countrymen had already settled. For a while I carried on in my profession of shoemaker, until better opportunities for earning money offered themselves in other occupations."

Hans A. Haaversen is undoubtedly one of the best-informed men among the Norwegians in this country. He is a highly trusted man who at present is engaged primarily in financial matters and has frequently been elected to various public positions. He speaks and writes English fluently and has acquired a fund of knowledge which entitles him to be called an educated man. Haaversen is a philosophically-inclined, reflective man, who has read widely in science, history, and philosophy. In several of these disciplines he has gained much insight, and this has struck me as all the more remarkable because among the Norwegian immigrants on Koshkonong few have applied their thoughts to anything beyond everyday matters—excepting, naturally, church disputes and a bit of politics for everyday use.

The firm of A. A. Flint and Co. is the largest business establishment in Stoughton. It deals in dry goods and has an annual turnover of somewhat more than $50,000—a respectable sum for a small town like Stoughton.

Our countryman Mathias Johannesen (Mathew Johnson) probably comes next after Flint & Co. in volume of business. His annual turnover amounts to about $40,000. Johnson operates a tailor shop, sells ready-made clothes, textiles, boots, and shoes, and also buys wool. Concerning his emigration from Norway and his experiences in this country he told me the following:

COURTESY OF STOUGHTON HISTORICAL SOCIETY

The Main Street in Stoughton, 1869. Mandt farm wagons are parked in the street.

"The farm Vea in Ringsaker was my childhood home. I learned the art of tailoring and worked at my profession in the community. Rumors about America had reached my district in eastern Norway, and stories about the wonders of the New World enlivened our imaginations. By the year 1853 my determination to emigrate had matured into action. In the spring of that year about fifty of us from Ringsaker left our birthplace and friends to try our fortune on this side of the ocean. In this group were many who had been landowners in Norway, but the majority were artisans, day laborers, and servants. We got ship accommodations from Christiania to Quebec, and continued our trip from there to Milwaukee. Some members of our group had relatives and friends on Koshkonong, so a number chose that settlement as their future home. I, however, went to Janesville, which already was a town of some size. I worked there about a year in a tailor shop and came in March, 1855, to Stoughton, where a town was in the making.

"I set up my own shop. Activity was slow at first; but as the town grew, my business increased and at present I employ about twelve people. They can earn from nine to eighteen dollars per week—an average of twelve dollars, or two dollars per day. There is no doubt that America offers people of the laboring class many advantages compared with Norway. Many of my countrymen are now living here in Stoughton. Even though few of them have grown rich, it can be said that many are in good circumstances, most of them have respectable incomes, and no one suffers want. Industry and endurance seldom go unrewarded in this country, and two skilled hands combined with good health give splendid promise for the future."

In the dry-goods business, the firm of Andersen and Lindas probably is the largest next to Flint & Co. John Lindas is an intelligent young man who was born on the island of Stord in Norway and came to America as a child. When the southern states rebelled, Lindas joined the ranks of the country's defenders as a volunteer and took part in many of the bloody battles which will be remembered as long as loyalty and love of liberty are respected. Some time after the end of the war he went into business in partnership with Nils Andersen. Andersen hails from Eidsvåg on the island of Stord, which he left about twenty years ago. He spent four years on Koshkonong, and when gold was discovered in Australia he went to that distant continent to try his luck in the mines. Four years later he returned with some capital which he invested first in a trading venture in Marshall, Dane county, and later in Stoughton. Thus Andersen has wandered from Norway to Wisconsin, from there to Australia, and then back again to America, where he settled as a citizen of this town.

Such a checkered career as Nils Andersen's does not lack parallels here in the Northwest. Even though not very many people have visited foreign continents, a large number, especially in the towns and cities, have tried several states of the union before settling down. Among the inhabitants of the small towns which spring up like toadstools here in the West we frequently meet men who joined the brotherhood of merchants in the East, were then employed in the South, and finally came north—enriched in experience if not in money—to establish a business. It is by no means exceptional that an artisan who has hung up his sign in the West may once have been a gold miner in California, and, if luck failed him there, may have worked several years in a factory in St. Louis or a shop in New Orleans or Philadelphia before he ends his days in one of the many flourishing new towns in the Northwest. One frequently meets men who have crisscrossed most of the country between the Gulf of Mexico and the Great Lakes. Here in the towns we seldom find those provincial types who are characterized by narrow-mindedness, arrogance, and exaggerated opinions of their own wisdom. Experience derived from practical life often makes up for a lack of academic training. Most of the men one meets have seen a good deal of the world, which has freed their minds of petty self-satisfaction and opened their eyes to an unprejudiced view of life. Let this be said in general about the townspeople out here in the West.

As in most American towns we find in Stoughton a number of different church affiliations. The following denominations each have one congregation and one church in town: Baptist, Methodist, Universalist, Catholic, Congregationalist, and Augustana Synod. In addition there are many people who have not joined any congregation, either because of lukewarmness or negligence, or because they harbor rationalist views. The great majority of Norwegians in Stoughton belong to the Augustana Synod; but two families are Methodists, three or four belong to the Wisconsin Synod, and a couple are said to be followers of Elling Eielsen.

As the population of Stoughton is divided among many different confessions, some people conclude that understanding and friendship between neighbors must of necessity rest on a very insecure foundation.* Undoubtedly sufficient fuel is found here to feed the fires of hate and religious fanaticism; but among the Scandinavians of Stoughton there is little of that intolerant spirit which in many other areas is flaunted as the only true Lutheranism and a sign of zeal for the faith of the fathers. No doubt there are people here, also, for whom Christianity is synonymous with ruthless hatred of everyone who does not belong to their denomination. But such individual intolerance is checked by the sound judgment of the majority. Hence one finds little here of that discord and strife which—to the shame of the Scandinavians—so often cause dissension among people who should work together in a brotherly spirit to enhance the reputation of the Scandinavians in America.

**Billed-Magazin*, June 25, 1870.

There is a literary society in Stoughton which has founded a city library where books can be borrowed in return for a certain annual fee. Peculiarly enough, among the members of the society are found only four Scandinavian names, a negligible number indeed compared with the proportion of Norwegians in the town and its environs. With very few exceptions it seems that books of educational value are "rare birds" among our countrymen in these parts. Apparently most of them feed their minds on the light reading material found in newspapers. There are no Scandinavian organizations here, no social gatherings for cultural advancement are ever staged, and educational lectures seem to be unknown. Such a lack of interest in the higher values of civilization must of necessity lead to spiritual apathy, egotism, and petty vanity. Slander and similar weeds grow luxuriantly in such a soil.

These statements should not be interpreted to mean that the Scandinavians here are on a lower cultural level than the rest of the population. It is my opinion that our countrymen in Stoughton, as elsewhere, can well bear comparison with their fellow citizens. As far as I know, even among the Yankees—who undeniably are the cultural leaders in most regions—there are comparatively few individuals here in Stoughton who through intelligence or education rise above the mass of the people. The poise that characterizes native-born citizens lends the Yankees a certain air of assurance in manners and outer appearance which, especially to a newcomer, gives an impression of intellectual and cultural superiority. But much of this often disappears when one penetrates beneath the superficial shell; and it will usually be found that the Norwegian, despite his often awkward manners, is in reality not inferior to his Yankee neighbor in intellectual maturity and depth of understanding. Insight gained through experience and adversity may frequently develop a seriousness of mind which serves to counterbalance a lack of systematic schooling. It seems to me that these qualities are found especially among the older generation of Scandinavians in this country; and if we disregard the religious quarrels which have clouded many otherwise clear minds, we can not deny that American institutions have had a beneficial influence on the intellectual development of the Scandinavian people. This may be said in general about the immigrants from the far North, though conditions in this respect vary widely from settlement to settlement.

In certain communities it is not at all unusual to find a collection of good books in farmhouses; the young people attend the district schools regularly and many families send their sons to high schools to let them enjoy the advantages of further education. In other Norwegian settlements, however, conditions are quite different: the habit of reading is undeveloped, young people do not attend school regularly, and parents pay little attention to their children's upbringing as enlightened citizens. In general the Yankees distinguish themselves—more than other nationalities in this country—by their concern for the education of their youth. They are generous when it comes to building schools, and even people of little means try to give their children as good an education as conditions permit. Their example has a beneficial influence on the European immigrants; as a whole, the inhabitants of our eastern and western states must undoubtedly be numbered among the world's best informed people.

The Irish Catholics cling devotedly to their prejudices and at times let themselves be misled by their priests to hate American institutions in general and the school system in particular because the papal church is, in essence, antagonistic toward the civilization of our century. Gradually, as the successors of St. Peter establish their authority on this continent, this opposition will increase. Sooner or later an open break must, of necessity, come between Americanism on the one hand, with its championship of liberty, tolerance, and progress, and the Church of Rome on the other, led by a supposedly infallible pope who, as a representative of the delusions of past ages, attacks the very foundations of nineteenth-century civilization.

There has for some time been talk of establishing a Norwegian Lutheran high school in Stoughton, and various steps have been taken toward the realization of this plan. Several people in the area have worked for the project with praiseworthy zeal, and there is a great likelihood that it will be carried to completion in the near future. According to the plan, the school building will cost about $15,000; I am told that part of this sum has already been raised through subscription. This amount of money is trivial for rich districts like Koshkonong and neighboring Norwegian settlements. Collection of funds to erect the building is, therefore, a surmountable task if the necessary goodwill is present. But it is a question whether the Norwegians on Koshkonong will be willing in the long run to make the sacrifices needed to keep a good school going. Experience has shown that academies and high schools in this country find it difficult to survive without annual income from endowments or other sources.

A couple of years ago the Wisconsin legislature offered to set up a normal school in Stoughton on condition that the town and surrounding district would contribute $30,000 to help pay for the construction of the necessary buildings. It was undoubtedly a mistake not to accept this offer because Stoughton will probably never have sufficient funds to operate an educational institution comparable to any of the state normal schools. Furthermore, the state pays the faculty salaries at the normal schools and takes care of all other expenses. Hence the people in the district are free of the continual requests for contributions which usually are connected with private institutions set up without sufficient funds to defray expenses not covered by student tuition.

The building which houses Stoughton's common school has a fine location on a hill near the town limits. Two grades have been added to the curriculum to care for those pupils whose parents wish their children to have instruction beyond the elementary classes. It can not be denied, however, that the town needs a high school. This need will presumably be met, one way or another, in the near future.

The Stoughton Reporter is published weekly. The paper recently came out in a new "dress" and has a very respectable appearance. The editor, Frank Allen, a respected attorney in the district, is said to be a well-informed man who enjoys the respect and confidence of his fellow citizens.

Ole Nilsen Falk from Amble in Sogn runs a drugstore in Stoughton. He came to America as a young man together with his parents. Through industry and thrift he has worked himself up to a prosperous station in life. During the late war he served in a Wisconsin regiment and was advanced to the rank of lieutenant. Shortly after the conclusion of peace, Falk established a drugstore in Stoughton and has dedicated himself to this profession with the energy and tireless vigor of a young man. With painstaking care he seeks to supply his store with good wares. His conscientiousness combined with a considerable knowledge of the qualities and uses of medicine insures his clients against the mistakes which are said to be made frequently by druggists in this country.

Christian J. Melaas owns the other Norwegian drugstore in Stoughton. He was born on Koshkonong, where his parents still live. After completing a course at Albion Academy he taught school several years and then became Falk's partner. More recently the two have run separate businesses. Christian Melaas is a gifted young man who has the insight and knowledge to run a successful drugstore.

Veterinarian Wettle O. Wettlesen came from Upper Telemark and has been in America twenty-five years. His father, who emigrated in 1845, has practiced as a veterinarian ever since he arrived in this country and is therefore well known on Koshkonong and in surrounding areas. The son, W. O. Wettlesen, has for some time lived in Stoughton and is considered very able in his field. Through a number of successful cures he has won the confidence which is a necessary prerequisite for a good practice.

J. Froshoug is said to have taken his veterinary examination in Norway. He has practiced in Stoughton only a short time and as yet I have not heard any reliable assessment of his qualifications. Recently Froshoug has taken a job as clerk in a drugstore where he will have an opportunity to observe whether the methods applicable in the animal kingdom are also suitable for sick human beings.

Jacob Wettlesen was born in the parish of Kviteseid in Telemark. He emigrated in 1843 with his parents, who settled in Pleasant Spring township as one of the first Norwegian families in the area. When rumors about the rich mines in the West reached Koshkonong, Jacob Wettlesen joined a group who decided to try their luck in those as yet little-known territories. After having roamed through Kansas, Utah, Idaho, and Dakota, he settled as a farmer in the Montana wilderness, engaging primarily in cattle-raising. The rush of people to the mines was great and the price of food soon reached fabulous heights. Good opportunities for moneymaking thus offered themselves and after a few years he could afford to leave a region where warlike redskins and equally dangerous whites often placed his life and property in danger. Since 1866 Wettlesen has been engaged as a grain dealer in Stoughton and is considered an able and reliable businessman.

Hans Pedersen from Tønsberg has since 1860 been established as a merchant in Stoughton. In proportion to the size of the town he has a considerable business. Recently he has also gone into the grain trade.

In the next issue of *Billed-Magazin* I intend to continue these sketches from old Koshkonong and Stoughton. Many settlers beyond the Mississippi formerly lived in this area and still have relatives and friends here. Koshkonong is the mother colony of many later settlements; and as people usually like to hear about conditions in a former home community, we dare assume that the current reports about the town and its businessmen will be of interest to many of our readers.

I will close this description of Stoughton by mentioning a few more of our countrymen who carry on business in this most Norwegian of all Norwegian-American towns in the Northwest.* As already mentioned, many of Stoughton's prominent businessmen are of our nationality; and it is demonstrated here as elsewhere that immigrants from the far North can hold their own in America not only as farmers but also as merchants and artisans, and in various other positions in society.

Besides the merchants discussed above I will mention Lars Tollefsen Dømbæ from Voss. He emigrated in 1844 and spent some time in the Norwegian settlement called Queen Anne, in Illinois, before moving to Koshkonong. He has now for some five years managed a store in Stoughton in partnership with Anders Nilsen Himle from Voss, who came to America about twenty years ago and settled on Koshkonong. The firm goes by the name of Lawson and Nelson and as both of the proprietors know many of the farmers in the surrounding area they can naturally count on a large clientele and a corresponding volume of business.

Ole Petersen, a baker by profession, traveled through Sweden, Denmark, Germany, and possibly other European countries as a journeyman during his

**Billed-Magazin*, July 2, 1870.

younger years. Then he settled in Christiania and for sixteen years was a baker in the Norwegian capital. Leaving his homeland, he first lived in Boston a while but then moved to Janesville and finally came to Stoughton thirteen years ago. Here he operates a bakery and carries on trade in foodstuffs. In 1866 Ole Petersen returned to Norway to see old friends and also visited his two sons in Denmark. He is the only baker in Stoughton and is well acquainted with many of the farmers in the district. Petersen therefore has many customers and a considerable business.

John Ingebrigtsen from the farm Hagenæs in Luster, in Sogn, came to America thirteen years ago. Here he usually goes by the name of John Brickson. Even though he has regarded Stoughton as his real home ever since he came to this country, he has from time to time also lived in other places both within and outside the state of Wisconsin. Of late he has for several years managed a grocery store in Stoughton.

We have already noted that the gardener Nils Jensen was the first Norwegian to settle in Stoughton. He was born on the manor of Thomb near Moss and was for a while an employee of Count Wedel on his Bogstad estate near Christiania. Rumors about America's wonders induced Jensen to leave his native land; and as his future home he chose Stoughton, which already gave promise of becoming a lively commercial center. But as a gardener he got very little business in his new hometown. People there had to think first of securing the basic necessities of life; they had to ignore everything which was superfluous or catered to a more refined mode of life. Jensen realized this and soon gave up his gardening for trade in ready-made clothes. He continued this business until his death in 1867. He had then resided in Stoughton twenty years.

Gardener Jensen's son, shoemaker Nils Jensen, operates his own shop in Stoughton besides trading in ready-made shoes, boots, and related wares. Firmness, reliability, and integrity are the virtues which the people of the community usually associate with this man.

Brynild Larsen Liland came to America from Voss twenty-one years ago. In 1867 he opened an iron foundry and blacksmith shop which generally employs twelve laborers. Mr. Liland's wagons, plows, and other agricultural implements find a profitable market not only in Wisconsin but to some extent also in Iowa and Minnesota.

T. G. Mandt and M. Getz have a wagon factory which employs ten to twelve laborers. Their wagons and other products are praised for their sturdiness and the factory is in good repute among the people of the surrounding area.

C. Larsen from the farm Haug in Bærum parish owns a plow factory which is said to be making good progress. His plows are held to be especially serviceable and the increasing sales augur well for the future.

S. H. Severson owns a lumberyard in Stoughton and is said to be doing a good business. He is a son of the late Helge Sivertsen Grimsrud from Tinn, the first Norwegian to buy land in the township of Dunkirk. When he was barely twenty years old, Severson went to Colorado, and later he spent three years in Minnesota. Then he returned to Stoughton and began his lumber business.

Knud Olsen from the farm Intelhus in Hemsedal emigrated eighteen years ago, worked a while for a saddler in Janesville, then dug for gold in Montana two years, after which he came to Koshkonong. For the last four years he has operated a saddle-making shop in Stoughton. He is the only saddler in town and consequently has many customers.

Gjermund Gjermundsen Bakke (G. G. Baker), from Tinn, was employed for a time by a merchant in Kongsberg, whence he emigrated to America and lived a while on Koshkonong where he engaged in farming; at present he is the agent for an express company and has his office in A. A. Flint's store in Stoughton.

Wilhelm A. Ferman, son of the former merchant P. C. Ferman in Trondheim, has lived about five years in Stoughton where he owns a photographic studio. The really beautiful and very expert pictures he produces can well bear comparison with the best photographic work in this country.

Among the buildings which are especially distinguished because of their tasteful architecture the Williams Block must be mentioned; its beautiful equipment and grandeur of construction remind one of cities like Milwaukee and Chicago. It is too bad that this structure so entirely overshadows the nearby buildings, which by comparison with this Goliath are given a peculiarly dwarfish appearance. The Highbee House hotel is likewise a respectable building for a small town. The commercial building set up by our countryman Jens Cold from Vardal is characterized by solid construction and up-to-date equipment. Cold came to America sixteen years ago, settled first in Janesville, then established a saddlery shop in Stoughton, where he did business for eleven years. Then he moved to Conover, Iowa, but after a stay of two years there he returned and a second time chose Stoughton as his home. He is a highly respected and enterprising man who is said to have acquired a considerable fortune while in this country.

Near the business section are found neat dwellings surrounded by beautiful gardens. And the inclination—especially characteristic of the Yankees—to furnish the home with those conveniences which create comfort and contentment is also evident here in numerous ways. Most of the houses are built of wood; but more solid materials will no doubt come into common use in the future because good bricks can now be bought at reasonable prices. Our countryman, Halvor Stenersen Jonsaas, has a brickworks scarcely a mile from the town limits and his products are said to be of excellent quality.

The Methodists, the Congregationalists, and the Presbyterians all have their own pastors in Stoughton. The other denominations—Catholics, Unitarians, and Baptists—are served at certain times by pastors from other congregations. Pastor Müller Eggen, who serves the Norwegian Augustana church here, formerly lived in Stoughton but now lives in Racine. As a rule he visits the Stoughton congregation every third or fourth week, as well as another church out in the country.

In local elections the two political parties do not present separate tickets, but from a joint ticket choose "the best man" irrespective of political affiliation. In recent years the Republicans have held a numerical superiority. At the last presidential election Stoughton gave Grant a majority of ninety-four votes.

The total wealth of the population, counting both real and personal property, is assessed by the tax commission at $350,000. If equally divided among the 1,400 inhabitants, we get a sum of $250 per individual; this number is used statistically to indicate the economic condition of the community. To serve as a realistic index of the people's financial status this sum should probably be increased by at least one-third. The tax rate last year was not quite one percent of the estimated property valuation.

What will Stoughton become in the future? There has been talk of thousands of inhabitants, magnificent factories, and commercial activity which would put the town in a class with its many rivals for greatness and power in this state. Progress is, of course, primarily dependent on the industry and initiative of the population. Stoughton actually enjoys many advantages which are important for growth and commercial development. There was talk about establishing a woolen mill; but this plan was abandoned because of lack of interest. An important question for the future of Stoughton is whether the inhabitants, on similar occasions, will be able to cooperate sufficiently to finance projects which exceed individual capabilities.

Dunn, Blooming Grove, Sumner, and Cottage Grove Townships

DUNN TOWNSHIP lies to the west of Pleasant Spring.*. The so-called Second Lake cuts into the northwestern part of the township, while First Lake forms a large bay which covers some of the area along the eastern border. Mud Lake fills a depression in the center of the township and Hook Lake is located toward its southwestern corner. Part of the terrain consists of a prairie of considerable size, while small marshy areas are scattered here and there among the woodlands.

About fifty Norwegian families live in Dunn township. Ingebrikt Johnson Helle from Kragerø talked to me about the arrival of the Norwegians and the founding of the settlement:

"I left Norway in April, 1845, crossing the ocean on a ship from Porsgrunn. There were, all told, 140 emigrants aboard. Many of us had received letters from friends who had left earlier, and since they praised America we also decided to look for homesteads beyond the big waters. As far as I could gather, it was these encouragements from America which had persuaded most of the emigrants to bid old Norway farewell. The trip across the ocean was full of dangers. The fierce gales which we encountered on the Atlantic threatened us with death and destruction. The boat was loaded with iron, and during one fearful storm the cargo got displaced, which nearly caused the ship to capsize. Even our experienced captain gave up hope of rescue. The terror and the cries of distress among the passengers were indescribable. After being tossed about on the ocean some fourteen weeks we finally reached New York harbor in a miserable condition. Then our immigrant group began the trip inland.

"Because of a lack of money I had to remain in Buffalo, where I got work

**Billed-Magazin*, July 9, 1870.

with a Quaker family. If genuine altruism and true charity are found anywhere in the world it is among these kind people. They treated me like a son, and never shall I forget their goodness toward me and my family. After a stay of four years in Buffalo I left for my intended destination in Wisconsin, and stopped first in Dunn township west of the Norwegian settlement on Koshkonong. My wife had two brothers, Nils and Lars Ellefsen Mastre, who had homesteads there near the center of the township. I looked them up and they sold me some of their land. This happened in the spring of 1849, and my wife's two brothers had already lived here more than five years when I arrived. They were the first Norwegian settlers in Dunn township. When they came, the only white people in the area were two or three Yankee families. Indians, however, were quite numerous: their young men roamed the woods searching for game while the old and weak caught fish in the lakes. Both Nils and Lars Mastre moved away several years ago; one now lives in Minnesota and the other in Iowa.

"The terrain consists largely of woods interspersed with swampy areas. Clearing the land was consequently a tough job for the early settlers; but the soil is fertile, and even now we can count on an average yield of twenty bushels per acre. We have good pasturage and easy access to water, so the township is well suited for cattle-raising. I have lived on this place ever since my arrival; no particular misfortune has struck either me or my family, and God has clearly blessed the labors of my hands in this country."

Thus far the man's own story. Ingebrikt Johnson is well-off; yes, he can even be called rich. His farm, with its well-kept buildings and well-cultivated fields, testifies that here lives a good farmer and an able tiller of the soil.

I will mention still another of the township's early Norwegian settlers, Ole Knudsen Dyrland from Seljord in Telemark, who left Norway in April, 1843. He told me the following about this migration and the accompanying circumstances: "Ole Knudsen Trovatten from Lårdal sent many letters from America to his friends in Norway. He praised the country and championed emigration. Throughout all Upper Telemark at this time we heard much about America and Ole Knudsen's letters. Many had their doubts; but then Knud Svalestuen from Vinje returned to Norway for a visit. He had lived in the Norwegian settlement at Muskego and his reports strengthened the faith of even the most dubious. Knud came back in the fall of 1843, and during the winter he was visited by representatives from various districts in Telemark seeking reliable information about the new land. The following spring great numbers of people from the upper mountain regions streamed toward the sea to secure passage across the ocean. Many families as well as single men and women left Seljord also. Three emigrant vessels sailed from Porsgrunn that spring. There were 211 emigrants aboard the ship I took. We went from Porsgrunn to Le Havre in

France. From there we secured passage on an American ship. After a successful voyage we landed in New York and immediately set out for the West. The whole group stayed together until we reached Milwaukee, but there we broke up and everyone went his own way. My wife and I first went to Muskego.

"There was much talk of Koshkonong at the time; many of the settlers had been west to have a look at the land, and they came back with good reports. After staying two weeks in Muskego I too decided to choose Koshkonong as my future home. That fall many of the older settlers left Muskego to seek new homesteads. I met Ole Trovatten and in accordance with his advice I bought land near the West Koshkonong church in Pleasant Spring township. Ole was guide and counsel for many of the newcomers in those days. I lived for six years on Koshkonong. Nils Mastre and his brother owned much land in the neighboring township of Dunn; and when Nils offered to sell me part of it, I moved to my present place. At that time the two Mastre brothers, Ingebrikt Johnson Helle, and some Yankee families lived in Dunn township. Ingebrikt Johnson had arrived in the spring of 1849, while I came to Dunn in the fall of that year. Besides me there were thus three Norwegian settlers living here. The next year Hans Gudbrandsen Mørkvolden from Numedal arrived; and still a year later the population increased considerably because of immigration."

People of Norwegian origin are most numerous in the township: next come the Irish, then the Yankees, and finally the Germans, who by comparison form a minority.

All the older Norwegian farmers here are well-off, some even rich. Knud Halvorsen Dale from Nissedal is held to be the richest farmer in the township, and next to him are mentioned Tollef Olsen Fossum and Ingebrikt Johnson Helle.

In the tax lists the average value of land in Dunn township is estimated at $18.37 per acre as compared with $19.50 in Pleasant Spring and $24.50 in Dunkirk. The reason for this lower estimate can presumably be found in the fact that a lower valuation is put on swampy land, which is rather extensive within the township.

The soil is fertile and the average yield of wheat per acre is higher than on Koshkonong; but the woodland, which constitutes the larger part of the tillable area, is difficult to clear; and putting it under the plow is very expensive for those who wish to enlarge their fields.* The township would seem to be especially well suited for cattle-raising because the grass grows luxuriantly and an abundance of good drinking water seems to be found on practically every farm. Sale of firewood is a fairly important source of income for the farmers. Some Norwegians have sold out and moved farther west, beyond the Mississippi.

**Billed-Magazin*, July 23, 1870.

The economic condition of the people seems to be about the same as in Pleasant Spring. Judging from the tax lists, one would assume that the value of land owned by Norwegians in the latter area is somewhat greater than in Dunn township. The nearest wheat market is found in McFarland, a station located within the township between Stoughton and Madison on the Milwaukee and Prairie du Chien Railway.

There are about fifty Norwegian farmers in the area, as well as twenty or so families living in McFarland. Thus there must be a total of about 400 Norwegians in the township. Practically all of them belong to the Norwegian Evangelical Lutheran Church (Wisconsin Synod). The congregation recently started building a church in McFarland. When completed, it will serve as an annex to the Koshkonong congregation.

In the past the district school was rather poorly attended by the Norwegian children; it is said that there are among the Norwegians some young people, past sixteen years of age, who are unable to read English even though they have grown up in this country. For seven or eight weeks every year parochial school is conducted to teach children the principles of Christianity. The level of education is probably lower in Dunn township than in many of the other Norwegian settlements. But there are said to be some happy indications of an awakening interest in the education of the younger generation.

All our countrymen in this township, with three or four exceptions, are Democrats. There is scarcely any other sizeable Norwegian settlement where the sentiment is as undividedly Democratic as in Dunn township.

Blooming Grove township

If one travels west from McFarland about four miles he will come to a little Norwegian community which is known locally as the Valdres settlement. The community is entirely surrounded by people of other nationalities and can therefore be looked upon as a Norwegian island whose shores are washed by non-Scandinavian elements. The following report will give a fairly clear account of the founding, development, and general condition of the settlement.

Nils Hansen Fjeld from southern Aurdal in Valdres was a farmer in Norway and was counted a wealthy man in his home community. But his family gradually increased and a series of poor harvests dimmed his prospects for the future. Despite work and worry, conditions grew worse rather than better. Thoughts of his children's future caused the father much anxiety. However, rumors about the fertile soil and cheap land in America also reached Aurdal; and there was much discussion of drawbacks and advantages of the New World as compared with Norway. Opinions were divided; some people viewed everything beyond the ocean through rose-colored glasses, while others crossed themselves in dismay on hearing that anyone might dare venture to a country swarming with poisonous snakes, voracious animals, and still more murderous men. No one had previously emigrated from Aurdal except a few bachelors, and nothing had been heard of their fate in the new land. The America fever soon spread to neighboring districts, but people's ideas about America rested primarily on loose hearsay, and conjecture took the place of judgment founded on reliable data. Finally a copy or two of Reiersen's book about Texas came to the community. "Now we have the printed word to go by," people declared, and many doubters were soon converted to the orthodox faith in the promised land beyond the waves. This book sent home from America encouraged countless individuals to leave community and homeland in order to partake of the much-lauded blessings of the New World.

Among them was Nils Hansen Fjeld. He sold his farm and other possessions in Aurdal and had somewhat more than 1,000 *speciedaler* in his pocket when he stood ready to set off for the distant land. To the best of my knowledge, he was the first family man from his parish to leave for America. As we might expect, his leaving gave rise to much talk; people felt that a man as prosperous as Nils Hansen should not tempt fate, since he could face old age with confidence if he would only remain in his native land.

In April, 1847, he came with his wife and seven sons to Christiania, where a ship loaded with iron lay ready to leave directly for New York. About 100 emigrants, mostly from Numedal, Toten, and Modum, were assembled there. But the ship was small, and a cargo disproportionately large in comparison to the size of the ship had ominously reduced the distance between deck and water. The passengers were packed like herring between the half-rotten walls of the ship which were to protect them from a watery grave. Everything went surprisingly well, however, during the first days; but when they reached the English Channel a storm arose so fierce that even the hardy crew were frightened. The passage there is very dangerous and the ship, failing to respond to steering, was tossed about by the storm-lashed waves. The cargo of iron broke loose from its moorings and beat violently against the planks of the miserable old vessel. Terror and despair were written on the faces of the sailors; and those passengers whom seasickness had not deprived of all sense and feeling reconciled themselves to the thought that the end of their days had come.

Finally the storm abated somewhat and the hope of rescue brightened every countenance. When the waves calmed sufficiently to enable the mate to direct the course of the ship, the captain ordered a return to Norway, as he preferred to repair damages in a Norwegian rather than an English port. "We anchored,'' said one of the passengers, ''in the harbor of Tananger near Stavanger, and after a few days again set our course westward across the Atlantic. The ship was slow and the trip was a long one. We had scarcely come halfway when the water gave out. Fortunately we met an American ship which gave us some water. We continued our westward course a couple of weeks, but then a large number of passengers ran short of food. Those who were best provisioned had to help their needy fellow passengers as long as their supplies permitted any sharing. Even the captain and the ship's crew were glad to receive the crumbs which came their way. In a most miserable condition, after a voyage of fourteen weeks, we finally reached the American continent and entered a port where we took on supplies. From there we got to New York without any mishap, and at once began our trip inland. The whole group stayed together until we reached Milwaukee, but there we were scattered like chaff before the winds. Some of the immigrants chose Koshkonong while many went to Rock Prairie or various other Norwegian settlements which had already been established.''

Nils Hansen Fjeld, with his family, went by way of Muskego to Koshkonong where he spent the first winter with a countryman of his in Albion township. After having inspected various parts of Dane county, he decided the following spring to buy land near Third Lake in Blooming Grove township. This became his permanent home, and as his sons reached maturity they also bought land in the neighborhood. Three of his sons still live in Blooming Grove, two have moved to Iowa, and two have died. Many Norwegians who once lived here have sold out and gone farther west. At present there are only eleven Norwegian farmers in the settlement, besides twelve landless families. There have been many of the latter here who worked for others until they earned enough money to move west and settle on homestead land. As these left, however, others took their places who in their turn, after a brief stay, sought new homes beyond the Mississippi.

Among other inhabitants of the township I will mention our countryman Andreas Nilsen Fjeld.* He is the third oldest son of Nils Hansen, the first Norwegian farmer in the Valdres settlement. Andreas Nilsen is a prudent, thoughtful man who through hard work and strict economy has acquired a considerable fortune. He owns, free of debt, 210 acres of land complete with buildings, implements, and livestock. Furthermore, he is said to have a fair amount of money invested at interest.

To the best of my knowledge all the Norwegians in Blooming Grove belong to the Evangelical Lutheran Wisconsin Synod. Some attend the Norwegian church in Madison, others have joined the congregation in Dunn township

**Billed-Magazin*, July 30, 1870.

which has built a new church in McFarland, while still others prefer to attend the West Koshkonong church.

The bulk of the population in Blooming Grove consists of Americans, Germans, and Irishmen. In general the Germans and Scandinavians who have come here from Europe seem to have acquired economic independence more easily than the Yankees from the eastern states. The hard work and thrift of the former lead to progress; unless some misfortune strikes them, their hopes for wealth and independence are realized. The latter, on the contrary, make many demands on life: the wife wants to live in style, while the husband's ideas of a decent existence often lead to expenses which do not correspond to their income. "They are anxious to fly before they have sprouted wings," a local Norwegian said recently, "and unless they have considerable capital to start with, they often fail at farming and suffer complete economic collapse."

The land in Blooming Grove is valued at an average of $20.37 per acre. The soil, on the whole, seems to be of rather mediocre quality and only certain areas can bear comparison with the better agricultural districts such as Albion or Christiana on Koshkonong. Large stretches are as yet not cultivated and they will likely continue to lie unused as long as there is a surplus of land farther west which will more generously reward people for their labor. The terrain is rather uneven and hilly and most of the area was originally covered by dense forest.

Blooming Grove is one of the most solid Democratic townships in Dane county. In the last presidential election the Norwegians—with possibly a couple of exceptions—cast a unanimous vote for the Democratic aspirant to the highest office in the land.

Sumner township

As already noted, the four townships which usually go by the name of Koshkonong form a rectangle constituting the southeastern corner of Dane county.* However, the settlement also extends into Sumner and Oakland townships in Jefferson county. The following paragraphs will give a brief account of the arrival of our countrymen in the first of these two townships.[33]

Thore Knudsen Nore from a farm and parish called Nore in Numedal emigrated with his family in 1842. He was then forty years old—a strong and industrious worker. After a short stay in Muskego, Thore Knudsen continued his trip westward and in the fall of 1842 arrived in the area later known as Sumner township, which at the time had no white settlers except for one Yankee family. Here he claimed land and began clearing it. The rude log cabin he built for himself and his family is still standing. Here also wealth proved to be a

*_Billed-Magazin_, August 27, 1870.

result of diligence: in a few years Thore Knudsen became a man of means, leading an independent life. He passed away last summer (1868) at the age of seventy-six.

Peder Larsen Svartskuren from Kongsberg was the second of our countrymen to choose Sumner township as a home for himself and his future family. He received aid to defray travel expenses from his friend Even Heg, who was then living in Norway township. In 1843, by way of Muskego, he came to the home of Thore Knudsen Nore, whose daughter he later married. He bought a piece of land in the neighborhood and began the process of homesteading. During the time he could spare from his farm work he followed his trade as a shoemaker.

"As far as I know," relates Peder Larsen, "I was the first person to leave Kongsberg for America. To be sure, I have heard that the previous year a laborer named Thomas Braaten emigrated, but I have no further knowledge of his departure nor of any circumstances connected with it. When I came here the whole township was covered with heavy forest, except for scattered small openings. There was an abundance of game in the woods, such as deer and prairie chickens, and the lake as well as the creek were full of fish. Indians roamed about in large bands. They did no one any harm, however, but were kind and willing to help. West of us, in the neighboring townships of Albion and Christiana, there were at the time only a few Norwegians, namely Bjørn Andersen from Vikedal, Amund Hornefjeld from Mosterøy, Gunnul Vindæg from Numedal, and Thorsten Olsen from Hå near Stavanger. Thorsten had come with the much-talked-of Stavanger sloop which brought the first group of emigrants from Norway to the New World.

"The year after my arrival in America I became sick and had to stay in bed five months. Fortunately I had by then saved some money which supplied me with the chief necessities of life. Help from others could not be expected because everyone had enough problems of his own. The goodwill might be there, but the means were lacking. I regained my health, however, and with time my prospects improved.

"Gradually more of our countrymen moved in from various parts of the country and at present there are twelve Norwegian as well as seven Swedish families in the township. The rest are Americans, Germans, and Englishmen. Among the Norwegians, six families belong to the Evangelical Lutheran Church, four are Methodists, and two have not joined any denomination. The local members of the Evangelical Lutheran Church belong to the East Koshkonong parish. During the winter of 1845 we united with that congregation to build a log house which was dedicated as a church the following spring. The building was small and plain; but the need for an assembly place was satisfied for the time being. It was our intention to construct a larger and better-furnished building as soon as the size and prosperity of the congregation would permit. This happened in 1858, when a spacious, cheerful, and pleasant limestone building was erected. But even this one is becoming too small for the needs of the congregation because the population has increased through both inner growth and additions from the outside. Our church has a steeple but no bell. A subscription is now under way for the purchase of an organ.

"Economic conditions among the Norwegians in the township are especially good. Some of the farmers can even be called rich; not only do they own free of debt extensive land holdings with necessary equipment but they also have considerable sums of money out at interest. During elections somewhat more than one hundred votes are cast. All the Norwegians, with two exceptions, are Republicans. Nothing deserving of special mention has happened since 1842 when the settling began. Conditions have developed quietly without any disturbing influences to hinder or delay progress. The population has grown steadily and wealth has accumulated gradually as the area under cultivation has increased and better means of communication have encouraged people's initiative by opening markets for the farmers' produce.

"Probably we should mention that the township was ravaged seventeen years ago by a band of thieves or robbers who openly perpetrated many deeds of violence before the authorities managed to stop them. They plundered houses as well as fields and no precautions could prevent their robberies. It was claimed that the band consisted of some Mormons chased out of Illinois; whether or not this was true I am unable to say. At least they accepted the Mormon teaching about polygamy and behaved like sworn enemies of the human race. The mills of justice ground slowly in those days and the law enforcers could do but little against such a large, organized group of desperadoes. Only after two years were the culprits caught and imprisoned to await trial. But the insufficiency both of jail facilities and of guards gave such experienced criminals an excellent chance to escape. As a result, when the day of trial arrived only two of the sixteen culprits remained in captivity. The rest had escaped. We were, however, free of them, and that was our main concern.

"You want to hear my opinion about America as a home for Norwegian immigrants. My answer must be that this is a good country, and here in the northwestern states it is much easier for a poor but industrious laborer to gain independence than in Norway. The institutions and laws are in many respects admirable but bribery and official corruption undermine much of our public life which could and should be better. As neighbors the Americans are helpful and easy to get along with, and in our neighborhood people of different nationalities have always lived well together."

Thus far Larsen's own report. I will merely add that Peder Larsen Svartskuren is considered a well-informed man who enjoys the confidence and respect of his fellow citizens. He has frequently been entrusted with local official positions and has several times represented his congregation (East Koshkonong) at synodal meetings. On the whole Peder Larsen has been favored by fortune in this country.

Cottage Grove township

This township is located north of Pleasant Spring, between Blooming Grove and Deerfield townships in Dane county.* The first Norwegian settlement on Koshkonong was in the northern part of Albion township. But shortly after our countrymen had arrived in this area they began spreading over the adjoining regions, especially northward and westward. When people's attention was attracted toward Koshkonong, after the founding of the less successful settlements in Illinois and Muskego, immigration soon increased considerably and many newcomers—in order to get more elbow room—staked out claims some distance away from the homesteads of their countrymen who had arrived earlier. Two years had scarcely elapsed since the first Norwegian set foot in the county before people of our nationality were found in the townships of Albion, Christiana, Pleasant Spring, Dunkirk, Deerfield, and Cottage Grove. These areas, together with several bordering communities, are looked upon as one settlement, which in extent and population is presumably still the largest Norwegian colony in the country.

Now the days of immigration to this region are long since past. If any newcomers do arrive to visit relatives or friends, their stay is usually brief. As soon as circumstances permit, they cross the Mississippi to find homesteads where land is cheaper and wages generally higher. Even older farmers may sell out here in order to buy land farther west. They feel that things are becoming too cramped on Koshkonong and that there is no reasonable relationship between land prices and the income from agriculture. Many of them therefore pull out and settle in distant parts where a short while ago the red men held undisputed sway. But now they are able to meet the difficulties of pioneer life in quite a different manner than in former days. For a second or possibly even a third time they start anew the clearing of virgin soil. They do not go into the wilds as poor newcomers, however, but arrive at their new homesteads armed with experience and some financial resources. Therefore the burdens are comparatively light and success is relatively assured. The present pioneers work under quite different circumstances than the immigrants during the 1840s. They are not forced to experience those trials and renunciations which were so characteristic of our early immigrant history. Though this is generally

Billed-Magazin, September 3, 1870.

true of the experienced and prosperous settlers who move west, it must be remembered that inexperienced and impecunious newcomers who stake out claims still labor under considerable difficulties.

Even though at present emigration and immigration in these regions about balance, the population is steadily increasing as a result of strong inner growth. "The Scandinavians in this country distinguish themselves by great fertility," say the Yankees, and a comparison between the birth rates in Norwegian and American families undeniably serves to corroborate this statement. But the Germans and certainly the Irish do not take a back seat to anyone in this respect. Consequently, Americans of the older generation admit that "the future belongs to the European immigrants of the present century." Already the Yankees of unmixed race constitute a decided minority in many areas.

As I tell in the paragraphs below about our countrymen in Cottage Grove, the reader should bear in mind that the present sketch is based on notes taken during a trip through the settlement in the summer of 1868. Any mention of recent conditions therefore applies to that year. This circumstance is of little or no importance, however, since the author's purpose here, as previously, has been to give an account of the early immigrants' life in Norway, their experiences while on the ocean, and their joys and sorrows in the new land, while discussions of present-day conditions have been regarded as mere side issues.

Our countrymen who first settled on Koshkonong belonged to the industrious and thrifty people still found in Norway's mountain valleys. Accustomed to privation and physical exertion in their native land, they were peculiarly suited to tackle the frontier and clear the way for later groups of immigrants. When these fathers of emigration tell about happenings of past days and their own experiences in this country we must admire the courage which defied all dangers and the endurance which has transformed a wilderness into flourishing fields. The difference between past and present is so great that only through a bold flight of fancy can we possibly visualize the change which has taken place. And when we consider that all this has transpired within three decades we can well understand why America has been called "the land of wonders."

The first Norwegians to settle in Cottage Grove township were Ole Knudsen Trovatten from Ødefjeld and Johan Bager from Christiania. Ole Trovatten came to Cottage Grove in the spring of 1843, but previously he had lived in Christiana and in Pleasant Spring township. Before emigrating he had served as sexton at Lårdal in Telemark and is referred to as a man equipped by nature with unusual gifts. Even though he generally led an irregular life and was especially addicted to drink, he was highly esteemed in his home community and was regarded by the people as a wise man who could dumbfound both pastor and judge when he so desired. He was eloquent, witty, and entertaining, kind, helpful, and resourceful. His matchless singing voice was famed far and wide, and the people of Telemark went long distances to consult with him concerning knotty questions. Eventually he was accused of counterfeiting money and the resulting complications and unpleasantness led to his departure. He settled on Koshkonong and sent his numerous friends back home many letters in which he eloquently made them acquainted with the glories of America. No one can doubt that Trovatten, to a large degree, caused the rapid upswing in emigration from the Telemark area. In this country he followed his old profession and served as sexton at the Liberty and East Koshkonong churches. He was ever ready to give newcomers a helping hand, and many of the early settlers speak with gratitude about his friendly services. But alcoholism gradually got the better of him, and the once highly active and richly endowed man became a useless member of society. Finally his vigorous constitution succumbed to the power of the "whiskey devil." Enfeebled in body and spirit he went to his grave.

The next Norwegian to settle in the township was Johan Bager, from Grue, who called himself John Olsen Hougen in this country. He had learned the art of baking in Christiania. He came to Cottage Grove during the summer of 1842, and later moved to Coon Prairie. I am not acquainted with the circumstances surrounding his departure from Norway, nor have I any information concerning his fate in this country. Bjørn Tovsen Vasberg settled in Cottage Grove at about the same time as John Hougen. He is said to have been endowed with rich natural gifts and as a youth raised high hopes for a brilliant future. In Norway he was a respected man until alcoholism overpowered him to the extent that, deprived of his good name and reputation, he found it advisable to leave for America. But he could not get rid of his evil inclinations here either and those gifts which could have become a blessing to society were used by him to defraud his fellowmen. After having committed several swindles in this township he moved to Minnesota where he also gained a bad reputation for dishonesty and fraudulent activity. At last they found him one cold winter morning lying dead on a highway. By the side of the corpse was an empty whiskey bottle which bore testimony to the cause of his miserable death. Such was the ending of a life which had brought shame and vexation to so many of his countrymen. For a while a rumor circulated that after his arrival in America Bjørn Vasberg, in association with two other vagabonds, forged Norwegian paper money. It was said that when a large number of bills had been prepared his two fellow culprits went to Norway to put the counterfeited notes into circulation; but the forgery was soon exposed and the two men concerned were arrested and condemned to imprisonment, one for nine and the other for five years.

In addition to what has already been told about Cottage Grove I wish to add the narratives of two men which give valuable information about conditions in the state two or three decades ago and also about the causes which induced the first emigrants from Telemark to leave their native land.*

Knud Svalestuen from Vinje left in 1839. He sent letters from America to his home community praising the fertility of the soil. Land which gave a rich yield could then be had at a low price. His letters stimulated much conversation and dispelled in part the misguided beliefs in such illusions as sea monsters and man-eating Indians. The last shreds of superstitious fear vanished when Knud finally returned home to give his friends verbal accounts of conditions on this side of the ocean. Undoubtedly there were, even after that time, certain individuals who vehemently defended the claim that America was a land of misfortune which brought death and destruction to immigrants. But these birds of ill omen could only in slight degree cool the emigration fever which from then on rapidly spread over Vinje and neighboring communities. Because of their obvious exaggerations they lost the confidence of the populace; only simple and credulous souls paid any attention to their warnings.

Among the leaders of emigration from Vinje we should mention Alexander Olsen Norman and Halvor Kostvedt, as well as Asmund Lunde and Ole Aanundsen Hodtvedt. Alexander Norman was a graduate of a teacher-training school and had served as a teacher in his home community. His annual salary was only twelve *speciedaler;* and even though he had a great desire to work for the education of the young, he felt that concern for the future demanded that he should enter some other, more rewarding profession. He therefore resigned from his teaching job. The local pastor, however, had a different opinion and was highly offended by his resignation. He even threatened to have the military authorities immediately draft Norman for service if he was unwilling to resume his teaching position. This threat made a very unfavorable impression on the young man who had looked with veneration on the teaching profession. The only reason he gave up his school position was that he feared he would have to become an intinerant beggar if he should, some time in the future, have a family to support. On the other hand, he had little desire to enter military service. In those days soldiers were driven back and forth on the parade grounds with blows and kicks as if they were cattle. Not infrequently it happened that out of sheer cockiness officers would attack privates merely to prove that they had the right to give orders and could demand absolute obedience. It was under these circumstances that Norman began thinking of emigrating; and in the spring of 1842 he left his homeland together with Halvor Kostvedt from Vinje. For a while he stayed in Christiana

**Billed-Magazin*, September 10, 1870.

township on Koshkonong, but later moved to Minnesota. With the same group came Asmund Lunde, a man richly endowed with natural gifts, who before emigrating had served as a sheriff's assistant in Vinje. He spent some time in Cottage Grove, whence he also went to Minnesota. Ole Aanundsen Hodtvedt, who likewise left in 1842, farmed a while on Jefferson Prairie, but now lives west of the Mississippi.

Alexander Norman, or Alexander Olsen Bækhus, as he was commonly known in his native community, first settled on Liberty Prairie and later lived in Pleasant Spring township. He left Wisconsin this year and is at present living in Minnesota. One of his sons has studied theology in St. Louis and is now a pastor. During his stay in this country Norman has acquired such a wealth of knowledge that he must surely be among the best-informed Scandinavians in the United States. He has been entrusted with various official positions, and was nominated by the Democrats for a county office a couple of years ago.

Aslak Olsen Bækhus (Gjerdjord) and Halvor Olsen, brothers of the above-mentioned Alexander Norman, emigrated in 1843, the year following their brother's departure. "There were hard times and much unemployment in Vinje," as Aslak told me. "In the best of circumstances a person could earn four to six shillings a day during the winter, but many people had no jobs and were willing to work for only their board.

"During the haying season in the summer a good worker was paid twenty-four shillings per day; but the windfall did not last long, and the money soon went to defray living expenses during periods of unemployment. Landed property was often heavily mortgaged and many farmers had to sell their inherited family farms. A numerous and poverty-stricken cottager class intensified the problem, and the need for public aid increased at an alarming rate. I suppose we must say that the community was overpopulated because there was not enough food and work for everybody. I was a shoemaker but I received only twelve shillings for making a pair of shoes. Despite hard work and perseverance I could earn very little beyond providing myself with food and clothing. Such were conditions, and the debt-ridden farmer as well as the unemployed working man listened attentively to stories about America. 'Cheap and fertile soil is all we wish for,' became the slogan. 'Then there will be hope for the future unless frost or other misfortunes destroy the fruits of our labors.'

"'In America I will at least be free of the ever-present fear of foreclosure' said the debt-ridden landowner; 'beyond the ocean I too can own a plot of ground which will belong to my family,' reasoned the impoverished cotter, while servants and day laborers comforted themselves with the thought that in the New World they would earn not only their daily bread but also wages for their labor. There were many who wished to leave, but it was no easy matter for some of them to obtain the necessary travel money. Those who could most readily have surmounted this difficulty were people who lived in somewhat easy circumstances and therefore chose to remain in the homeland.

"My brother Halvor and I came to Muskego in the late summer of 1843.* We worked there as day laborers, and settled in Cottage Grove in the fall of 1844. The sexton Ole Knudsen Trovatten had already lived here three years. Bjørn Tovsen Vasberg from Lårdal, Johan Bager from Solør, and Halvor Kostvedt from Vinje had arrived in 1843. There were no other Norwegians here at the time. My brother and I bought a piece of land in partnership. We had to buy food in Beloit, forty-four miles from Cottage Grove; there was nothing to be bought locally, since all our neighbors were poor newcomers who did not have anything more than we did ourselves. The Indians were friendly and helpful and aided the immigrants to the best of their abilities. I lost my only cow, and that was a tragedy for me and my family. I was also attacked by the climate fever and was bedridden for thirteen weeks. It happened more than once that there was no food in the house; what this meant can well be understood, considering the circumstances. Hunting relieved the situation somewhat because there was lots of game in the woods and abundant fish in the streams. Our condition improved steadily. The population of the township increased gradually through immigration; and in time we got good roads, a schoolhouse, a church, and all the conveniences which are the fruits of civilization.

"At present there are twenty-five Norwegian farmers in Cottage Grove. The rest of the people are Yankees, Germans, and Irish. All the Norwegians, with a couple of exceptions, belong to the Evangelical Lutheran Church. The English school is well attended by the Norwegian farm children, and every year we also have six to eight weeks of parochial school where the young people are given religious instruction. Newspapers are found in every home and good books are not uncommon among our countrymen. The economic situation is good and a few farmers can even be called rich. The moral condition is about as in the neighboring townships. About two-thirds of the Norwegians hereabouts are Democrats; the rest endorse Republican principles."

Aslak Olsen's brother, the above-mentioned Halvor Olsen Gjerdjord, is a popular man in his circle. The writer of these accounts visited him during a trip through the township about two years ago (1868). Based on some notes I then jotted down I will relate the following:

"My brother and I," said Halvor, "decided to try our luck in America and

Billed-Magazin, September 17, 1870.

secured passage over the ocean on a ship from Skien. There were about ninety people in our emigrant group—most of them from Telemark and Numedal, and a few from Lier. We landed in New York on the Fourth of July, America's famous independence day. From there we continued to Milwaukee. I got a job with a Yankee, receiving six dollars per month during harvest time. When I had saved some money, and part of what my brother had borrowed for ocean passage was repaid, we bought land in Cottage Grove and moved out there in the fall of 1844. Aslak had a wife and child to care for; but I was unmarried and therefore hired out as a day laborer whenever there was a chance to earn some money, while my brother stayed at home and worked on our land. During the winter of 1845 I went off to work in the woods but took sick and was rather weak for about a year. We first bought only eighty acres of land. This was soon increased to 160. The area contained prairie, marshes, and woodland in those days. In time our condition improved so much that we could buy still more land and since then I have lived on my own farm."

Thus far the man's own account. Apparently the Bækhus or Gjerdjord family had distinguished itself for initiative and education in the home community. One of the three brothers, Alexander, graduated from a teacher-training establishment and taught school. Aslak was skilled in gold and silver work; and the youngest, Halvor, was held to be a gifted man of whom much was expected. The mother, Anna, was the daughter of Aslak Næstestua, a respected and prominent man in Vinje. His son and Anna's brother, Asmund, was known in Norway as a mechanical genius who hardly had an equal in the whole country. King Carl Johan, who happened to see a gun made by the talented Vinje man, acknowledged his respect publicly and sent the artisan a silver cup as a sign of the royal favor. The brothers Gjerdjord have been fortunate in this country also. After the hardships of pioneer days were overcome, no special ill luck has struck the family. Aslak is a rich farmer. Halvor now lives in Marshall, and interest on the capital he has saved insures him against want of any kind. He is a veterinarian and as such has helped his countrymen and neighbors greatly. For a number of years he has represented his congregation at the synodal meetings and has always enjoyed the respect and confidence of his fellow citizens. In politics Halvor Gjerdjord is a moderate Democrat. "As far as economic opportunities are concerned," Halvor told me, "I like America very much. We can not complain of the laws—in many respects they are excellent—but respect for the laws leaves much to be desired. Over here there is also much disrespect for the Word of God."

The above-mentioned gifted mechanic from Vinje, Asmund Aslaksen Næstestua, also lives in Cottage Grove. "I emigrated," he said, "in company with my two nephews, Aslak and Halvor, in 1843 and came to Milwaukee in August of that year. Before my departure I was a farmer in Vinje.

But my property was burdened with some debt and a large pension owing my parents after I took over their land. The income from the farm was scarcely sufficient to support a family. The letters I read from my countrymen in America praised the country highly. Consequently I undertook the long journey accompanied by my wife and six children. At the same time ten families and some single people emigrated from the parish of Vinje. During the first winter I stayed in Muskego, where I worked as a blacksmith for a Yankee until both my wife and I became sick and were incapable of doing any work for seventeen weeks. In the spring of 1844 I went to Cottage Grove, where we lived in a dugout belonging to my countryman Halvor Kostvedt. The next three years I worked for others as a day laborer, but then I bought a piece of land and had a home of my own. Since then fate has been good and kind to me. I have achieved the temporal success and the prospects for the future of my children which were my aim in coming to America. Knud Teisberg from Vinje emigrated the same year as I and now lives in Christiana township. The same is true of Halvor Donstad from Kviteseid and Bjørn Olsen Hustvedt from Vinje. Both are farmers in Cottage Grove, live in easy circumstances, and are highly respected men."[34]

Footnotes

INTRODUCTION

1. For further information about Svein Nilsson see especially D. G. Ristad, "Svein Nilsson, Pioneer Norwegian-American Historian," in *Norwegian-American Studies and Records*, 9 (Northfield, Minnesota, 1936), 29–37. Pertinent material is also found in J. B. Wist, "Pressen efter borgerkrigen," in *Norsk-amerikanernes festskrift 1914* (Decorah, Iowa, 1914), 47–52, 182, 183; and Theodore C. Blegen, *Norwegian Migration to America: The American Transition* (Northfield, 1940).

2. E. Hagerup Bull, "Friele, Christian," in *Norsk biografisk leksikon*, 4 (Oslo, 1929), 271–275.

3. Wist, "Pressen efter borgerkrigen," 51. That Nilsson remained something of a political spy after coming to America is evident from a letter he wrote to Mathias Lindas in May, 1869. See Beulah Folkedahl, trans., "Norwegians Become Americans," in *Norwegian-American Studies*, 21 (1962), 124.

4. Blegen, *Norwegian Migration to America: The American Transition*, 584.

5. Wist, "Pressen efter borgerkrigen," 183. *Billed-Magazin* is now a collector's item. Only a few complete files are in existence. The archives of the Norwegian-American Historical Association at St. Olaf College have one complete and two incomplete files. Complete files are also in the archives of the Minnesota Historical Society and in the Luther College Library.

6. *Billed-Magazin*, January 23, 1869. The later articles appeared in the issues of January 23, 30, February 6, 13, March 13, 20. Johnson played a prominent part in educational, political, and business affairs. See Agnes M. Larson, *John A. Johnson: An Uncommon American* (Northfield, 1969).

7. *Billed-Magazin*, February 19, 26, March 5, 1870. These articles are translated in C. A. Clausen, ed., *The Lady with the Pen: Elise Waerenskjold in Texas* (Northfield, 1961), 76–80.

8. For information about *Skandinaven* see Wist, "Pressen efter borgerkrigen," 45–56. For political views expressed in *Skandinaven* see also Jon Wefald, *A Voice of Protest: Norwegians in American Politics, 1890–1917* (Northfield, 1971).

9. Wist, "Pressen efter borgerkrigen," 52.

10. The common school controversy among Norwegian Americans has been well discussed by numerous writers. See for instance Lawrence M. Larson, "*Skandinaven*, Professor Anderson, and the Yankee School," in *The Changing West and Other Essays* (Northfield, 1937), 116–146; and Frank C. Nelsen, "The School Controversy Among Norwegian Immigrants," in *Norwegian-American Studies*, 26 (1974), 206–219.

11. Ristad, "Svein Nilsson," 37.

BILLED-MAGAZIN

1. A translation of these introductory paragraphs also appears in Ristad, "Svein Nilsson," 30.

2. When, in accordance with the law of primogeniture, the oldest son took over the ownership of the farm he was obligated to provide his parents with a pension (*føderåd*) during their lifetime.

3. The book referred to was undoubtedly Ole Rynning's *Sandfærdig beretning om Amerika* (Christiania, 1838). The book has been translated and edited by Theodore C. Blegen under the title *Ole Rynning's True Account of America* (Northfield, 1926).

4. The *speciedaler* was the main monetary unit of the Scandinavian countries from the early sixteenth century until the mid 1870s when it was replaced by the *krone* (crown) at the rate of four *kroner* per *speciedaler*.

5. Gitle Danielsen joined the Mormon Church and left his family.

6. A paragraph is omitted here which explains the American system of dividing land areas into counties, townships, and sections.

7. Søren Bache kept a journal during his stay in Wisconsin. The journal has been translated and edited by Andreas Elviken and C. A. Clausen under the title *A Chronicle of Old Muskego* (Northfield, 1951).

8. James Denoon Reymert (1821–1896) was a very versatile man. He edited the first Norwegian-American newspaper, played a part in Wisconsin politics, became a very successful lawyer in New York and was involved in business ventures there as well as in Chile and in Arizona, where he also practiced law and published a newspaper. See Martin L. Reymert, "James Denoon Reymert and the Norwegian Press," in *Norwegian-American Studies and Records,* 12 (1941), 79–90; and Carl G. O. Hansen, "Pressen til borgerkrigens slutning," in *Norsk-amerikanernes festskrift,* 9–13.

9. Hans Nielsen Hauge (1771–1824) was a very influential lay religious leader in Norway. He and his followers were harassed by church and civil officials and frequently ridiculed by the public with such terms as "readers" or "hang-heads." Much has been written about Hauge and the Haugean movement. See, for instance, Joseph M. Shaw, *Pulpit under the Sky: A Life of Hans Nielsen Hauge* (Minneapolis, 1955).

10. Colonel Hans Heg organized and led the 15th Wisconsin Regiment, "the Scandinavian Regiment," until his death in the battle of Chickamaugua. A considerable literature has grown up about him both in English and in Norwegian. See Theodore C. Blegen, *The Civil War Letters of Colonel Hans Christian Heg* (Northfield, 1936), and Waldemar Ager, *Oberst Heg og hans gutter* (Eau Claire, Wisconsin, 1916).

11. Numerous books and articles have been written about Elling Eielsen and his followers. For a brief scholarly account see E. Clifford Nelson and Eugene Fevold, *The Lutheran Church Among Norwegian-Americans,* 1 (Minneapolis, 1960), 71–81, 126–150.

12. The Augustana Synod or, more exactly, the Scandinavian Evangelical Lutheran Augustana Synod of North America, was organized by Norwegians and Swedes in 1860. In 1870 they parted amicably and the Norwegians then joined with the Danes to form two new bodies: the Norwegian-Danish Evangelical Lutheran Augustana Synod and the Conference for the Norwegian-Danish Evangelical Lutheran Church in America, which were respectively known as the Norwegian Augustana Synod and the Conference. These various Augustana Synods aimed to steer a middle way between the low-church Eielsen movement and the high-church Norwegian Evangelical Lutheran Church in America which was organized in 1853. The latter body was usually referred to as the Norwegian Synod and was accused by its antagonists of being tainted with "Missourianism" and "Wisconsinism" as taught by German seminaries in Missouri and Wisconsin. Consequently Norwegian Americans frequently referred to it as the Missouri Synod or the Wisconsin Synod. Readers should be careful not to confuse these terms with Lutheran synods by those names founded by German Americans. The tangled debates between the various shades of Norwegian-American Lutheranism are well expounded by Nelson and Fevold in their two-volume work, *The Lutheran Church Among Norwegian-Americans.*

13. During the Age of Absolutism (1665–1814) the Dano-Norwegian kings, in accordance with the ideas of mercantilism, frequently granted monopolies to owners of foundries and sawmills to purchase timber from the Norwegian *bønder* (farmers) in the surrounding areas. Among the families which were able under this system to exploit the farmers were the Blairs, the Cappelens, and the Løvenskiolds, who became wealthy merchants as well as owners of land, foundries, and mills. Certain aspects of this system lasted until 1860. For a brief discussion see Olav Kaarstein, "Einevaldstida og dei norske skogane," in *Årbok for Telemark, 1961* (Skien, 1961).

14. Severin Løvenskiold (1777–1856) was a prominent landowner and foundry operator as well as an influential conservative politician who was appointed to prominent positions by the Swedish-Norwegian kings of the time. See Arne Bergsgaard, "Løvenskiold, Severin," in *Norsk Biografisk Leksikon*, 8 (Oslo, 1938), 600–606.

15. During the economic depression following the Napoleonic Wars Norwegian paper money declined greatly in value. A Norwegian silver *daler* or *speciedaler* was worth 120 Norwegian *skilling,* making a *skilling* worth about one American cent. Norway returned to the silver standard in 1842.

16. The fever and ague, or malaria—known among Norwegian immigrants as *agern*, *klimatfeber* (climate fever), or *sumpfeber* (swamp fever)—was regarded as a most dreaded affliction. Although the disease was seldom fatal, it left the settlers for long periods too weak to work.

17. Knud Langeland (1813–1888) came to America in 1843. He became an influential journalist among the Norwegian Americans, at various times editing *Nordlyset, Democraten, Skandinaven,* and *Amerika.* He was an ardent anti-slavery man and took an active part in Wisconsin politics. Next to Svein Nilsson he made the first attempt to

write a history of the Norwegians in America: *Nordmændene i Amerika* (Chicago, 1889). See Arlow W. Andersen, "Knud Langeland: Pioneer Editor," in *Norwegian-American Studies and Records,* 14 (1944), 23–38.

18. About Hans Barlien see D. G. Ristad, "A Doctrinaire Idealist: Hans Barlien," in *Norwegian-American Studies and Records,* 3 (1928), 13–22.

19. Søren Jaabæk (1814–1894) was a Norwegian politician who served in the *Storting,* the Norwegian legislative assembly, from 1845 to 1890. The reference is to his consistent policy of economy and, as a consequence, his notorious vote of "no" on all state appropriations for salary and pension increments to government officials.

20. For a discussion of Gjert Hovland's influence on Norwegian immigration see Theodore C. Blegen, *Norwegian Migration to America, 1825–1860* (Northfield, 1931), 65–70.

21. Mercantilistic laws and guild rules regulating trade, industry, and handicrafts in town and country were abolished by the Scandinavian governments during the middle decades of the nineteenth century. See B. J. Hovde, *The Scandinavian Countries, 1720–1865,* 1 (New York, 1948), 229–275; and T. K. Derry, *A History of Norway 1814–1972* (Oxford, 1973), 93–135.

22. An extensive and controversial literature has grown up about the character and achievements of Cleng Peerson. For bibliographical references and a scholarly appraisal see Blegen, *Norwegian Migration to America, 1825–1860*, 24–56, and Kenneth O. Bjork, "Introduction," in Alfred Hauge, *Cleng Peerson,* 1 (Boston, 1975), vii–xviii.

23. Concerning Bjørn Anderson Kvelve's connection with the founding of the ill-starred Beaver Creek settlement, the son of Bjørn Anderson, Rasmus B. Anderson, makes the following comments in his *The First Chapter of Norwegian Immigration, 1821–1840* (Madison, Wisconsin, 1896), 161, 246–247.

"Bjørn Anderson had never been at Beaver Creek, but his severe criticisms on La Salle county naturally influenced the immigrants of 1837 to seek another locality. Blame has been cast on Bjørn Anderson's name in connection with the Beaver Creek fatalities, but this is utterly unjust. While he disparaged La Salle county, he did not recommend Iroquois county, which he had never seen." And again: "It seems to me that the story told above about my father and the succeeding scene, either Mr. Ole Nattestad, or the scribe Professor Svein Nilsson, must have been drawing somewhat upon his imagination. The facts as I have them from my mother, from Mons Aadland, and even from Ole Nattestad himself, do not warrant the painting of so weird a picture. All the prose there is in the romance is that my father met these people in Chicago and was unwilling to recommend the Fox River settlement, with which he was not pleased, and as is easily seen, he had no hand in recommending the immigrants to go to Beaver Creek."

24. Rasmus B. Anderson (1846–1936) was a well-known, versatile, and controversial figure among the Norwegian Americans. He was a prolific writer, university professor, diplomat, and journalist. See Lloyd Hustvedt, *Rasmus Bjørn Anderson; Pioneer Scholar* (Northfield, 1966); Paul Knaplund, "Rasmus B. Anderson, Pioneer and Crusader," in *Norwegian-American Studies and Records,* 18 (1954), 23–43; and *Life Story of Rasmus B. Anderson* (Madison, 1915), an autobiography written with the assistance of Albert O. Barton.

25. For a discussion of Johannes Nordboe's role in the migration movement see Arne Odd Johnsen, "Johannes Nordboe and Norwegian Immigration," in *Norwegian American Studies and Records*, 8 (1934), 23–38, and Einar Hovdhaugen, *Frå Venabygd til Texas* (Oslo, 1975).

26. For brief biographical sketches of Norwegian-American pioneer doctors see Knut Gjerset and Ludvig Hektoen, "Health Conditions and the Practice of Medicine Among Early Norwegian Settlers, 1825–1865," in *Norwegian-American Studies and Records*, 1 (1926), 1–59. A briefer account is found in Blegen, *Norwegian Migration to America: The American Transition*, 54–68.

27. "Mother Sather" was a noted quack healer in Norway.

28. A discussion of Trovatten's influence as a letter writer is found in Blegen, *Norwegian Migration to America, 1825–1860*, 197–200. See also C. A. Clausen, ed. and tr., "The Trials of an Immigrant: The Journal of Ole K. Trovatten," in *Norwegian-American Studies and Records*, 19 (1956), 142–159.

29. An extensive literature has grown up about the work of pastors C. L. Clausen and J. W. C. Dietrichson. See Nelson and Fevold, *The Lutheran Church Among Norwegian-Americans*, 1:82–119; E. Clifford Nelson, ed., *J. W. C. Dietrichson in Wisconsin* (Northfield, 1973); Carlton C. Qualey, ed. and tr., "Claus L. Clausen, Pioneer Pastor and Settlement Promoter: Illustrative Documents," in *Norwegian-American Studies and Records*, 6 (1930), 12–29; and R. Anderson, *Pastor Claus Laurits Clausen* (Brooklyn, 1921).

30. The text does not make clear whether the sign of the cross was cut by Dietrichson when he delivered his sermon or whether it was cut at the time of the memorial service in 1869. As Dietrichson makes no mention of such a ceremony we assume that the sign of the cross was cut into the trunk of the oak tree during the memorial celebration.

31. A complex and inconsequential paragraph about the shape and topography of Pleasant Spring township is omitted here.

32. The concluding part of this paragraph is omitted, which consists of a long, complicated description of the topography of the township and some generalizations about the early settling of Wisconsin which have no bearing on the history of Norwegian immigration.

33. A long paragraph follows which relates how the township was named in honor of Senator Charles Sumner of Massachusetts, who in May, 1856, while delivering an anti-slavery speech entitled "Crime Against Kansas," was physically assaulted and beaten with a cane by Congressman Preston Brooks of South Carolina.

34. The rather abrupt ending of this final article in the series might indicate that Svein Nilsson intended to contribute further articles; but despite the fact that eleven later issues of *Billed-Magazin* were published, no more articles about the Scandinavian settlements appeared.

Index*

*All places not otherwise identified are in Norway.